NEWPORT'S MUNICIPAL BUSES

Andrew Wiltshire

On the afternoon of 24 May 2008 77 (P177 VDW) an Alexander Strider-bodied Scania N113CRL of 1997 is seen crossing Newport Bridge.

(Andrew Wiltshire)

Front cover

154 (NDW 605) a Longwell Green-bodied Daimler CVG6 looks quite smart in the 50:50 livery. It is passing the former Arts College in Clarence Place.

(Cliff Essex)

Back cover

An Enviro200 in the latest livery. 304 (YX11 AGY) is seen at the new Mon Bank estate on 24 August 2018 with the 11.00 service from Friars Walk bus station.

(Geoff Gould)

INTRODUCTION

Thirty-nine years have now passed since Edward A Thomas and David B Thomas brought us *Trams and Buses of Newport 1845 to 1981*, a splendid piece of work published in 1982. Edward A Thomas was a Senior Traffic Clerk with Newport Corporation Transport. Both gentlemen have now sadly passed away, and fortunately I had the great privilege of getting to know David (Dave to all his friends), for many years up until his untimely passing in 2015. As for Newport's buses, there have been tremendous changes to the fleet since 1981, but as I write in 2021, Newport Transport is still at work serving the people of what has now become the City of Newport.

My earliest memories of Newport buses were as a very small boy living in Llanrumney, Cardiff. We lived less than five minutes' walk from St. Mellons village, and from there we could catch a number 30 to either Cardiff or Newport from outside the Bluebell Inn. With encouragement from my father, I gradually became conversant with the different types of motor buses in the Cardiff fleet, and consequently those in other local fleets including Newport.

Newport has not grown as much as its neighbouring city Cardiff, and its bus fleet has developed in a completely different way to that in Cardiff. There have been several changes of livery and vehicle policy over the years. It has gone from being a predominantly double-deck operation from the 1930s to one of largely single-deckers by the mid-1990s.

Leyland Titans and later Atlanteans dominated the motor bus fleet for many years but from 1971, in a surprise move, Newport turned to Scania and built up a relationship that has lasted for several decades. Deregulation in October 1986 saw the fleet become an arms-length company, of which Newport Council still retained ownership.

Newport town became a city in 2002. In 2019 Newport Transport became the first bus operator in Wales to place an electric bus in service and 2020 saw a further fourteen enter service. By 2020 Newport Transport served nearly eight million customers per annum and are committed to delivering customer service excellence, while transporting passengers to their chosen destination in comfort, safety and on time. The Newport Transport motto is "make the switch".

With the publication and success of my earlier book *Cardiff's Municipal Buses* in 2016, in 2018 I decided that it would be fitting to complete a similar piece of work for neighbouring Newport Transport.

This book takes a chronological look at the types of vehicles operated by Newport's municipal fleet and its successor up to the present day covering both the trams and in particular the motor buses. In order to do this, we need to briefly consider how the history of local public transport services in Newport evolved, and how the municipal undertaking came into being.

ACKNOWLEDGEMENTS

Without the help of many friends and acquaintances this work would never have been completed to a standard with which I would be happy. A very large thank you must go to Ivor Homfray, John Jones and Mike Taylor for their endless support and enthusiasm for the project. Ivor has painstakingly answered dozens of queries and also provided many images from his collection. John has made available his archive files in addition to his photograph and slide collection; and both Ivor and John have spent much time proof reading the text. Mike has made available many images from the Cardiff Transport Preservation Group (CTPG) archive, as well as letting me borrow and undertake research from the extensive archive of both his late father Chris and the late Dave Thomas to whom I would like to dedicate this book.

I would also like to thank the very helpful staff at Newport Central Library and Chris Hogan who provided some rather interesting facts and figures mainly from the 1960s. And then there are the other enthusiasts who have let me use their photographic material including Cliff Essex, Geoff Gould, Peter Relf, Peter Keating, David Beilby and Peter Smith. I must also thank the The Omnibus Society, who have once again let me reproduce some images taken by or from the late Roy Marshall collection. Bernard McCall has once again given his enthusiastic support and backing for this major project, while my wife Tracey continues to encourage me as I research and compile yet another transport book.

Andrew Wiltshire   Cardiff   March 2021

CONTENTS

ISBN : 978-1-913797-04-1

Published by Bernard McCall, 400 Nore Road, Portishead, Bristol, BS20 8EZ, England.
Website : www.coastalshipping.co.uk
Telephone/fax : 01275 846178. Email : bernard@coastalshipping.co.uk.
All distribution enquiries should be addressed to the publisher.

Printed by Gomer Press, Llandysul Enterprise Park, Llandysul, Ceredigion, Wales, SA44 4JL.
Telephone : 01559 362371   Fax : 01559 363758
Email : sales@gomer.co.uk   Website : www.gomerprinting.co.uk

FOREWORD

I was very humbled to be asked to create a foreword for Andrew's latest publication, this time on a well embedded organic business that is Newport Bus, across its varied and long history of serving the public of Newport, a business that has constantly reinvented itself to ensure it met the needs of its customers.

As Managing Director since 2010 the company has morphed from a local bus operator into a regional transport provider, allowed solely by the impressive base built up over many years. It is vital that we never forget where we came from and the many innovations of the past that have laid many foundations to allow this company to be what it is today. This publication clearly and accurately records the many phases of power mode used by this company and the numerous choices many before us have made in fleet specification, type, manufacturer, networks, and ticketing.

From horse driven trams to most recently electric zero emission buses this company has always stayed with the mode of its time. You can still see the horse troughs where the horses bedded down and fed, the massive internal cranes used to maintain the electric trams and the tram lines in the depot today. These are all the history of the company that this publication carefully records for all to learn or reminisce.

You may think this is a publication for people with just transport interest, but it is so much more than that, it uniquely records the history of Newport and how public transport was used in over 100 years in such a way that should give immense pride to all those that delivered or used the service. I am sure you will enjoy this publication as much as I have and hope that if you are ever able, come and travel with Newport Bus!

Scott Pearson FCILT, Managing Director, Newport Bus

CHAPTER ONE
A TRANSPORT SYSTEM FOR NEWPORT

The origins of Newport

The Romans built a fort at Caerleon to guard the crossing of the River Usk at that point, and by 1093AD, the Normans successfully built a castle and a bridge much further downstream. A town began to grow around this settlement on the west bank of the Usk, which was to become Newport. Newport was still a market town in 1800 and somewhat smaller than the county town of Monmouth. It had a population of around 1,100 and comprised two main streets, High Street and Stow Hill. Transport links at this time were basic. There were some stagecoach services including one to London for those who could afford it, as well as a number of sailing boat services to Bristol.

By 1832 the population of Newport had grown to 4900, and ten years later, on a site between Commercial Road and the river, the Town Dock opened. The first railways were operating through Newport by 1850, the year in which a station was opened on the High Street site. Another significant event was the opening of a large dock to the south of Pillgwenlly in 1875 by the Alexandra (Newport) Dock Company followed by the South Dock in 1893. Pillgwenlly is often referred to as just Pill or Pill (Dock) as will become obvious throughout this book. There soon became a need for another bridge across the River Usk, and so the Newport Transporter Bridge was constructed. This impressive structure was officially opened on 12 September 1906 and is still in working order in 2021.

Newport was by 1906 the largest town in the county of Monmouthshire, and was a county borough between 1891 and 1974. As a result of local government reorganization in 1974, the Borough of Newport was now within the county of Gwent, while in 1996 Newport became a unitary authority responsible for all local government services within its area. After submitting a bid in July 2001, Newport was granted city status on 14 March 2002.

Geographically much of Newport is low-lying close to the River Usk and River Ebbw to the west. There are also adjacent hilly areas including Brynglas, Christchurch, Gaer, St Julians, and the Ridgeway at Allt-yr-yn, which all offer excellent views over Newport on a clear day.

An early transport system using horse buses

On 2 January 1845 a Mr George Masters commenced operating a horse bus service in Newport from his wine and spirit vaults at 2 Bridge Street, to the Devonshire House Inn on Church Street in Pillgwenlly. It ran four times a day, but was abandoned during 1846. Bristol-based Robert Williams also began running a horse bus service in 1845 from the Bristol Steam Packet Company's berth on the River Usk, to Caerleon, Usk and Abergavenny. This was not without problems as Williams was from outside the county, and this caused a certain amount of resentment locally.

Thomas W Phillips began a service in November 1845 from King William the Fourth Inn on Commercial Street, to The Bell at Chepstow. In 1854 Charles Phillips, a popular local character started a horse bus service that connected the railway stations in High Street and Dock Street. There were other horse bus services in the 1850s and 1860s, but all would appear to have been poorly patronized and therefore short-lived.

C Hale was running between the Steam Packet Inn in Newport and Caerleon from 1875, while a Mr Pobjoy was operating to Cardiff from the Prince of Wales Inn on Cardiff Road. From the above it can be concluded that many of the recorded services ran between inns and hotels, while it would seem to be that on the whole the population of Newport at this time preferred to save their money and travel on foot.

Despite the introduction of a new horse tramway in 1875 horse bus services would continue in and around Newport until 1902. The Newport Tramway Company introduced two services in 1879 to complement their tramway service. One of these ran from the Custom House, Dock Street to the Alexandra Dock Head, while the second ran from the Queen's Hotel to Kensington Place, Maindee. The Alexandra (Newport) Docks and Maindee Omnibus Company Limited began running a service from Alexandra Dock Hotel to Kensington Place from 1 December 1883. In 1886 a Mr Eastman from Maindee began operating a horse bus from the Cross Hands Hotel on Chepstow Road into the town centre.

There followed a period of intense competition between the various horse omnibus companies and the Newport Tramway Company. The latter had taken over the Town to Pill section of Perry's horse bus route, and in 1886 three buses to Andrew's patent design were purchased which featured a staircase and knifeboard seating on the upper deck.

The Alexandra (Newport) Docks and Maindee Omnibus Company went out of business in late 1886. Some of the buses were sold to Edmund Perry while Solomon Andrews also took one. Perry recommenced operating horse buses in 1887 with a service from Westgate in the town centre to Maindee. The Westgate departure point changed to the Queen's Hotel in 1889, while Perry gave up running horse buses in 1894.

One of three Andrews patent horse buses as purchased by Newport Tramways in 1886 to work between the Alexandra Docks at Pill and High Street station.

(The late Dave B Thomas collection)

On 15 March 1895 Solomon Andrews began a horse bus service from Westgate up Stow Hill as far as the Handpost Inn which required a second horse for the initial run up Stow Hill. In July 1901 Newport Corporation took over operation of this service along with those of the horse tramway. The Stow Hill service was withdrawn in March 1902 mainly due to poor patronage and this area was left without public transport until 1904 when the electric tramway began to serve Stow Hill.

Horse tram proposal

In 1870 the population of Newport was estimated to be in the region of 26,000, and there were in the order of 4,000 inhabited dwellings in the town. Street tramways were already operating successfully in many towns and cities around Great Britain, and it was thought that a growing town like Newport would benefit from a tramway that could offer a cheap and quick mode of travel to tired pedestrians.

At a meeting of Newport Town Council on 22 November 1870, Councillor J Murphy sought permission of the Council to introduce a street tramway to Newport. A group of townsmen had in the meantime formed a private company to promote such a proposal. If permission was granted, the company proposed to apply to the Board of Trade for a Provisional Order to construct a tramway. The plan was for a single line to a gauge of 4ft 8½in, to run from the Queen's Hotel, Station Street to Commercial Road, Pillgwenlly via Tredegar Place (now the lower part of Bridge Street) and Commercial Street. It would include three passing places. The proposal also included three branch lines that included a loop serving Ruperra Street, Dock Street and Bolt Street; another serving Llanarth Street and Dock Street and finally a spur into Portland Street. The last two proposals were soon withdrawn. There were many objections, but finally, at a meeting on 30 August 1872, Councillor Murphy's motion was approved, and Newport Town Council gave consent to the introduction of a street tramway in Newport.

Tramway given the go ahead

Consent was needed from Newport Town Council to apply to the Board of Trade for a Provisional Order which was granted at a meeting on 19 December 1872. On 13 March 1873 at Newport Town Hall a Board of Trade Enquiry was held, conducted by Colonel Hutchinson, and attended by the Town Clerk and a number of other interested bodies. Hutchinson then produced a report which was approved by the Board of Trade (Railway Department) on 18 March 1873 in accordance with Section 5 of the Tramways Act 1870. The Provisional Order authorising Newport Tramway Company to construct and operate a street tramway was adopted at a Town Council meeting on 22 April 1873.

The Provisional Order also gave approval for extensions to the system. These included a line along High Street, Clarence Place and Caerleon Road to the junction of Church Road and Duckpool Road, Barnardtown. Authority was also given for a second extension along Chepstow Road to Kensington Place, Maindee. However, a clause stated that for a tramway to run along High Street, the roadway would have to be widened to at least 24 feet. The Newport (Mon) Tramways Act 1873, confirming the Board of Trade Provisional Order, was passed in the House of Commons in July 1873. In December 1873 the company invited tenders for the construction of one and a half miles of single track line with passing places. The contract was subsequently awarded to Messrs Speight and Sons of Leeds. Construction of the horse tramway commenced on 24 April 1874, and the route from the town centre to Pillgwenlly was completed in just three months. The accommodation to house the trams and stables was built in a corner of Friars Field which was just off Commercial Street and accessed via a short spur along Friar Street.

The tramway opens

On 10 December 1874 a successful trial run took place over the new tramway and on 14 December Colonel Hutchinson from the Board of Trade, C Kirby the borough surveyor and a number of others inspected the system. The Newport Tramway Company was then granted a certificate to commence operating, but this was considerably delayed due to difficulties obtaining the required number of suitable horses. The official opening eventually took place on 1 February 1875.

The extension beyond Frederick Street level crossing on Commercial Road to the end of Commercial Road could not be completed at this stage, as this section of road was owned by the Tredegar Wharf Company. Consent was finally given to the Newport (Mon) Tramway Company in May 1876, and the last section was constructed and opened in December 1877. The Ruperra Street section was to be short-lived and was closed in the autumn of 1877, due to a downturn of trade at the Town Dock following the opening of Alexandra Dock in April 1875.

The widening of High Street took place in 1879, but a tramway was not actually laid along High Street until 1894.

The original horse-drawn tramcars were single-deck with seating for around sixteen passengers, and purchased from the Starbuck Car and Wagon Company of Birkenhead. Open-top double-deck cars had replaced these by the end of the century. In the early days the Company used their own horses, but in 1877 a Mr Edmund Perry took over responsibility for providing them.

A new operator

In April 1881, the contract for actually running the tramway expired, and the Newport (Mon) Tramways Company would have to decide if they wanted to continue running it themselves or invite tenders from those interested in leasing this aspect of the operation. The lines were subsequently leased to a Mr Edmund Perry for a period of five years. He would pay £820 rental per annum and be responsible for working expenses and track maintenance. However, after a number of setbacks including bankruptcy, and criticisms from the Town Council, Perry was forced to terminate his lease in March 1885. At this point operation was once again taken on by Newport Tramways Company. In 1886 the original tramcar shed in Friars Field was closed having been replaced by a new facility in Mountjoy Street which could house ten tramcars. A second much larger shed in Clarence Place could hold twenty-eight trams.

Double-deck horse tram number 11 is seen in Commercial Street just opposite the Westgate Hotel in the 1890s.

(Ivor Homfray collection)

Enter Newport Corporation

The Newport Corporation Bill received royal assent in July 1892, and within this Bill were powers that enabled Newport Corporation to purchase the existing horse tramway from the Newport (Mon) Tramways Company for £4,500. In March 1894 the Newport Town Clerk sought offers from businesses to operate the existing tramway, and also the proposed extensions mentioned above to Church Road and Kensington Place via High

Street. Three offers were received and on 28 July 1894, it was decided to grant a 21-year lease to Solomon Andrews and Son, who would be acting on behalf of the South Wales Property, Machinery and Carriage Company Limited, who had tendered £1,860 annual rental. The South Wales Property, Machinery and Carriage Company Limited commenced operation of the tramway on 30 July 1894.

Meanwhile work on the extensions to Church Road, Barnardtown and Kensington Place, Maindee and improvements to the line along Commercial Street had commenced in April 1894. These were all completed by the end of the year, but operation of them was delayed as Solomon Andrews did not have sufficient tramcars available. Andrews also replaced most of the earlier double-deck cars with more modern vehicles.

Horse tram number 14 poses for the photographer at the Cross Hands terminus on Chepstow Road.

(Cardiff Transport Preservation Group collection)

There duly followed an extension to the Cross Hands Hotel, Beechwood on Chepstow Road, which was opened on 28 September 1895. Further extensions took the horse tramway to Somerset Road on Caerleon Road and Prospect Street on Malpas Road. In addition, the line was doubled from High Street Post Office and out over Newport Bridge to Clarence Place. All this work was completed for an opening on 22 March 1899.

The horse tram routes	Commenced
Town Centre (Bridge Street) to Pillgwenlly	1 February 1875
Town Centre to Kensington Place on Chepstow Road	7 December 1894
Town Centre to Duckpool Road on Church Road	7 December 1894
Town Centre to Prospect Street on Malpas Road	22 March 1899
Town Centre to Somerset Road on Caerleon Road	22 March 1899

In 1898 the fleet comprised 22 tramcars and 118 horses. There were up to eighteen tramcars in daily service, and all required two horses per tram apart from the Church Road service which managed with a single horse.

Newport Corporation takes over

In November 1900, the South Wales Property, Machinery and Carriage Company Limited gave notice to Newport Corporation, of their intention to terminate the lease on the tramway. As a result of this Newport Corporation took over operation of the horse tramway on 30 July 1901. It paid £9,000 for land and buildings in Clarence Place plus the stables in Mountjoy Street. A sum of £6,295 was paid for 137 horses, 26 tramcars and items of associated equipment. The Corporation also purchased three secondhand tramcars from Liverpool Corporation. In August 1901 a sub-committee of the Electricity and Tramways Committee took control of the tramway system which also included the Stow Hill horse omnibus service. In September 1901 the new tramway along Corporation Road was opened, and was double-track layout running to the junction with Spytty Road.

Electrification proposal

Newport Corporation began investigating electrification of the town's tramway. On 21 March 1900, the Lighting and Traffic Committee discussed a surface contact system. This required a skate under the tramcar to pick up current from metal studs located in the road. This avoided the cost of installing and maintaining an overhead pick-up system, but its reliability was dubious should the studs become damaged or coated with road dirt and such like. Then there was the safety aspect. In theory the stud was only live when the tram skate passed over it, but there was the risk of leakage in heavy rain, snow or flooding. Consequently, the Borough Engineer, Horace Parshall recommended the overhead wire system for Newport.

On 25 June an Act of Parliament was passed for the conversion to electrical operation of the tramway in Newport. This allowed for double-track extensions, and was based on existing lines along Caerleon Road, Chepstow Road, Malpas Road and along Alexandra Road to Watch House Parade which was close to the dock entrance. In addition, a brand new line was constructed up Stow Hill as far as Risca Road. On 4 September 1900, Horace Parshall was appointed as the Engineer responsible for constructing the electric tramway, building a new power station on a site between Corporation Road and the River Usk with an adjacent tram shed and works. The existing Corporation Power station in Llanarth Street was deemed inadequate to supply the new tramway.

Purchasing new electric trams

In 1900 George Frederick Milnes set up a factory in Hadley, Shropshire, constructing electric tramcars. By 1903 G F Milnes & Co was in financial difficulty and the Hadley works eventually became part of United Electric Car Co Ltd in June 1905. Between 8 and 10 January 1902, the Electricity & Tramways Sub-Committee visited the works of British Westinghouse at Trafford Park, Manchester, the British Electric Car Company and the Hadley works of G F Milnes. After inspecting a tram at the Milnes factory, the Committee agreed that the new Newport trams should be to a similar specification. A tender for thirty electric tramcars at a total cost of £14,691 was accepted from British Westinghouse. The fifty-five-seat trams were built by G F Milnes with British Westinghouse electrical equipment and G F Milnes open-top bodies mounted on 4-wheel Peckham cantilever trucks.

Building an electric tramway

The Council's Electric Committee was reformed as the Electricity and Tramways Committee on 27 November 1900. In 1901 construction of the new power station and tram sheds on Corporation Road commenced. The tram sheds would be capable of housing approximately fifty tramcars, plus a further twelve in the workshops. On 31 July 1902 authorization was granted for the construction of five miles and three chains of track (one chain is 22 yards). Tenders for the construction opened in August, and the work to double the tracks and extend existing lines to the Borough boundaries was awarded to A Krauss & Son of Bristol, but did not include the Stow Hill extension. Construction of the overhead wire system was undertaken by W T Glover & Company, while Henley's Telegraph Works produced the necessary cables, which were laid in cable ducts by Callenders Cable and Construction Company.

In November 1902 work commenced on doubling tram tracks in readiness for electrification and constructing extensions out to the Borough boundaries at Chepstow Road, Caerleon Road and Malpas Road. In January 1903 work on the new East Power Station was virtually complete, while the adjoining tramcar depot was completed in March. This consisted of a twelve-road shed made up of nine roads for stabling tramcars, a repair shop, a motor repair shop and a paint shop. In April 1903, Mr H Collings Bishop was appointed Tramways General Manager and Engineer. He had been the Borough Electrical Engineer since August 1902.

Commissioning the new electric tramway

Drivers began training on the electric tramcars on Sunday 29 March 1903. This took place on Corporation Road and it had to be a Sunday as they were driving horse trams Mondays to Saturdays. There followed a Board of Trade inspection on 8 April, and subsequently a certificate was issued enabling the electric tramway to commence operations. On 9 April the horse trams ran until 10.00am. Then at 11.00am electric trams numbers 7 and 13 arrived at the Town Hall on Commercial Street. With tram number 13 leading, the Mayor John Holman Dunn plus civil dignitaries travelled by tram to Lysaght's steel works, returning along Corporation Road to the power station which they inspected. They then travelled forward to Pillgwenlly where the Mayor declared the line open. Tram 13 was driven by H Collings Bishop, with the Mayor also taking a turn at the controls.

Tram number 18 in High Street in 1903. Passing the Old Post Office and Corn Exchange at the top of High Street (now demolished). The original position of the destination box and headlamp is noteworthy.

(The late Dave B Thomas collection)

The now rebuilt 16 heads into town at the Caerleon Road/Duckpool Road junction with tram 34 behind heading out to the terminus in 1937. 135 Caerleon Road behind the tram still stands and in 2021 is a Boots pharmacy.

(R V C Richards courtesy Cardiff Transport Preservation Group collection)

The first batch of electric tramcars were numbered 1-30 and seated fifty-five passengers. Each tram had a pair of 30hp Westinghouse electric motors and featured Westinghouse 90 controllers. Each controller had seven notches for power and five for the electric brake. It is thought that three trams were experimentally fitted with patent Newell brakes, possibly in conjunction with the opening of the Stow Hill route in 1905.

The lower saloon had three windows on each side with six top lights. The four middle top lights were of the opening hopper type, while the remaining two hinged outwards. The wooden seats in the lower saloon were arranged in a longitudinal fashion, whilst the upper deck featured reversible garden-type seats either side of a central gangway. Each garden seat incorporated a hinged flap seat to the "Never-Wet" design. If the seat was wet, then the passenger could flip it over revealing a dry side. This novel feature cost an extra £11 per tram, but was considered worthwhile if passengers could be encouraged to use the top deck in wet weather.

When new they had destination boxes mounted above the upper deck netting and headlamps in the upper deck panels. The destination boxes were later moved to the lower part of the upper deck netting and the headlamps to the platform-level panels. The platform lattice gates were considered a hazard and were later removed and replaced by brass chains.

Let the service commence

The first electrified route opened to the public at 2pm on 9 April running between Pill and Corporation Road via the town centre. It is thought that the first car to run in passenger service was number 13. A second route from Pill to Chepstow Road via the town centre commenced on 27 May 1903. This was in turn followed by new routes from Pill to Caerleon Road on 27 June and Pill to Malpas Road on 27 July, also running via the town centre. All three termini were situated at the borough boundary. The tram stops were situated approximately 200 yards apart and there were a number of compulsory stops for safety reasons.

Following the introduction of the electric trams from 9 April 1903, most of the horse trams services had ceased running by July. The exception being the service along Church Road between Duckpool Road and Caerleon Road, a distance of just 400 yards. However, this service was not profitable and was abandoned on 3 November 1903.

In the first full month of operation of all four routes, 457,989 passengers were carried by the electric tramcars. Receipts from fares were given as £2,149. Up to and including 31 March 1904, the trams had covered approximately 635,000 miles and had carried in the region of five million passengers. They had made a profit of £275 which was considered satisfactory, given that this was a new tramway system.

Table of fares charged	
Caerleon Road route	
Caerleon Road terminus to Pill (full journey)	2d
Caerleon Road terminus to Duckpool Road	1d
Somerset Road to Town Centre (Westgate or General Post Office)	1d
Clarence Place to Cardiff Road	1d
Town Centre to Pill	1d
Town Centre to Caerleon Road terminus	1½d
Chepstow Road route	
Chepstow Road terminus to Pill (full journey)	2d
Chepstow Road terminus to Maindee Post Office	1d
Kensington Place to Town Centre	1d
Clarence Place to Cardiff Road	1d
Town Centre to Pill	1d
Town Centre to Beechwood Road	1½d
Corporation Road route	
Corporation Road terminus to Pill (full journey)	2d
Corporation Road terminus to Town Centre	1½d
Corporation Road terminus to Power Station	1d
Railway Bridge to Town Centre	1d
Clarence Place to Cardiff Road	1d
Town Centre to Pill	1d
Malpas Road route	
Malpas Road terminus to Pill (full journey)	1½d
Malpas Road terminus to Town Centre	1d
Town Centre to Pill	1d
Workmen's special cars	
Any distance, any route by workmen's cars	1d

The Stow Hill route

When the Council met on 12 January 1903, one item on the agenda was the introduction of a motor bus service serving Stow Hill. However, in December 1903 a report was published that recommended the use of electric trams for this route. It would be a single line tramway and the gradient of the hill would require modifications to the roadway near the Clifton Road junction, as well as the demolition of two cottages and acquisition of part of the vicarage gardens. The estimated cost of such a tramway was in the region of £17,000.

The original plan was to use single-deck bogie tramcars on this route, but to keep costs down, and after approval from the Board of Trade, tenders for ten double-deck trams similar to the first thirty were sought. In early 1904 G F Milnes quoted £478 each for trams for the Stow Hill route, but Milnes was in liquidation and unable to supply them. Newport then placed an order on 14 March 1904 with Dick, Kerr & Co for a total of ten trams at a cost of £5,046 10s. They featured Christensen air-brake equipment at an additional cost of £450, deemed necessary due to the steep gradients encountered on Stow Hill. They were fitted with Brill 21E trucks with a 5ft

6in wheelbase, and Dick Kerr 25A motors. They would be constructed in Preston at the works previously occupied by The Electric Railway and Tramway Carriage Works Ltd (E R & T C W) They were delivered as 31-40 in June 1904 before the Stow Hill route was ready and were therefore initially put to work on other routes.

Tram number 37 was built by Dick, Kerr & Co for the Stow Hill route. It is seen on Newport Bridge in 1904 in original condition.

(The late Dave B Thomas collection)

A major difference with trams 31-40 was that they featured Bellamy reversed staircases to the upper deck. This was to prove awkward for tall drivers as they hit their heads on the staircase. As with the first batch they had destination boxes mounted above the upper deck netting and headlamps in the upper deck panels. The destination boxes were later moved to a lower position below the canopy, and the headlamps to the platform-level panels. However, tram 38 managed to avoid these modifications until much later in its working life.

In addition to the air brakes, each tram was fitted with a Spencer mechanical slipper brake. This was operated by a wheel fitted to a shaft on the outside of the chain brake spindle. They could all be applied at the same time if necessary.

On 1 November 1904 a trial run was undertaken over the Stow Hill route which was one mile and one furlong in length. A number of brake tests were carried out on the return journey. On 4 November 1904 the tramway was inspected by the Board of Trade and passed it fit for operation. The service was opened to the public the following day, with a frequency of ten minutes, and all the trams running through to the Chepstow Road terminus. The new service was reported to be well patronised with over 4,000 passengers on the first day alone.

A disaster was narrowly avoided on the first afternoon of operation, when tramcar 40 failed to slow down when turning from Clifton Road onto Stow Hill while making a descent to the town centre. Wet greasy rails caused the tram to slide and gather speed, but the driver was able to bring it under control and to a standstill in High Street. An interesting requirement for all trams employed on the Stow Hill route was that they had to leave the depot with No.1 end towards Westgate Square, or the trolley boom would become de-wired on a particular curve. No.1 and No.2 ends were clearly marked on the canopy above the driver's head.

The Stow Hill route was the only proper incline on the system and the section between Westgate Square and St. Woolos Cathedral reached a gradient of 1 in 11. This route was the preserve of senior drivers, who got an extra 2/- per week. The section of tramway between Westgate Square and Clarence Place was the busiest as it was used by trams on every service.

Tram number 37 is seen at the Risca Road/Preston Avenue terminus of the Stow Hill route, which at this time was the town boundary. It has now had its destination indicator and headlamp repositioned.

(The late Dave B Thomas collection)

The water cart

The decision was made to acquire a service vehicle for the tramway and in May 1906 a tender of £751 was accepted from Dick, Kerr & Co for the supply of a single-deck water cart/rail-grinder. It was built by The United Electric Car Co Ltd, the new name given by Dick, Kerr & Co to the former E R & T C W works at Preston. It could not carry passengers and it entered service as number 41 in a red livery. It was fitted with Dick, Kerr 3A motors and a Spencer slipper brake. It had been proved that by watering the rails their lifespan could be increased. A carborundum block could also be fitted between the wheels on the truck to undertake rail-grinding. Number 41 could also be used for towing broken down or damaged tramcars back to the depot. During the First World War it received a grey livery which it then retained for the rest of its active life

In 1907 Collings Bishop advised that the tram's chilled iron wheels would be replaced with steel wheels, to increase tyre life from six months to three years. Approval was also given to re-equip the tram fleet with new Westinghouse 90M controllers and Westinghouse Newell magnetic track brakes. This gave the driver much better control as well as reducing the amount of energy required to apply the brake. Early recipients were tramcars number 22, 29 and 30. Some of the tramcars were also fitted with rail-cleaning apparatus to help clear dirt from the rail grooves. In March 1907 time clocks were installed at each terminus at a cost of £35 each, while drivers and conductors were issued with uniforms for the first time.

In 1907 the Tramways Manager Mr Collings Bishop made three proposals for improving the system:
(a) that the Stow Hill route be converted to double-track from Westgate Square to Charles Street.
(b) construction of a siding to hold ten cars in Rodney Road off Clarence Place.
(c) extension of the Corporation Road service as far as the new Transporter Bridge.

The doubling of the tramway on Stow Hill was completed and in use from July 1909. A loop was provided in Clarence Place which served the purpose of the Rodney Road siding proposal. By the end of 1908 an eight-minute service existed on all routes except that between Pill Gates and Clarence Place where a four-minute composite service operated.

A trolleybus report

In 1908 Collings Bishop produced a report that recommended operation on Sundays to avoid capital lying idle for 52 days per year. This proposal was rejected. He also proposed the use of one-man operated trackless trolley vehicles as feeders to the tramway system on the following routes:

Pill Gates to New Pier Head;
Corporation Road tram terminus to the Transporter Bridge;
Church Road to Woodland Road via Fairoak Avenue;
Albert Avenue to Summerhill Avenue;
Cromwell Road to Nash Road.

He also suggested routes outside the borough of Newport to locations such as Rogerstone, Bassaleg, Caerleon and Malpas. The report was not adopted. Bishop estimated the running cost of a trackless trolley vehicle to be 7.58d per mile compared to 11.48d per mile of an electric tramcar.

Tram number 6 in original condition is seen at the Caerleon Road terminus in c1909 with Driver D Bale at the controls.

(The late Dave B Thomas collection)

Moving forward

Three additional tramcars were required for the Stow Hill route in 1909 after the doubling of the track.Tenders were received from three suppliers in March 1909 as follows:

Preston	£1,973 15s 0d
British Thomson-Houston (BTH)	£2,153 0s 0d
Dick, Kerr & Co	£2,140 0s 0d

The Dick, Kerr & Co tender was accepted and an order placed on 14 May 1909. They would supply three trams on Brill 21E trucks and would be more powerful than the earlier trams to make them more suitable for the Stow Hill gradients.

Numbered 42-4, these trams were generally similar to cars 31-40 of 1904, but had finer netting on the upper deck balcony. They had a pair of 35hp Dick, Kerr & Co 3A motors and DB1 Form E controllers. They were also fitted with Spencer mechanical slipper brakes.

On 29 February 1912 Mr Collings Bishop retired as manager of the Tramway undertaking and was succeeded on 1 March by N J Young. Mr Young took the

Car 43 in original condition is seen descending the lower part of Stow Hill.

(The late Dave B Thomas collection)

title of General Manager of the Tramways and Electricity Department, while a Mr A Nichols Moore became the new Electrical and Tramways Engineer. Also in 1912 an electrical signalling system was installed on Stow Hill at the junction of Charles Street and Clifton Road. This was removed about five years later when the track layout was modified. Signals were also installed to control the single line section of High Street from the National Provincial Bank to Station Approach.

By 1912 a fair number of tramcars were showing signs of their age and were in need of rebuilding. The first tram to be dealt with was car number 2 which was completed on 14 June 1912. Its body was rebuilt and strengthened with steel angle framing, while the lower saloon ventilation and general lighting throughout was improved. Its destination box and headlamp repositioned as described earlier. Electrical engineer A Nichols Moore anticipated that this work would extend the life of tram number 2 by four to five years, and was keen to see the other 29 trams in this batch similarly treated in the following two years. Route number indicators were fitted in the former headlamp position, as shown in the table. However, the use of route numbers was abandoned after a short period. Route letters were then introduced, but for some reason were not displayed on the trams.

Route 1	Chepstow Road
Route 2	Caerleon Road
Route 3	Corporation Road
Route 4	Malpas Road

In April 1913, the average number of electric tramcars available for service stood at 36 out of a total fleet of 43. By now eleven had been refurbished, and A Nicholls Moore is quoted as saying the average cost of rebuilding a tramcar was £180. By March 1914 nineteen had been dealt with. This rose to 28 by March 1916.

On 21 April 1913 the fares were increased and a few days later, a new siding was opened outside the General Post Office in High Street. From 1 May the tram routes were revised and frequencies increased. This resulted in a three-minute frequency to Pill, and the number of trams required to maintain this level of service rose from 27 to 29. See table below:

Route	Frequency	Trams required
Chepstow Road to Pill (Docks)	6 minutes	9 cars

The terminus was at Beechwood Park Road (Somerton Road) and extras ran from Westgate Square to Beechwood Park Road.

Caerleon Road to Pill (Docks)	6 minutes	8 cars

The terminus was at St. Julians Park (Borough Boundary) and extras ran from Westgate Square to St. Julians Park (Borough Boundary).

Stow Hill to Malpas Road	6 minutes	8 cars

Corporation Road to High Street (General Post Office)	7 minutes	4 cars

This service had previously run through to Pill (Docks) but was now truncated. A special laying-over siding had been constructed at the General Post Office in High Street.

Motor bus proposal

In 1913 a joint report submitted by the General Manager (N J Young) and the Electrical Engineer (A Nichols Moore) recommended that powers be obtained to run motor omnibus services to areas of Newport that were not presently served by the electric tramway. This also included places outside the Borough such as Caerleon, Pontnewydd and Crosskeys. It also mentioned a summer service to St. Brides lighthouse. Unfortunately, this report received the same negative response as Bishop's trolleybus report five years earlier.

World War One

The Newport Corporation Act 1914 did however authorise the operation of motor omnibuses within the Borough and two miles outside. The outbreak of war the same year meant no further action was taken. Staff shortages were a major problem following the outbreak of the First World War as many male staff had taken up military service. Women conductors were employed from 1916 and women tram drivers from 1917.

There was now a requirement to transport large numbers of people to the munitions factory at Alexandra Dock, Pill, but there were not always enough trams available to do this as there were often as many as five under repair at any one time. More tramcars were needed and as new trams were not available, the undertaking would have to look at using trailers or obtaining second-hand trams. The trailer option was ruled out by the Tramway management and so used trams would be pursued.

The Bath Tramways Company and The Gravesend and Northfleet Tramways Company each had two cars available, but at a prohibitive cost. On the other hand, the London County Council (LCC) had a large number of four-wheel tramcars on offer which were in good condition. London County Council was attempting to standardise on bogie tramcars and wished to dispose of around one hundred earlier truck cars which at first glance were deemed suitable for use at Newport. They were London County Council class B-type, single-truck double-deck cars that had been new in 1903 as open-top trams. They were fitted with covered tops at some point after 1906, but retained their open platforms.

In July 1917 it was agreed to purchase six of these in a deal that included transportation costs plus dismantling at the London end by Dick, Kerr & Co, and re-assembly in Newport. The final cost was a £4,069 10s 8d. They arrived at Newport by rail and were partially assembled near Cardiff Road level crossing before being towed to the tram depot. Here they were overhauled and modified for use in Newport and started to enter service from 31 August 1917 numbered 45-50. They were the first covered-top tramcars in Newport. These trams were fitted with standard LCC two-line destination boxes, and ran as such in Newport for a number of years before being replaced by standard Newport destination boxes.

They were restricted to service between Clarence Place and Pill Docks as their overall height was a problem. They could not pass under the railway bridges on Chepstow Road, Corporation Road and Caerleon Road, and were also unsuitable for the Stow Hill route. The road under Chepstow Road and Corporation Road bridges was later lowered to allow their use on these routes. At some point car 47 was reduced in height to allow its use on the Caerleon Road service. This was successful and 45/6, 48-50 were later reduced in height.

Thirteen conductresses pose for the camera with Traffic Superintendent C W Evans and his dog.

(The late Dave B Thomas collection)

Number 49 was a former LCC tram and has now been rebuilt with a vestibule. It is seen in the depot yard at Corporation Road in the 1930s.

(The late E A Thomas collection)

On 3 December 1917 the tramway was extended beyond Commercial Road in Pill to a new terminus at the gates of the Alexandra Docks, a distance of three furlongs (a furlong is one eighth of a mile). People were now able to travel right up to the dock entrance whereupon they could board a steam train or motor bus which would take them to their place of employment on the dock estate. The motor bus was operated by the port owner, the Alexandra Docks and Railway Company. A new service was then introduced from Clarence Place to the Dock Gates to meet the heavy traffic on this section of line. The former London trams 45-50 gradually settled down to work this route. There was a plan in 1918 to fit the earlier trams with protection screens in front of the driver's position. By 1919 this had not materialized. In March 1919, Arthur Ellis the General Manager of Cardiff Corporation Tramways proposed that the tramway systems of Cardiff and Newport should be linked. This never got any further due to an objection in 1920 by G Vernon Jones of Castleton who had begun operating a Newport to Cardiff motor bus service.

By 1920 all trams apart from 38 had been rebuilt. In the same year it became apparent that Newport Bridge over the River Usk was showing signs of its age and needed to be replaced. On 11 April 1921 work started on constructing a replacement wooden structure which was completed on 2 November 1922. This carried a double track tramway and remained in use until the new bridge was completed on 23 May 1927. The new Newport Bridge was officially opened on 21 June 1927.

The last new tramcars

The General Manager and Borough Electrical Engineer produced a joint report in January 1920 in which they recommended the purchase of an additional eight tramcars, in order to be able to maintain an efficient level of service. They proposed eight double-deck covered top trams. Four were to the usual 4-wheel single-truck layout, while the other four were high capacity trams on bogies. Tenders were duly received for the above eight trams. As both tram builders had a large number of back orders, Newport was told there would be a wait of around twenty months for their new trams.

On 14 April 1920, orders were placed for the bodies as follows:		
Four single-truck car bodies	Hurst Nelson	£7,200
Four bogie car bodies	Brush	£9,000

On 15 April 1920, orders were placed for the running gear as follows:		
Eight Preston bogies and four Preston single trucks	English Electric	£3,320
Eight sets of electrical equipment (excluding controllers)	English Electric	£5,980

In December 1921 bogie tramcars 51-54 were delivered by rail and placed onto the tramlines at the Commercial Road/Ebenezer Street level crossing. After further preparation at the tram depot, they entered service just before Christmas. These were Newport's first new trams for twelve years and were built by the Brush Electrical Engineering Company Limited of Loughborough. These large and impressive covered-top totally-enclosed trams had seating for eighty, and could also carry forty standing passengers. They had a front entrance and rear exit layout.

51-54 featured English Electric Preston (Brill type) 22E bogies, while the electrical equipment included a pair of English Electric DK30B 40hp motors and Brush (English Electric/Dick Kerr DB1K3) controllers. They had glazed vestibules and garden-type seating in the lower saloon as well as on the top deck. They were regularly used on the Chepstow Road route where their high seating

Brush-built bogie car tram number 53 is seen when quite new at the town boundary terminus on Chepstow Road, which was about ½ mile from Royal Oak.

(The late Dave B Thomas collection)

capacity was particularly useful, and were considered to be very good crowd-clearers.

In February 1922 it was reported that bogie cars 51-54 were running well, but had received a certain amount of abuse from drivers as the brakes were powerful. This caused the trams to slide on the rails, resulting in wheel-flats which of course led to a rough and noisy ride until the wheels could be dealt with. When it was fairly new number 51 was decorated with working lights, to advertise an electricity exhibition at Stow Hill skating rink, which later became the Pavilion Theatre. For this role it was coupled to a 4-wheel tram as 51 had no track brakes. It thus remained the only covered top car to work on the Stow Hill route.

The last new trams for Newport followed in February 1922 and were numbered 55-58. These were 4-wheel tramcars constructed in Scotland by Hurst Nelson of Motherwell on English Electric Preston (Brill-type) 21E trucks. Electrical equipment included a pair of DK 29 30hp motors and Brush (English Electric/Dick, Kerr & Co DB1K3) controllers. In appearance they were similar to 51-54 but were of course much shorter. They also had a front entrance and rear exit layout. And so the total number of electric tramcars operated by Newport came to 58 which included the water cart 41.

Hurst Nelson tram number 57 at the Lysaght terminus on Corporation Road.

(The late Dave B Thomas collection)

What could work where

As these eight new trams (51-58) were all covered top, the clearance under the Chepstow Road railway bridge was increased. By 1922 there were six routes out of the town centre and only the Chepstow Road, Corporation Road and Alexandra Dock (via Pill) route could be worked by any tram. The table on the next page sets out which route the various types could normally be found running on by 1922.

Fleet Nos	Route
1-30	Caerleon Road, Chepstow Road, Corporation Road to Alexandra Docks;
31-40, 42-44	Stow Hill route;
45-50 (ex L C C)	Caerleon Road to Alexandra Docks;
51-58	Chepstow Road route and later the Corporation Road route.

From 1922, an effort was made to use the sixteen covered top cars as much as possible in the interests of passenger comfort. After many attempts over a period of fourteen years, in 1922 Sunday working was finally agreed. On 28 May 1922 trams began operating on Sundays for the first time between the hours of 14.00 and 22.00.

The overhead equipment

As mentioned earlier, construction of the overhead wire system was undertaken by W T Glover & Company, while Henley's Telegraph Works produced the necessary cables, which were laid in cable ducts by Callenders Cable and Construction Company. The original overhead was supported from 21ft high poles with galvanised steel span wires. Poles with bracket arms were used on the Stow Hill route. In 1913 a heavier gauge of trolley wire was introduced across much of the system. Overhead junctions were originally hand-operated, but by 1913 had become automated.

A horse-drawn tower wagon was acquired in 1903 but it was decided that a motor driven vehicle would be more economical so one of these was obtained in 1904. This vehicle was involved in a serious accident later that year when it ran out of control on a hill. It was repaired and ran for many more years. By 1916 a horse-drawn tower wagon was in use once again, and this was replaced in 1920 by a battery-driven example purchased from Ransomes, Simms and Jefferies registration DW 2066. The final tower wagon at the end of tram operation in 1937 was of Daimler manufacture.

Tram 42 is travelling along Risca Road towards the terminus in the mid-1930s. It has just passed St. John the Baptist church at the junction with Oakfield Road.

(R V C Richards courtesy Cardiff Transport Preservation Group collection)

Permanent way

All the tramway track was standard gauge of 4ft 8½in. The rails were laid on a concrete foundation, and either granite or wooden blocks were used between and on either side of the rails. At its peak the electric tramway in Newport consisted of 7.32 miles of double and interlaced track and 1.32 miles of single track. There was a section of interlaced track that ran between High Street and the junction with Commercial Street. This was known as a gauntlet section, and was controlled by signals at each end mounted fifteen feet above the ground. Lower red and upper green lights were controlled by a man positioned half way along the section.

There were four level crossings on the system; those on Cardiff Road and George Street were removed in the 1920s. The other two were on Commercial Road at Frederick Street, and Alexandra Road. The terminus at the dock gates consisted of a scissors crossing. The main facing points at Westgate Square, Shaftesbury Street and Clarence Place (four in all) were mechanically operated from 1912. All other points were changed by rods that were carried in each tram. Following complaints about

the condition of the track, a lot of repairs to track and foundations as well as track renewal was carried out in 1912/13. This continued after the First World War at considerable expense to the undertaking.

Changes and oddities

Tram number 16 received a Hurst Nelson 21E truck in 1921. 31 later received electro-pneumatic track brakes in place of its air brake, which meant it was no longer used on the Stow Hill route. 31 also received a Hurst Nelson 21E truck, but this was fitted with Metrovick electrical equipment which made car 31 more powerful than its contemporaries. Tram 43 was rebuilt with a vestibule in 1927 followed by numbers 38 and 49 by 1930.

Tram 34 was rebuilt as a closed top in April 1928 and with vestibule ends and trolley retriever. This cost a total of £320 and the tram now had a reputation for being noticeably slower. The air-brake from 34 was transferred to car number 31 which could then work the Stow Hill route once again. 34 was then put to work on the Caerleon Road route.

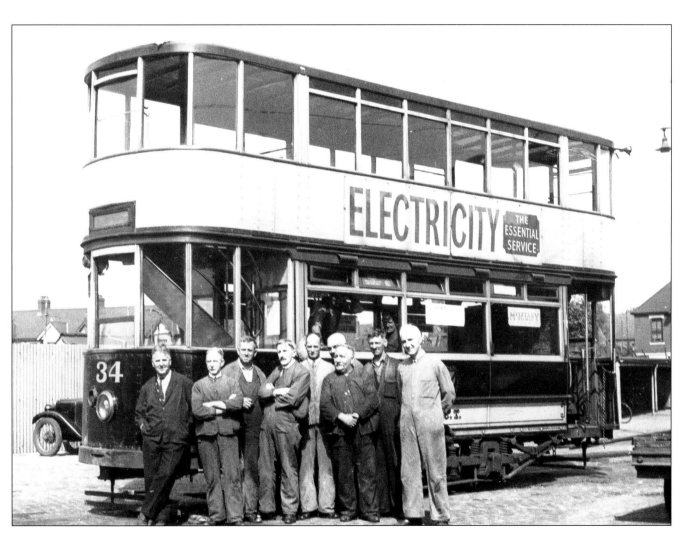

Now rebuilt with a closed top and vestibules, tram 34 poses in the depot yard with a group of maintenance staff in 1937. Tram services had now ended.

(Phil Hurford courtesy Cardiff Transport Preservation Group collection)

CHAPTER TWO
MOTOR BUSES AND THE END OF THE TRAMS

Existing motor bus services in Newport

Motor omnibuses were no strangers to Newport in the early 1920s, and had been operating in the Newport area since 1906. On 1 January that year, The Alexandra Docks and Railway Company started a motor bus service from the Commercial Road tram terminus in Pill, to the Pier Head on the dock estate. These were sometimes extended to the Great Western Railway station at High Street in the town centre. They were initially operated by a pair of fourteen-seat Milnes-Daimler buses but from 1908 were replaced by a Simms single-decker. When the Corporation's tram route was extended to the Dock Gates in 1917, the motor bus service confined itself to work entirely within the dock estate.

Other motor buses could be seen working up to the outskirts of Newport between 1913 and 1922, and were employed on services further afield. These included R W Robins Bus Service who plied between Cardiff and Newport from 1913 until 1919. He was succeeded in 1920 by G Vernon Jones of Castleton, who had begun operating a Newport to Cardiff motor bus service. Ironically this business passed to Cardiff City Tramways in April 1924. After the First World War, Usk Motor Service (W R Kendrick) of Usk began running four journeys per day from Usk to Caerleon commencing on 7 June 1919. At Caerleon the bus connected with trains to Newport, but on 6 December this service was extended from Station Approach, Caerleon, to Caerleon Road, Newport, to connect with the trams. At this point in time Newport Corporation continued to protect the revenue generated by the electric tramway, by refusing to allow motor buses to penetrate the Borough boundary. South Wales Commercial Motors Ltd began operating between Newport and Chepstow in April 1921. Lewis and James of Newbridge commenced trading as Western Valleys Omnibus Services in June 1921. They operated between Crumlin and Newport and soon after between Cwmfelinfach and Newport. In August 1921, W and H Barrett of Pontnewynydd commenced trading as Eastern Valley Motor Services with a service between Pontypool and Newport.

Progress with motor buses

On 31 July 1914, an Act of Parliament gave the Corporation powers to run motor buses within the Borough and also in St. Mellons Rural District. With the outbreak of the First World War, any plans to take up this opportunity were quietly placed on the back burner. In October 1923, Mr N J Young the General Manager recommended that consideration be given to introducing motor buses to two residential areas not currently served by trams. These were:

i)   Bridge Street to Edward VII Avenue, Clytha.
ii) Clarence Place to the Borough boundary on Christchurch Road.

A fifteen to twenty-minute frequency was proposed for each service, both of which involved some hilly terrain. The Council agreed to this, and the type of vehicle to be used would be determined after the Manager and Electrical Engineer had inspected what was on offer at the 1923 Commercial Motor Show at Olympia in London.

The Corporation's first motor buses

The first motor buses to be acquired by Newport Corporation were a batch of six Karrier CY single-deckers. Karrier Motors Limited was formed in 1920 in Huddersfield from what had up until then been Clayton and Company Huddersfield. They specialised in building petrol-driven vans, wagons and lorries, many of which would be destined for the municipal sector. They also built charabancs and some of their chassis would be completed as buses. They later built trolleybus chassis, and after getting into financial difficulties, Karrier was acquired by the Rootes Group in 1934.

The CY model was a chassis of normal-control layout that Karrier built between 1924 and 1927 primarily for completion as a public cleansing vehicle. The Newport examples numbered 1-6 were completed as twenty-seat buses with solid tyres, and were acquired at a cost of £817 16s each. They featured sprag gear due to the hilly nature of the route on which they were to be deployed, and this was fitted at an extra cost of £87 per bus. Bodywork would be provided by Short Brothers Limited of Rochester. Short Brothers was founded in 1908 and was involved in the manufacture of aircraft. The 1920s were a difficult period for the aircraft industry and so Short Bros diversified into the production of lightweight tram and bus bodies. They had roof-mounted number boxes at the front of the bus and side boards for the destination, and were equipped for one-man operation. It is thought that they had Dorman 4JU petrol engines when new, which were later replaced by Dorman 4JJL 30hp engines in the late 1920s. The solid tyres were replaced by pneumatic from about 1926.

The first of the new motor bus services commenced on 7 April 1924 and operated between Clarence Place and Christchurch Road where the terminus was situated at the junction with Gibbs Road. On the outbound run, the route deviated via Rodney Road, St. Vincent Road and Corporation Road, before following Caerleon Road. It then climbed Summerhill Avenue, Woodland Road, and then deviated along Crescent Road and Victoria Avenue onto Christchurch Road. The inbound route omitted Rodney Road.

3 (DW 3492) was one of the six Karrier CY motor buses with twenty-seat body built by Short Bros.

(The late Dave B Thomas collection courtesy Cardiff Transport Preservation Group collection)

This is 8 (DW 4452), one of the unpopular Karrier JHS models of 1925 with unusual-looking full-fronted bodywork by Vickers. It is seen just prior to delivery.

(The late Dave B Thomas collection)

The second of the planned services started operating on 12 April, and ran from Smith's wine merchants on Bridge Street to Edward VII Avenue. It took a route via Godfrey Road, Serpentine Road and Fields Road. On both of these services the driver collected the fare, issued tickets using a Bellpunch ticket machine and completed a full waybill. For these additional duties, and taking into consideration the hilly nature of the two services, the driver was rewarded with an extra 2/6d a week.

A third new service, this time from Clarence Place to Lliswerry commenced on 15 September 1924 and operated via Livingstone Place, Archibald Street, Balmoral Road and Somerton Road. With a frequency of 40 minutes, it initially operated afternoons and evenings only, with a full service on Saturdays. The terminus was near Lliswerry school on Nash Road, close to the Lliswerry Road/Nash Road junction, but was later extended along Lliswerry Road to Black Lane (renamed Moorland Avenue in 1938). This new route meant that five out of the six Karriers (1-6) were in service Monday to Friday, and all six were required on Saturday. Consequently, there were no spares in the event of a breakdown, so another two Karriers were purchased. These buses used the larger JHS forward-control chassis. They had thirty-seat forward-entrance full-fronted bodywork by Vickers Ltd of Crayford, Kent. Delivered in July 1925 as fleet numbers 7 and 8, number 7 had a Dorman 4JJ 32hp petrol engine while number 8 was powered by a Dorman 4JOR 45hp engine. Their rather angular box-like shape earned them the nickname "the bacon boxes", while during the warmer weather, the heat from the engine in the cabs earned them a further nickname "chip shops". These were not particularly popular buses.

On 31 July 1925, another Act of Parliament gave Newport Corporation powers to run motor buses up to three miles beyond the Borough boundary. This act did not however grant the permission that the Tramways Department had requested which was to run bus services to Abersychan, Crumlin and Abertillery. Nor did it provide for proposed excursion services to the likes of St. Brides, Peterstone, Symonds Yat and the Wye Valley.

On 1 August 1925, the original two services to Christchurch Road and Edward VII Avenue were joined up to form a through service, which was extended to Allt-yr-yn Avenue, Ridgeway, on 16 November. This extension was withdrawn from 22 August 1925 when a brand new service to Glasllwch Lane, High Cross commenced which ran from Bridge Street via St Marks Crescent and Allt-yr-yn Avenue. In March 1926 a rival operator Mr G Fisher was granted permission to run a motor bus service from Rodney Road to Goldcliff, a small village beyond Nash. However, on 22 May, operation of this was taken over by the Corporation. Further new services included one to the Angel Hotel, Caerleon, and another to New House at Nash. There was also a Wednesdays and Saturdays only service to Llanfrechfa and all three departed from Skinner Street in Newport town centre.

Further new buses were received in March 1926 numbered 9-13. These Karriers JHS models were very similar to 7 and 8, and also had Dorman 4JOR 45hp engines. They were followed in August by another three identical vehicles numbered 14-16.

Karriers 6 (DW 3495), 16 (DW 5082) and 3 (DW 3492) inside the depot in about 1930.

(Roy Marshall collection courtesy of The Omnibus Society)

In 1927 Karrier launched the Super Safety Six Wheel Coach and an example was loaned to Newport Corporation in July 1927, for use on a special service to the Royal Agricultural Show at Tredegar Park. Also delivered in time for this show were another pair of Karrier saloons, 17 and 18. This time they were smaller JKL models of the forward control layout with 42hp petrol engines and pneumatic tyres. They had Vickers twenty-six-seat bodies and were the first half-cab vehicles in the Newport fleet. Their destination box was attached to the underside of the canopy and a route board was mounted on the waist rail.

17 (DW 5586) is a twenty-six-seat Karrier JKL of 1927. One of a pair, they were the first half-cab motor buses in the fleet and the last Karriers purchased.

(The late Dave B Thomas collection)

Newport's first Leylands

In August 1927 the Transport Department received the first of many Leylands that would join the fleet before the Second World War. They were a pair of Lion LSC1 models with Leyland's own twenty-six-seat forward-entrance bodywork and were numbered 19 and 20. The Leyland Lion LSC1 was a passenger chassis introduced by Leyland in 1925 with a wheelbase of 14ft 6in, and went into production from 1926. It was joined in 1926 by the LSC3 which had a longer wheelbase of 16ft 5in and both were very successful. The Lion LSC series had a four-cylinder petrol engine of 43.5bhp and was available as a chassis, or like the Newport examples, complete with a Leyland body.

In September 1927 the Council considered a proposal to acquire the operations of Lewis and James plus those of Barratt's but no action was taken. In February 1928 the Transport Department agreed to purchase the services of Mr T Beavis who operated from the Handpost Hotel on Risca Road to Rogerstone, Machen and Cefn Mably. However, the Transport Department soon backed out of this agreement, due to certain conditions issued as a result of objections from Magor and St. Mellons Rural District Council.

In January 1928 the Glasllwch Lane motor bus service was withdrawn, with some journeys on the existing

Edward VII Avenue service extended to serve Glasllwch Lane once again. The same month a new service from Bridge Street to the Barracks on Barrack Hill off Malpas Road commenced with a thirty-minute frequency.

The first of many Leyland buses delivered to Newport, 19 (DW 5636) is a Lion LSC1 model new in 1927 with Leyland bodywork.

(The late Dave B Thomas collection, as restored by Wye Valley Studios, Caldicot)

Decline of the tramway

In 1925 there was a proposal to widen Malpas Road which would mean relaying the tramway at great expense. In 1927 the widening was given the go ahead but the cost of relaying the tramway was considered prohibitive. So the decision was made to replace the Malpas Road trams with a motor bus service. This materialised as a new cross town service linking Pillmawr Road, Malpas, and Cardiff Road, Maesglas, to a six-minute frequency.

Tram 36 at Lysaght's Institute terminus on Corporation Road in about 1934. The Institute building seen in the background was opened in 1928 providing facilities for staff at the nearby Orb steel works. In 2020 the restored building serves as a venue for events and functions.

(R V C Richards courtesy Cardiff Transport Preservation Group)

The Westgate Square to Malpas Road portion of the tram service from Stow Hill ceased to operate after Tuesday 31 January 1928 and marked the beginning of the gradual decline of Newport's electric tramway. The tram depot in Corporation Road then became the eastern terminus of the route from Stow Hill though by the end of the system in 1937 it had been cut back to the General Post Office in High Street.

The new replacement bus service began on 1 February 1928 and was provided by ten new Leyland Lion LSC3 saloons with thirty-two-seat Short Bros bodies. They were numbered 21-30 and were purchased at a cost of £1,342 each. These buses had a large roof-mounted route number box at the front, a destination box attached to the underside of the canopy and route boards mounted on the waist rail on each side of the bus.

22 (DW 5801), a Leyland Lion LSC3 of 1928 has a Short dual-door body. It was one of ten similar buses that gave up to eleven years' service with Newport.

(Roy Marshall collection courtesy of The Omnibus Society)

With the bus fleet now standing at thirty vehicles, a total of £6,500 was invested on upgrading the depot facilities for motor buses. Consideration was also given at this time to the future purchase of three-axle forty-seat motor buses.

The rest of the motor bus network was allocated route numbers in 1928 as follows.

Route no.	Areas served
1	Christchurch Road to Edward VII Avenue
2	Town Centre (Skinner Street) to Caerleon
3	Malpas to Maesglas
4	Town Centre (Skinner Street) to Lliswerry
5	Town Centre (Skinner Street) to Goldcliff
6	Town Centre (Bridge Street) to Barracks
7	Town Centre (Skinner Street) to Llanfrechfa

Construction of the Maesglas housing estate to the west of the town and off Cardiff Road was started in 1929 and building was still ongoing in 1935.

Further thoughts on trolleybuses

It was now 21 years since the idea of running trolleybuses was first considered. In 1908 it had been rejected but on 29 October 1929, the Council adopted a report that proposed to replace the Westgate Square to Chepstow Road tram service with trolleybuses. It was also proposed to extend this route right through to the Royal Oak Inn at the Chepstow Road/Christchurch Hill junction. On 4 June 1930 an Act of Parliament authorised the running of trolleybuses in Newport. However, by then it had been decided not to proceed with trolleybuses for the time being as the planned widening of Chepstow Road would not take place for another two years. It was predicted that trolleybuses would cause congestion to other road users when turning at Westgate Square in the town centre where Dock-bound passengers would need to transfer to another form of transport. It was therefore decided that motor buses would be ordered to replace the Chepstow Road tram service.

Newport's first double-deck buses

Sixteen Leyland Titan TD1 double-deck buses were ordered to replace trams on the Chepstow Road route. Fitted with forty-eight-seat Leyland bodies to lowbridge layout, costing £1,668 15s each, they were delivered between April and August 1930 as numbers 31-46. They had an unladen weight of around 5tons 14cwt and would be Newport's only lowbridge layout double-deckers.

The Leyland Titan double-deck chassis was first announced in late 1927 as one of two high-specification designs by G J Rackham, the other being the single-deck Tiger. The Titan TD1 would have an overall length of twenty-five feet, a wheelbase of 16ft 6in and feature a 6.8-litre 6-cylinder overhead valve petrol engine of 90hp. Other components included a 4-speed crash gearbox, all-round vacuum servo brakes and an underslung worm-drive rear axle. It could be offered as a complete package with a lowbridge forty-eight to fifty-one-seat Leyland body and open staircase. From 1929 this combination also became available with an enclosed staircase and completed to a highbridge layout, although some customers preferred to source their own bodybuilder.

The Chepstow Road bus service was allocated route number 8 and commenced running on 18 August 1930. It comprised a six minute frequency to Hawthorn Avenue and a twelve-minute frequency to the Royal Oak Inn below Christchurch. At the same time trams were withdrawn from the Chepstow Road to Pill (Docks) route resulting in the tram route from Corporation Road to the town centre being extended to the docks at Pill until the end of the system in 1937.

Leyland TD1 number 37 (DW 7160) is seen before delivery in 1930 with the four prominent side destination boards and piano front. These sixteen buses were the only examples of the lowbridge layout double-decker ever to be purchased by Newport.

(Roy Marshall collection courtesy of The Omnibus Society)

The first tram withdrawals

In 1930 seventeen of the original tramcars were taken out of service and subsequently scrapped. These were numbers 1-8, 12/4, 19-21, 25/8, 30 and Stow Hill car number 40. In 1931 tramcars 15 and 22 together with Stow Hill cars 32 and 35 all met a similar fate. This left thirty-six passenger carrying trams in service.

Until now buses had been painted dark maroon and cream, but in 1931 a bus appeared in an experimental blue and cream livery. Apparently the Corporation was not impressed, and the idea of any livery change was abandoned. From 1 August 1931 it became compulsory under the 1930 Road Traffic Act for any bus with more than twenty seats to have a conductor on board. This brought an abrupt end to one-man operation in Newport. In 1931 two of the original Karrier CY motor buses, numbers 4 and 6, were withdrawn from service and broken up by the Corporation. In January 1932 the

Tramways Committee considered the withdrawal of the Stow Hill service as this was currently returning a loss of £1,600. However, the cost of introducing a replacement bus service together with other factors, resulted in a temporary reprieve for this route.

In April 1932 the Transport Department received another four new buses. Numbers 47 and 48 were a pair of Leyland Titan TD2 double-deckers with forty-eight-seat Leyland bodies to normal height featuring, for the first time, nearside destination boxes. The TD2 model was a revision of the TD1 which first appeared in 1931 and, thanks to the 1930 Road Traffic Act, was built to an overall length of 26 feet. It had an up-rated engine and brakes and was superseded by the TD3 in 1933.

The other new buses were a pair of Leyland Lion LT5 saloons 49/50, fitted with Weymann thirty-two-seat rear-entrance bodies. They had the route number and destination blind displays built into the front roof dome.

47 (DW 7754) was one of the two all-Leyland-bodied TD2s built to highbridge layout. It is seen when new in 1932 and served Newport until 1949.

(Roy Marshall collection courtesy of The Omnibus Society)

They were the first of many bodies supplied by this coachbuilder up until 1948. The Leyland Lion LT1 chassis had replaced the LSC models in 1929, and the LT5 model first appeared in 1932. It had a Leyland T-type 4-cylinder petrol engine and a 4-speed sliding-mesh gearbox. It also had servo brakes and was succeeded by the LT5A model in 1933.

49 (DW 7756) a Leyland Lion LT5 of 1932 with a Weymann body. It was one of a pair, and the first Weymann bodies for Newport. The integral route number box in the front roof dome and also the folding doors should be noted. Both buses lasted until almost the end of World War Two and were sold for further service.

(Roy Marshall collection courtesy of The Omnibus Society)

The introduction of oil engines

In April 1933 the Transport Department received a Titan TD2 demonstrator on loan from Leyland Motors. Registered TJ 1514, it was fitted with a Leyland E43 oil engine and was only a month old. It was fitted with a forty-eight-seat Leyland highbridge body of very similar appearance to 47 and 48. In August it was purchased for

The former Leyland TD2 demonstrator TJ 1514 was purchased in September 1933 after a period on loan. It was the first oil engine vehicle in the fleet and was numbered 51.

(Roy Marshall collection courtesy of The Omnibus Society)

£1,400, and given fleet number 51. Its unladen weight was 5tons 17cwt. This vehicle proved so successful that it was decided to purchase a number of E43 oil engines to replace the petrol engines in the Leyland Titan TD1s, TD2s and Lion LT5s (see table below). It took over four years to complete the conversions.

Conversion date	TD1	TD2	LT5
8/33	33		
9/33	34		
10/33	39		
5/34	35		
6/35	42 44		
8/35	45 46		
11/35		47	
3/36		48	
6/36	31		
8/36	38		
12/36	32		
2/37	43		
6/37	37		
7/37	36 40 41		
10/37			49
11/37			50

Replacing the trams

On 26 June 1934 the Electricity and Tramways Committee met to discuss the question of future transport policy in Newport, and the replacement of the remaining tram routes. This required twenty-eight new vehicles and they had three options: trolleybuses, oil-engine motor buses or petrol engine motor buses, though the latter was not favoured. Capital expenditure was estimated as shown in the table:

28 trolleybuses	15 @ £1,850 each	
	13 @ £1,650 each	£49,200
Overhead equipment, cables, poles		£24,000
Conversion of car sheds		£1,000
	Total estimated cost	£74,200
Estimated net revenue per year		£11,153
28 oil-engined buses	15 @ £1,850 each	
	13 @ £1,650 each	£49,200
Conversion of car sheds		£500
	Total estimated cost	£49,700
Estimated net revenue per year		£11,079

Two routes were proposed: Corporation Road to Pill (Docks) and Caerleon Road to Stow Hill. The number of vehicles required was later adjusted to thirty, and so the total estimated costs rose to £78,698 and £52,050 respectively.

The final option to be considered was to convert just the Caerleon Road to Stow Hill route to trolleybus operation which would require just fourteen vehicles.

The Joint Report on Tramway Conversion dated October 1936 highlighted the following:

Advantages of the trolleybus:
 i)   Silent and smooth operation;
 ii) Rapid acceleration;
 iii) Absence of smoke and fumes;
 iv) Power under control of Corporation.

Disadvantages of the trolleybus:
 i)   It is route-bound;
 ii) The erection of standards and wires in streets.

Advantages given for the motor bus were that it could be used on any route with ease. This also rendered it available for football and dog-race traffic as well as shows and such like. There was a lot of support for trolleybuses, but their disadvantages were highlighted which led to their ultimate rejection.

From September 1934 service number 3 from Malpas to Maesglas was extended to Tredegar Park where a turning circle had been constructed. This extension only operated at certain times of the day between spring and autumn, to cater for visitors to the park.

In the years 1933/34, the last four Karrier CY motorbuses (1-3, 5) of 1924, and one of the two Karrier JHS motorbuses of 1925, number 7, were taken out of service for disposal. Number 7 had covered a total of 145,649 miles in seven years.

The joint board proposal

This rather interesting proposal came to light in February 1935, when the Electricity and Tramways Committee received a letter from the Western Welsh Omnibus Company. It suggested that as Newport Town Council had at that time decided for financial reasons not to proceed with the replacement of the remaining tramway system with motor buses that the Electricity and Tramways Committee meet representatives of Western Welsh to discuss the possibility of the latter taking over the running of passenger transport services in Newport.

The Committee agreed to such a meeting, but on 12 March 1935 the Town Council overruled this. A further letter was received from Western Welsh in June 1935, stating that it was not their intention to take over the tramway services, but to close down the tramway and replace them with bus services under the control of a joint board. No further action was taken.

For the first time Newport's population exceeded 100,000 in 1935.

A significant event in 1936 was the opening of the Kingsway by-pass between Cardiff Road and Town Bridge. Also that year route 4 to Lliswerry was combined with route 6 that ran to the Barracks.

The end of the trams

On 10 November 1936, the Town Council decided by 22 votes to 12 to abandon the remaining tram routes, and replace them with motor buses. As a result, thirty new Leyland buses were ordered for delivery in 1937. These would comprise sixteen Titan double-deckers and fourteen Tiger saloons, all with Weymann bodywork. In January 1937, the Electricity and Tramways Department was renamed the Electricity and Transport Department. One of the Leyland TD1s new in 1930 was elaborately decorated for the coronation of King George VI in May 1937.

A rather shabby tram number 10 at the Caerleon Road terminus towards the end of operations in 1937.

(The late E A Thomas collection)

The new buses were received between July and September 1937. The Leyland Titans were TD5 models with fifty-two-seat highbridge bodies and cost £1,380 10s each. They were numbered 66-81 and had an unladen weight of 6tons 13cwt. The Leyland TD5 model was introduced in 1937 as a development of the TD4. The TD4 had introduced vacuum/hydraulic braking and the option of the Leyland E102 8.6-litre oil engine. This engine became a standard feature of the TD5.

67 (BDW 20) was one of the sixteen Leyland TD5s new in 1937 with attractive 5-bay Weymann bodywork. They had Leyland oil engines.
(RHG Simpson from Cardiff Transport Preservation Group collection)

The Leyland Tigers were TS8 models numbered 52-65 and costing £1,331 each. Their thirty-three-seat Weymann bodies were to dual door layout, with a sliding door at the front and also behind the rear axle. They had an unladen weight of 5tons 9cwt. The Leyland Tiger TS1 design introduced in 1927 was closely related to the Titan. It had a 17ft 6in wheelbase, an overall length of 27ft 6in and incorporated a 6.8-litre petrol engine. There followed the TS2 model in 1928 and TS3 in 1930. Later models featured a bigger 7.6-litre engine, a new gearbox and rear axle, and triple-servo vacuum brakes. An oil-engine version was announced in 1933. The TS8 model was derived from the Titan TD4 and TD5 models and featured a Leyland 8.6-litre oil engine as standard and a 24V electrical system.

52 (BDW 5) was the first bus to carry the new green and cream livery and is seen in the depot yard when new. It was one of the fourteen Leyland Tiger TS8 saloons new in 1937 with Weymann bodies to dual-door layout.

(The late E A Thomas collection)

The new buses started to enter service from 30 August 1937 and introduced a new green and cream livery to the fleet. They replaced the trams on the Caerleon Road and Stow Hill routes that day when a new bus service, number 4 with a four-minute frequency was introduced. This ran between the Beaufort Road junction on Caerleon Road, via the town centre to the Fields Park Road junction on Risca Road at the Stow Hill end of the route.

The last tram to run from Caerleon Road was number 34, while the last on the Stow Hill section was number 38. This just left the Corporation Road to the Docks route, which made its final run on Sunday 5 September. Number 51 was the very last to operate from the Docks via the Town Centre. A large crowd had gathered outside The Westgate Hotel in Westgate Square to see number 51 depart at 10.50pm bound for the depot. The driving on this final and historic run was shared between former tramway inspector J Evans and two long-service drivers, F Weeks and J Bull. At the depot tram 51 was then stripped of all removable parts by souvenir hunters, who had packed the car on its last journey. However, the honour of the last tram to enter the depot after tram 51 fell to number 53 which came up from the Corporation Road terminus.

A large crowd has turned out for the occasion of the last tram 51 on 5 September 1937. This view shows tram 51 outside the Westgate Hotel having come up from the dock gates. It will work the 10.50pm journey to the depot.

(The late Dave B Thomas collection)

On Monday 6 September 1937 motor buses commenced operating route number 9, a new service that ran between Lysaght's works on Corporation Road and the Dock gates in Pill. As for the redundant tram system most of the trams were taken away to Cashmore's scrapyard for breaking up, while many of the traction poles remained in situ for many years as lamp posts. The tram lines were gradually lifted or covered over.

This is a notice from the South Wales Argus *informing readers that service 4 would be operated by motor buses from 30 August 1937.*

(The late Dave B Thomas collection)

Bogie tram 52 being taken away from the depot behind a Wynn's steam wagon, bound for the scrapyard of Matthews and Ward.

(Phil Hurford courtesy Cardiff Transport Preservation Group collection)

Former L C C tram 50 awaits its fate at Cashmore's yard in Newport.

(Cardiff Transport Preservation Group collection)

New in 1938, Leyland TS8 number 85 (BDW 924) lays over in "the pull-in", Dock Street in the 1950s, with the Central Market behind. The sliding entrance door is worthy of note.

(Roy Marshall collection courtesy of The Omnibus Society)

Town centre improvements

In January 1938 major changes occurred in Newport town centre when traffic lights were installed at Westgate Square. Skinner Street was then made one-way for traffic leaving the square. The one-way section of Dock Street between its junctions with High Street and Skinner Street was extended south to the junction with Corn Street. There were also numerous changes to bus stops and termini in the town centre in early 1938.

October 1938 saw the delivery of ten new Weymann-bodied Leyland buses. Numbers 82-86 were a further five Tiger TS8 model saloons, but this time they had thirty-six-seat forward-entrance bodies. Numbers 87-91 were TD5 models and virtually identical to the sixteen (66-81) delivered the previous year.

The remaining Karrier JHS motorbuses, number 8 of 1925, and the entire 1926 batch numbered 9-16 were taken out of service during 1937/38, and were all scrapped by the Corporation.

Fleet summary for January 1939		
Type	**Fleet numbers**	**Year new**
SALOONS		
Karrier JKL	17 18	1927
Leyland LSC1	19 20	1927
Leyland LSC3	21-30	1928
Leyland LT5	49 50	1932
Leyland TS8	52-65	1937
Leyland TS8	82-86	1938
		Total = 35
DOUBLE-DECKERS		
Leyland TD1	31-46	1930
Leyland TD2	47 48	1932
Leyland TD2	51	1933
Leyland TD5	66-81	1937
Leyland TD5	87-91	1938
		Total = 40
Fleet strength was seventy-five motor buses.		

This is 87 (BDW 926) one of the five Weymann-bodied Leyland TD5s delivered in 1938.

(RHG Simpson from the late Dave B Thomas collection)

CHAPTER THREE
WORLD WAR TWO AND THE AUSTERITY YEARS

The outbreak of war

Following the outbreak of war on 3 September 1939, there was a drastic curtailment of bus services within Newport owing to fuel restrictions. Frequencies were reduced on all routes, with priorities given to those that carried workmen. People were encouraged to walk and only use buses for longer journeys. They were also encouraged to travel at off-peak times if they could.

From August 1939 Leyland Tiger TS8s 52-61 were temporarily converted to ambulances for evacuation purposes by the National Defence Emergency. The cost of this was met by the Welsh Board of Health. Up until September 1940, buses had to stop running during air-raid warnings which caused a lot of disruption and loss of revenue. After this date buses could operate during these warnings, but only if anti-aircraft guns were not in use or bombs were not being dropped.

91 (BDW 930) in wartime drab livery in the late 1940s. This Leyland TD5 is seen on High Street on route 8 to Chepstow Road.

(Roy Marshall collection courtesy of The Omnibus Society)

By June 1940 there were around eighty members of uniformed traffic staff serving with the forces, and so General Manager Mr N J Young was given powers to reintroduce women conductors when the need arose as had been the case in the First World War. Initially twenty-eight (aged 21 to 23) were employed from February 1941, but more followed as the situation grew worse. In May 1941 it was announced that at the end of the war, the Cardiff to Newport service would be jointly operated. Sunday services were reduced even further from July 1941 and in 1942 the number of bus stops on each route was reduced, and the last departures from the town centre were brought forward to 10pm. From

October 1942 some vehicles were parked overnight away from Newport at Lodge Road, Caerleon, to reduce the risk of damage to the Corporation's buses during air raids. Each bus was in the care of a driver.

Sadly, the Borough Electrical and Transport Engineer Mr Arthur Nichols Moore died in post on 10 October 1943, aged 67, after more than thirty-one years' service. In January 1944, the Electricity and Transport Department was split into two separate departments. The General Manager Mr N J Young retired in May 1944 after an impressive thirty-two years as General Manager of the Electricity and Transport Department. He was succeeded by Mr Charles W Baroth, aged 44, who took over as General Manager, having previously held a post with the Birmingham and Midland Motor Omnibus Co Ltd (Midland Red).

Unfrozen buses

In April 1940 tenders were invited for the supply of fourteen buses and an order was placed for ten Leyland Titan double-deckers and four Leyland Tiger saloons. This was followed in March 1941 by a similar order, but this time there were five saloons in addition to the ten double-deckers. All received bodywork by Weymann, and the following month it was announced that an additional ten buses would be purchased at a cost of £26,336.

At the outbreak of war, production of buses had more or less stopped as manufacturing concentrated on the war effort. Newport was no longer able to standardise on Leyland, and had to take what it was offered. However, there were still large numbers of components in stock at some manufacturers. The government gave permission to use these parts, and for production to continue of "unfrozen" buses to exhaust these stocks. Examples of unfrozen double-deckers were AEC Regent, Bristol K5G and Leyland TD7, while saloons included the Bristol L5G, Dennis Lancet II and Leyland Tiger TS11.

The first buses received were four Weymann-bodied Leylands in January/February 1942, which were theoretically part of the 1940 order mentioned above. These were classed as "unfrozen" chassis as they had been built some time prior to 1942 and stored by the government. 92-94 were TD7s while 95 was a Tiger TS11 with a thirty-six-seat forward entrance body, and the only TS11 to be bodied by Weymann. Their Weymann bodies were built to the late 1930s outline, and were of all-metal construction, with no obvious wartime features. TD7s 92-4 were therefore very similar in appearance to the 1938 deliveries (87-91).

96 (DDW 24) was the very last TD7 and did not enter service until October 1942, very late for an unfrozen vehicle. This view was taken at the Clarence Place stop on Corporation Road opposite St. Vincent Road.

(The late Dave B Thomas collection)

The fifth bus was TD7 number 96 which did not arrive until October 1942, some considerable time after production of Utility buses had commenced. Its body was of composite construction with simplified wood fillet window glazing, and the upper deck front windows had hinged ventilators of "utility" specification.

All five vehicles were delivered in an overall grey livery and had leather upholstery from new. It is thought that a further Leyland TD7 was actually diverted elsewhere, becoming Devon General DL239 (HTA 302).

The two petrol-engined Karriers (17/8) together with Leyland Lions (19/20) were taken out of service on 30 September 1939 due to petrol rationing, and were sold for £50 each, for further use as lorries. These were followed on 30 November by Lions 21-30 which had clocked up between 362,000 and 425,000 miles in service with Newport.

Many of the Leyland Lions found further use during the war and 23 and 27 were eventually purchased by the War Department in 1941. The seats from many of these withdrawn buses were reused for the new wartime Utility buses.

What are Utility buses?

The Utility bus was a wartime specification vehicle to a design drawn up in 1941 and authorised by the Ministry of War Transport and Ministry of Supply. It was a low cost common-specification bus, available as a normal-height body seating thirty upstairs and twenty-six in the lower saloon, or as a lowbridge layout seating twenty-seven on the top deck and up to twenty-eight in the lower saloon. The body would be of composite wood-framed construction, with no interior lining and minimal features. To cut costs there were few shaped panels and opening windows, while steel was used widely in place of aluminium.

The Weymann bodies on Guy Arabs 97 and 98 were built on Metro-Cammell frames and were originally destined for Manchester Corporation for fitting on Daimler COG5 chassis. They were painted green with three cream bands. These Guys were obtained for £2,328 10s each and were to the Manchester's pre-war streamline design. The buses originally allocated to Newport as 97 and 98 were Guy Arabs with Park Royal bodies. However, these were diverted to London PTB in 1942 as G1/2 (GLF 651/2). Number 99 and all subsequent buses in the table had bodies to wartime utility specification.

Newport Corporation's Utility buses				
Fleet no.	Registration no.	Chassis	Body	Year
97/8	DDW 33/4	Guy Arab I 5LW	Weymann	1943
99	DDW 42	" 6LW	"	"
100	DDW 46	Daimler CWG5	Duple	"
101/2	DDW 60/1	Guy Arab II 5LW	Weymann	"
103	DDW 62	" 6LW	"	1944
104-6	DDW 64/6/9	" 5LW	"	"
107/8	DDW 71/2	" 5LW	"	"
109-12	DDW 83/110-2	" 6LW	"	"
113-6	DDW 113-6	" 5LW	Park Royal	"
117/8	DDW 117/8	" 6LW	"	1944/45
119-21	DDW 119-21	Daimler CWA6	"	1945
122/3	DDW 122/3	" CWD6	"	"
124-7	DDW 124-7	" "	Brush	"
128	DDW 128	" "	Duple	1946

All had seating to H30/26R layout.

98 (DDW 34) was one of a pair of Guy Arab I 5LWs with a Weymann body on Metro-Cammell frames to Manchester Corporation's streamline design. It is seen on High Street in July 1949.

(Roy Marshall collection courtesy of The Omnibus Society)

100 (DDW 46) was the only Daimler CWG5 in the Utility fleet, and was new in 1943, with a Duple body. Here it is at the "pull-in" in the mid-1950s.

(Cardiff Transport Preservation Group collection)

Seen out on Chepstow Road is 115 (DDW 115), a Guy Arab II 5LW with a Park Royal body new in 1944.

(Cardiff Transport Preservation Group collection)

The Daimler CWG5, 100, had an unladen weight of 7tons 7cwt and the complete bus cost £2,540. Guy Arab IIs 101-6 had an unladen weight of 8tons 1cwt. It is believed that 99, 106/7 had leather upholstery from new while 105 had moquette. The remaining Guys were fitted with wooden-slatted seats from new. 99-102 were painted in all-over grey, but in 1944, 106 and all vehicles from 110 onwards were painted green with two cream bands, with older vehicles in the fleet soon following suit. Daimlers 119-21 featured leather upholstered seats, improved interior lighting, aluminium panelling, domed roof panels, sliding window vents and metal handrails. This was a sign that wartime restrictions were being eased slightly. In August 1944 it was announced that the green and cream livery would be reintroduced to replace the wartime grey.

120 (DDW 120) was one of three Park Royal-bodied Daimler CWA6 buses new in 1945. After laying over, it would work to Alway estate on route 6.

(Roy Marshall collection courtesy of The Omnibus Society)

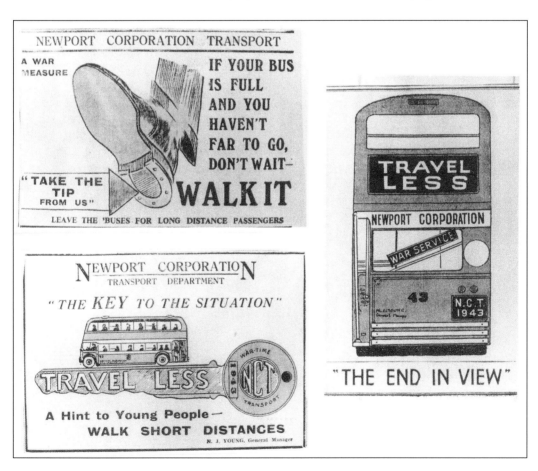

A selection of wartime notices that appeared in the local press during 1943.

(Ivor Homfray collection)

Network expands as war draws to a close

The 4A was a new cross-town service introduced from Monday 2 October 1944 and running from the top of St. Julian's Road to Bassaleg Road, Gaer Park. Its launch was accompanied by much pomp and ceremony, with the Mayor of Newport, the General Manager Charles Baroth and a number of councillors, undertaking the first journey to Gaer. Further improvements were implemented in December 1944 and the last bus departure time from the town centre was extended from 10 to 10.30pm, and frequencies on some services were improved. The new service was extended from Highfield Road to Gaer Park Avenue on 12 December 1947.

On Sunday 1 July 1945 Newport Corporation began to operate service 30 to Cardiff jointly with Cardiff Corporation. Cardiff had previously operated this alone from a stop on Cardiff Road at the Commercial Road junction, until it was suspended upon the outbreak of war in September 1939. As a joint operation its Newport terminus was moved to Bridge Street and, after just one month, Newport Corporation considered this service to be a success. Construction of the Alway housing estate commenced in 1945 and all roads were named after famous composers. The Gaer housing estate was also being built around this time, using the names of famous poets and writers for street names.

Summary of the buses withdrawn during the war years			
	1939	1944	1945
Karrier JKL	17 18		
Leyland Lion	19-30	49 50	
Leyland TD1		31-34	35 36 41
Leyland TS8			52 53 56 58 60 63

The Second World War officially came to an end on 2 September 1945 though staff shortages continued to be a problem and hampered further service development. Unlike the situation in 1918, the employment of female platform staff continued after the war ended. The order placed in March 1941 for fifteen new Leyland buses was eventually cancelled in February 1946.

Below is a summary of services in early 1946. It should be noted that six out of the thirteen routes are cross-town services.

Summary of services in 1946		
Route	Area served	Comments
1	Ridgeway Ave-Town Centre-Gibbs Rd or Christchurch	(a)
1A	Barracks-Town Centre-Gibbs Rd or Christchurch	(a)
2	Newport to Caerleon (The Common or Lodge)	
3	Malpas (Pillmawr Road)-Town Centre-Maesglas	(b)
4	Caerleon Road-Town Centre-Western Avenue	(c)
4A	St. Julian's Road-Town Centre-Bassaleg Road	
5	Newport to Goldcliff/New House	
6	Town Centre-Lliswerry-Alway Estate	
6A	Town Centre-Lliswerry-Nash Road	(d)
7	Newport-Caerleon-Ponthir-Llanfrechfa	
8	Town Centre-Chepstow Road	(e)
9	Corporation Road-Town Centre-Docks	
30	Newport-Castleton-St. Mellons-Cardiff	(f)

(a) Some journeys extend to Christchurch.
(b) Some journeys extended to Tredegar Park in summer months.
(c) Runs from Caerleon Road/Beaufort Road junction.
(d) To Nash Road junction with Traston Road.
(e) To Chepstow Road, Hawthorn Avenue or Royal Oak.
(f) Jointly run with Cardiff Corporation.

From June 1946, the number of standing passengers allowed was reduced to just five at all times. In August 1946 the General Manager and Engineer Charles W Baroth departed for a new post at Salford City Transport where he was credited with transforming a very rundown fleet into one of the finest in the north west. His place was taken by Mr Lee Wilkes who had previously held posts at Chester City Transport and before that at Darwen Corporation Transport.

In July 1946 the Goldcliff service was extended from Porton Corner to Whitson Court Farm. In December the Malpas terminus of service 3 was extended to the top of Whittle Drive. In order that double-deckers could be introduced in 1947, services 1 and 1A were re-routed via Godfrey Road and Serpentine Road, and joined up to the Alway Estate and Nash Road services as 6 and 6A respectively. The 3A would then follow as a new service to Brynglas Avenue in May 1947. Other new services in 1947 were one to Marshfield (Groes Corner) which was confusingly given the service number 30, as it followed the Cardiff service for part of its journey. Route 10 was a new service to West Nash Camp at the end of the year running via Corporation Road and Cromwell Road. In 1952 this was extended to serve the new Uskmouth Power Station, which had recently been commissioned.

Newport Corporation Transport made an application to the Traffic Commissioner to operate vehicles exceeding 7ft 6in wide on seven routes. It was reported in Notices & Proceedings No.268 of 1 October 1947 that permission had been granted for routes 3, 16, 17 and 22, but not for routes 8, 19 and 20. Towards the end of 1947 Newport Corporation was granted a twelve month permit to operate a bus service from Newport to the large Girling Works on Grange Road, Cwmbran. This was because the private operators, who had up until then operated this service, were suffering from a vehicle shortage. The Lucas/Girling factory manufactured automotive brakes and shock absorbers and was a major employer in the area. Operation by Newport ceased in 1950.

Post-war fleet renewal

The Daimler CV range had been introduced in 1946 and was made available with AEC, Daimler and Gardner (5LW or 6LW) engines, coupled to the usual fluid flywheel and pre-selector gearbox. Daimler was keen to promote the CVD6 with its own engine, but this option was discontinued in 1954, sometime after the CVA6, leaving the popular CVG5 and CVG6 models.

Eight smart fifty-six-seat Weymann-bodied Daimler CVG6s arrived in June and July 1947 and were built to peacetime specifications which would be welcomed by the travelling public. They were powered by Gardner 6LW engines which had proved themselves to be very rugged and reliable in the wartime Guy Arabs of 1943-45.

The Newport Daimlers were very early examples of the CVG6 model for the home market and were numbered 129-36, using registrations that had been booked by the Transport Department in 1944. They had an unladen weight of 7tons 15cwt. They were in the pre-war livery of green with two cream bands and a cream roof although for some reason 133 had a green roof when new. They also had painted radiators and became regular performers on service 30 to Cardiff in place of wartime Daimlers 119-21. On 19 January 1948, number 129 was damaged when it skidded on ice and overturned at Tredegar Park with forty-five passengers on board.

In 1945 Leyland announced the Titan PD1 model, a new and completely revised version of their Titan double-deck chassis featuring the 7.4 litre E181 engine. The PD1A was a slightly updated version of the PD1 and appeared in late 1946. It was 26ft long and 7ft 6in wide and Newport had a batch of nine on order for delivery in 1947. However, these were delayed, and this led to a temporary vehicle shortage in December 1947 as a result of which up to six coaches had to be hired from local private operators, to assist during peak periods.

The new Leyland PD1As were numbered 137-45 and started to arrive in late December and into January 1948, but due to problems with their springs, they did not enter service until March. Technically 137-40 were further buses from an outstanding order for Leyland double-deckers, placed by Newport in April 1940. The chassis had cost £1,658 10s each while the Weymann bodies were £2,152 11s 10d each. They were the last Weymann bodies to be purchased by Newport, and for some reason this batch of buses was destined to spend most of its working life at Newport on routes 8 and later 16. The new Daimlers and Leylands featured leather upholstery and had a rear-mounted chrome-finished bumper. The Daimlers had half-drop opening windows while the Leylands had sliding vents. 137/8/40/1 originally had chromed radiators while for some reason 139/42/4/5 had their radiators painted green. In June 1958 number 137 was rebuilt with rubber-mounted windows, while 142/4 were similarly dealt with in 1962 using parts from the Davies bodies on Daimlers 123-5.

132 (DDW132) was one of the eight Weymann-bodied Daimler CVG6s new in 1947. It is seen here at the bus pull-in in original condition.

(R H G Simpson from the late Dave B Thomas collection)

In 1947 Leyland TD1 number 43 was withdrawn together with the former Leyland TD2 demonstrator, number 51. Number 51 had clocked up around 441,400 miles in service at Newport. Three further TD1s, numbers 37/9, 40, were taken out of service in 1948.

Fleet summary for January 1948		
Type	**Fleet numbers**	**Year new**
SALOONS (total = 9)		
Leyland TS8	54 55 57 59 61 62 64 65	1937
Leyland TS11	95	1942
DOUBLE-DECKERS (total = 73)		
Leyland TD1	37-40 42 44-46	1930
Leyland TD5	66-81	1937
"	87-91	1938
Leyland TD7	92-4, 96	1942
Guy Arab I	97-99	1943
Daimler CWG5	100	"
Guy Arab II	101/2	"
"	103-117	1944
"	118	1945
Daimler CWA6	119-21	"
Daimler CWD6	122-7	"
"	128	1946
Daimler CVG6	129-36	1947
Fleet strength was 82 motor buses.		

Newport took advantage of relatively few demonstrators during its first forty years of motor bus operation. However, in 1949 GHP 259, a Daimler CVG6 with fifty-six-seat Northern Coachbuilders bodywork was inspected.

Newport's first bus station

To help relieve traffic congestion in the town centre, a major one-way traffic system was introduced on 22 August 1949. Part of the overall scheme was to reduce the number of buses waiting at roadside bus stops, and hence keep the traffic moving.

On the same day a new bus station for the sole use of Newport Corporation was opened. Known as the "pull-in", it was constructed at the northern end of Dock Street and opposite the Central Market. So from 22 August all NCT services operating from the east side of town and also from the Malpas Road direction were routed via the new bus station. The other nine NCT services continued to depart from the following stops.

Departure Point	Service
Baneswell Road	5 to Goldcliff
Baneswell Road	10 to West Nash Camp
Cambrian Road	1 to Christchurch Road
Cambrian Road	6 to Alway Estate
Cambrian Road	6A to Nash Road
High Street	3 to Malpas
High Street	4 to Beaufort Road
High Street	4A to St. Julian's Road
High Street	9 to Corporation Road

Fleet renewal was set to continue on a grand scale between 1948 and 1951 and consisted of thirty-six double-deckers, all with seating for fifty-six. In April 1947 tenders were invited for the supply of forty double-deckers and an order for just thirty-six was placed in the following July. This comprised twenty Guy Arab IIIs with Meadows engines and sixteen Leyland PD2/3 models.

Honesty boxes

In September 1949 honesty boxes were securely installed on twenty-four of Newport's buses. They were aimed at passengers who made short trips, and whom the conductor failed to reach in time. After just three weeks they were deemed to be relatively successful, although on the down side some passengers used them as used ticket bins and a number of attempts were made to steal the boxes.

Rugged and reliable buses

During the Second World War the Guy Arab had demonstrated itself to be a simple rugged and reliable chassis and consequently after the war there was much more interest in the products of Guy Motors. The Guy Arab III model appeared in 1946 and was essentially a peacetime version of the Arab II, a 7ft 6in wide and 26ft long chassis later available as 8ft wide. It was lighter than the Arab II and the radiator and bonnet were 4in lower, offering the driver better visibility of the kerbside. From 1950 the 27ft long Arab III was introduced. Power units were the usual Gardner 5LW or 6LW engine, but a third and fairly uncommon option was the Meadows 6DC-630, a 10.35-litre diesel which developed up to 130bhp. The standard gearbox for the Arab III was the 4-speed Guy constant-mesh, but a 4-speed Wilson pre-selector gearbox was specified by a number of municipal fleets including Newport.

The first sixteen buses saw the fleet numbering commence a new series starting from 1. The first to arrive were ten Guy Arab III models fitted with Meadows 6DC engines and Wilson pre-selector gearboxes. They were received between December 1948 and March 1949 as 7-16. Their bodies consisted of Park Royal framework that was completed by Guy Motors and each bus had an unladen weight of around 7tons 11cwt.

Number 7 was exhibited at the 1948 Commercial Motor Show. Unlike 8-16, it featured a rather small front destination aperture, which was replaced by a standard Newport-style indicator before entering service. Number 7 also had fluorescent lighting in the lower saloon.

The remaining six buses arrived in April 1949 and were Leyland Titan PD2/3s with Leyland bodies. The Leyland Titan PD2 was first introduced by Leyland Motors in 1947, as a development of the 1945 PD1 model. It was initially available as a 26ft chassis with 7ft 6in (PD2/1) and 8ft width options (PD2/3). Newport's PD2/3s were numbered 1-6 and were the first 8ft wide buses in the fleet with an unladen weight of 7tons 13cwt and each cost £3,843 9s. Due to their extra width they were initially confined to services 3, 4, 9 and 30.

8 (FDW 42) is seen in Greyfriars Road, Cardiff not long after entering service in 1949. The flat dash panel is below the windscreen and the radiator is flush with the front of the bus.

(S N J White courtesy Ivor Homfray collection)

5 (FDW 55), a Leyland PD2/3, was one of the first eight-feet wide buses in the fleet.

(John Jones collection)

Gardner-powered Guy Arab III 17 (FDW 841) is turning out of Harrow Road onto Corporation Road on its way back into town.

(Cardiff Transport Preservation Group collection)

32 (GDW 99) is seen on Cardiff Road returning from Maesglas and bound for Malpas.

(R H G Simpson from the Cardiff Transport Preservation Group collection)

A further twenty double-deckers arrived between January 1950 and April 1951 and consisted of another ten Guy Arab III models and ten Leyland PD2/3s, but there were a number of differences compared to the earlier deliveries. The Guys numbered 17-26, were to have been identical to 7-16, but it was decided to cancel the order for Meadows engines, and go for the 102bhp Gardner 6LW power unit. This meant that in order to accommodate the longer 6LW engine, 7-16 had a more pronounced dash panel below the windscreen and a slightly different offside wing. The bodies would however be the same and were built by Guy Motors on Park Royal frames.

The Leyland PD2/3s followed from September 1950 as 27-36, and their rather protracted delivery was not completed until April 1951. This was due to difficulties at the bodybuilder Bruce Coach Works of Cardiff. When ordered in July 1947, five were due to receive Welsh Metal Industries bodies and the remainder were built by Air Dispatch in Cardiff. In January 1948, it was decided that all ten would be completed by Bruce Coach Works, the successor to Air Dispatch (using East Lancs frames). Their chassis cost £1,726 10s each and the bodies came in at £2,135 each. The Leyland PD2/3s were regular performers on the Cardiff service 30 from 1949 until

about 1958 when newer Leyland double-deckers were taken into stock.

The last Leyland TD1s numbers 38, 42, 44-6 were withdrawn in 1949, together with Leyland TD2s 47 and 48. Taken out of service in 1951 were Leyland TD5 number 80 and TD7s 93-5. 44 and 80 became driver training vehicles in the ancillary fleet for a brief period. 95 was used as a cash office at the depot after all mechanical units had been removed. All the remaining pre-1937 vehicles had by now been replaced and the fleet had grown to 124 buses, its largest yet.

Rebuilding buses

With such a large number of new buses now in service, the transport department could turn its attention to the overhaul and rebuilding of older buses. The condition of the bodywork on many of the remaining pre-war buses was of concern, and so a major overhaul programme commenced in 1949 under the supervision of Engineering Superintendent Mr A H Thickens.

There follows a summary of all pre-utility vehicles rebuilt/overhauled during the period 1949 to 1954:

Pre-war buses		
Type	**Fleet number**	**Overhauled by**
Leyland Tiger TS8	54 55 59 62 64 65	Newport Corporation
Leyland Tiger TS8	57	H Richards & Co Ltd, Newport
Leyland Tiger TS8	61	D J Davies, Treforest
Leyland Titan TD5	67 68 69 72 74 78 80	Newport Corporation
Leyland Titan TD5	82	H Richards & Co Ltd, Newport
Leyland Titan TD5	66 70 71 73 75 76 77 79 81	D J Davies, Treforest
Leyland Titan TD7	92 93 96	H Richards & Co Ltd, Newport

Some of the dual-door TS8 saloons were converted to front-entrance only as follows: B34F (64), B35F (55 59 61) and B36F (54 57 62 65). Leyland TD5s 87 and 90 were re-seated to fifty-four-seaters in 1949 with the addition of two extra seats on the upper deck. Also 54 and 57 had their offside emergency exits moved to the rear of the bus. Leyland TD5s 67 and 69 had their upper deck seating increased to thirty in 1949.

To give some examples from the table above, Leyland TD5 number 77 was stopped on 24 July 1950 on the instruction of the Ministry of Transport. It had covered 304,528 miles since its last overhaul in 1942. 77 was sent to D J Davies who charged £725 to rebuild its Weymann body. It returned to Newport where it was repainted before entering service once more on 1 June 1951.

By comparison, Leyland Tiger TS7 number 65 was stopped on 22 October 1949 on the instruction of the Ministry of Transport. It had covered just 115,542 miles since its last overhaul in 1941. All body and cab pillars were found to be defective and so the bus was taken into Newport's own workshops on 28 July 1950 for a complete overhaul. This was completed on 29 November, and a Certificate of Fitness was issued on 26 January 1951.

The thirty-two "utility" buses were a little more complex as some were rebuilt or partially rebuilt, while others received new bodies, and in one case received a rebuilt body from an older bus.

Utility buses		
Type	**Fleet number**	**Overhauled by**
Guy Arab	99 103 104 105 108 110 111 113 117	Newport Corporation
Daimler CWG5	100	Newport Corporation
Daimler CWD6	126	Newport Corporation
Guy Arab	98 107 114	Bruce Coach Works, Cardiff
Guy Arab	112	H Richards & Co Ltd, Newport
Guy Arab	106	Weymann

110 received a new D J Davies 4-bay body incorporating Metal Sections parts, and was completed by Newport Corporation in February 1956. 106 was extensively damaged on the offside following a collision with a steam locomotive at Newport Docks, resulting in its return to Weymann to be rebuilt.

Park Royal-bodied Guy Arab II 113 (DDW 113) as rebuilt by Newport in 1955 with rubber-mounted glazing. It is seen in the Dock Street pull-in and is advertising a local brew.

(RHG Simpson from the late Dave B Thomas collection)

119 (DDW 119) received the Weymann body from 1937 Leyland TD5 79 in June 1955. This body had been rebuilt by D J Davies in 1951.

(John Jones collection)

121 (DDW 121) was the Daimler CWA6 utility re-bodied by D J Davies in 1954 as a thirty-two-seat saloon. It is seen in the depot yard. It has a sliding door and unusual nearside destination box.

(Cardiff Transport Preservation Group collection)

121 received a new D J Davies single-deck body to B32F layout in August 1954. This incorporated Metal Sections parts, and was the last half-cab saloon to be bodied by Davies. The bus had a chrome-plated radiator and was used for much of its subsequent life working on services for the Christian charity Toc H. Daimler CWD6s 123-5/7/8 had their old bodies removed in about 1952 and their chassis were overhauled.

In 1954 they received new D J Davies 5-bay bodies incorporating Metal Sections parts at a cost of £1,580 each. Much of the work was completed by Newport Corporation using interior parts from older buses. They entered service in the 1954 livery as shown in the photograph of 128.

Daimler CWD6 128 (DDW 128) in post-1954 livery with cream around lower saloon windows. The bus is seen on Corporation Road opposite St. Vincent Road, with its new D J Davies body dating from 1954.

(Cardiff Transport Preservation Group collection)

Weymann-bodied Leyland PD1A 137 (DDW 137) is seen on Corporation Road. It has been rebuilt with some rubber-mounted windows and sliding ventilators.

(Peter J Relf)

Other work carried out	
103-5/11/3	Rebuilt with rubber-mounted windows in 1954-6;
104/6	Fitted with Gardner 6LW engines in 1949;
102	Fitted with a Gardner 6LW engine in 1954;
103/9	Fitted with Gardner 5LW engines in 1951 and 1959 respectively.

A number of the unrebuilt Guy Arabs had their wooden slatted seats replaced by cushioned seats from withdrawn buses, but some kept wooden seats to the end of their life.

A second bus depot

By 1949 the Corporation had purchased an old aircraft hangar from the Air Ministry, and a plot of land in Kimberly Terrace off Malpas Road, on which to erect it for use as a bus depot. The work was completed and it was fitted out for use in early 1950.

In March 1950 the General Manager and Engineer Mr Lee Wilkes was forced to retire due to ill health. His place was taken in June by Mr R A Hawkins who had come from Burton-upon-Trent Corporation. Mr Hawkins was not in favour of the old hangar being used as a bus depot, and instead would like to have seen the existing depot yard roofed over. From January 1952 the hangar was let out to various tenants and was still believed to have been owned in 1972.

On 12 September 1950, the Town Council decided that advertisements would not reappear on Newport's buses for the time being. However, this method of income was re-instated following a press advert in May 1952.

In June 1952 advertisements started to re-appear on Newport's buses after a gap of about seven years. From now on these were applied in-house by the Corporation's own paint shop staff.

The bus that never was

Guy Motors completed one of its own bodies on an Arab III chassis (FD70599) for display at the 1950 Commercial Motor Show.

As it was not destined for a customer, Newport Corporation agreed that it could be exhibited in their livery with fleet number 37. After the show the bus was retained by Guy for experimental duties and eventually the body was removed and stored. The chassis continued in use as a slave to transport body parts from Park Royal in London to Guy's own bodyshop in Wolverhampton.

In 1952 East Kent placed an order for thirty Arab IV chassis and Guy Motors wished to exhibit one of these as a complete vehicle at the 1952 Motor Show. Chassis number FD71546 was then fitted with the stored "Newport" body from the 1950 Motor Show and repainted into East Kent colours. It was eventually delivered to East Kent as GFN 908 and unlike the other twenty-nine buses in the order, this one would never receive platform doors.

Service revisions

In 1951 revised timetables were introduced and there were a number of changes to existing services. The 3A which ran from the town centre to Brynglas Avenue was extended in the opposite direction to the Ridgeway. The 6 lost its town centre to Ridgeway section as a result and now only ran to Alway. Service 11 was a new route from the Dock Street pull-in, a relatively short distance to the new Civic Centre, while the 12 was a new one to Caerau Crescent via Bridge Street and Clytha Park Road. The 11 was not a success and a new service 11 commenced in October 1952 from the Dock Street pull-in to Masefield Vale on the new Gaer Estate. This ran out via Caerau Crescent and returned via Stow Hill.

Workmen had enjoyed the privilege of reduced fares for travel since the days of horse tram operation but this was finally withdrawn from January 1952. The withdrawal of through fares on cross-town services in October 1947 had proved to be very unpopular with passengers, so the Corporation eventually relented and they were re-instated in 1952.

An open top bus

Wartime Guy Arab 99 was rebuilt as an open-top bus in 1953 to celebrate the coronation of Queen Elizabeth II in June that year. It was painted cream with green mudguards and fitted with new leather upholstery. As such this popular vehicle put in another five years' service.

Converted to open-top layout for the coronation celebrations in 1953, wartime Guy Arab 99 (DDW 42) is seen at Tredegar Park.

The very unpopular saloon

In May 1953 Leyland TS8 number 62 of 1937, having been rebuilt, was placed in service as a standee bus with a centre doorway. It now featured twenty-six perimeter seats with standing room for twenty-four. Its chassis was lengthened and modified to cope with the increased weight. It was normally used on the Christchurch Road service and was not a popular vehicle with passengers, being nicknamed the "Cattle truck". The Transport Department received many complaints about number 62, and people living in the Christchurch Road area of Newport signed a petition against the use of this bus on the Christchurch and Gibbs Road route.

The vehicle was said to be uncomfortable and dangerous when on the move, and the wide doorway and cut-away steps were also a hazard. By October 1953 it had been re-seated to carry thirty passengers in a conventional manner, but the problem of the doorway and steps persisted.

In 1951/2 five Leyland Tiger TS8s were rebuilt to front-entrance. 82/3/5 became thirty-five-seaters while 84/6 became thirty-four-seaters.

In the years 1952/53 five buses were taken out of service for disposal. They were Leyland Tiger TS8 numbers 57 and 83, Leyland TD5 89 and Guy Arab utilities 97/8 of 1943. 57, 83 and 97 became driver training vehicles in the ancillary fleet.

Below is a summary of the buses withdrawn between 1946 and 1953.

	TD1	TD2	TD5	TD7	TS8	TS11	Arab I
1947	43	52					
1948	37 39 40						
1949	38 42 44 45 46						
1951			80	93 94		95	
1952					83		
1953			89		57		97 98

There were no withdrawals in 1946 and 1950. Leyland Tiger 95 became a cash office at the garage until scrapped in about 1955.

CHAPTER FOUR
FLEET RENEWAL AND STANDARDISATION

Dennis single-deckers

Between 1954 and 1957, Newport Corporation purchased a motley, but nonetheless interesting collection of fourteen Dennis saloons. Dennis were promoting fuel economy and Newport were obviously keen to give them a try. 1954 witnessed the arrival of six, comprising no less than three different models all with D J Davies bodywork.

Number 37 was a Dennis Lancet III J10C, a 30ft long, 8ft wide bus. 38 on the other hand was a Dennis Falcon L9 and the only one completed as a bus for the home market. Both were of forward-control layout with fully-fronted bodywork seating thirty-eight passengers. A forward entrance was installed serviced by a sliding door while the cabs also featured sliding doors, the first for the Corporation. 37 had an unladen weight of 6tons 15cwt, while 38 was 5tons 7cwt. When it entered service in January 1954, 37 was the last Lancet III completed for the home market and it had cost a total of £3,486.

The Dennis Lancet was a pre-war design that was first introduced in 1931, and was generally regarded more successful as a coach than a service bus. Originally offered with a petrol engine, a four-cylinder diesel was later made available as an option. The Lancet III variant appeared after World War Two and was fitted with a 7.58-litre Dennis 0.6 diesel of 100bhp.

The Dennis Falcon was introduced in the late 1930s when Dennis was rationalising its bus and coach range. It inherited the driveline of the old Ace and Mace chassis, and was a lightweight vehicle with a low frame. Engine options were usually the Gardner 4LK or Perkins P6 and it was available as either normal or forward control. However, Newport 38 had the same engine as the Lancet 37, and the complete bus was purchased for £3,295. With a choice of two lengths of wheelbase, most post-war Falcons were normal-control layout.

With its somewhat outdated looks, the Dennis Lancet III number 37 (JDW 89) lays over at the pull-in.

(Roy Marshall collection courtesy of The Omnibus Society)

The slightly smaller Dennis 38 (JDW 90) was a Falcon, also with a D J Davies body. It is working the semi-rural service to Goldcliff.

(R H G Simpson from the Cardiff Transport Preservation Group collection)

The underfloor engine saloon was now becoming very popular, and so Dennis developed a horizontal version of their 110bhp 7.6-litre 0.6 engine and fitted to a new chassis named the Dominant. This had an Eaton 2-speed rear axle and a Hobbs automatic gearbox. In 1952 a lighter model appeared as the Lancet UF chassis with a low driving position. It had a Dennis 5-speed overdrive gearbox and featured the Dennis double-reduction axle, which was supposed to improve the ride quality as well as reducing fuel consumption. It could be completed as a bus or coach and remained in production until 1961.

The last four Dennis saloons to arrive in 1954 were Lancet UF models. They were numbered 39-42 and had front-entrance D J Davies bodies with seating for forty-four and an unladen weight of 6tons 9cwt. They had platform doors and 39/41/2 had a roof-mounted destination box above the nearside third-bay window. The chassis cost £2,078 each (without tyres), while the bodies were £1,720 each. These were the only Lancet UFs to be operated by a municipal fleet, and Newport was the second largest operator of the type after East Kent.

39 (KDW 259) is one of the Dennis Lancet UF with D J Davies front-entrance bodywork. It is seen at the bodybuilders' premises prior to delivery.

(Eric Warrilow courtesy Ivor Homfray collection)

Whilst engaged on a private hire duty, Dennis Lancet UF 40 (KDW 260) is noted parked on Museum Avenue in Cardiff with 41 behind.

(Cardiff Transport Preservation Group collection)

39-42 entered service at the rate of one a month from July 1954 and 42 was exhibited at the 1954 Commercial Motor Show in October. 39-41 had identical amounts of body trim, 42 having additional polished strip on the body sides at wheel arch height. Over a period of time the trim on all four buses was gradually lost due to accident damage, repairs and repainting. All six Dennis saloons carried a revised livery of cream with green below the waist rail.

In August 1953 following the unsatisfactory performance of its Meadows engine, Guy Arab III number 13 was fitted with a Gardner 6LW power unit. The 6LW was a longer engine which resulted in the radiator being moved forward at least six inches giving the buses a pronounced "snout". All ten buses were so fitted and the last dealt with was number 8 in February 1956.

On 22 September 1954, the *South Wales Argus* reported that faced with a £14,000 deficit, the Transport Department had applied to increase fares, stating that only 40% of routes were profitable.

Outdated saloons

A further eight D J Davies-bodied Dennis Lancet UF saloons were delivered between January 1956 and February 1957. As with the earlier batch, they had Metal Sections body frames. Numbered 43-50, they were quite different in that they had forty-two-seat bodies with hinged cab doors and an open-platform rear entrance. This somewhat outdated layout was deemed preferable from the passenger's viewpoint, and allows the bus to pull up at a stop in the same manner as a double-decker. It did however leave Newport with a batch of buses that could not be used for one-man operation. Newport's Lancet UFs were the first and only underfloor engine saloons bodied by D J Davies. It is worth mentioning that these buses introduced route number displays to the left of the front destination aperture.

From 1954 the livery applied to rebuilt double-deckers was modified to include cream around the lower saloon windows. Deemed an improvement, this was then adopted as standard for new double-deckers too. A good example can be found on Daimler CWD6 128 on page 40.

The last Guys for Newport

Birmingham City Transport received the first of its own special Guy Arabs in 1950 that incorporated a "new look" bonnet dubbed "tin front". This dispensed with the traditional exposed radiator and front nearside wing. A pre-select gearbox and a Gardner 6LW engine were standard. Guy then modified the specification to make it more attractive to a broader customer base. A constant-mesh 4-speed gearbox was offered and a Gardner 5LW engine could be fitted if desired. In 1953 to further its appeal an exposed radiator version was made available.

Guy Arab III number 12 (FDW 46) now has a Gardner engine and features a revised front including the protruding radiator. It is seen on Corporation Road bound for Nash Road, Liswerry on a 6A.

(Peter J Relf)

45 (LDW 503), one of the rear-entrance Dennis Lancet UFs of 1957, in the bus station when fairly new. The small window in the nearside front panel was to help the driver judge the kerb.

(Ivor Homfray collection)

A good close-up view of the unusual rear entrance arrangement on Dennis Lancet UF number 48. There is a the substantial step on the platform.

(Cardiff Transport Preservation Group collection)

Newport was successfully operating a number of Guy Arab III models and so perhaps it was not surprising that they should try the Mark IV Arab. Four Guy Arab IV double-deckers were received in 1955/56 and these had 4-bay D J Davies bodies. They were numbered 146-9 and entered service between August 1955 and January 1956. For some reason 146 had seating for fifty-eight, while the other three seated fifty-nine passengers. They were powered by the Gardner 6LW engine coupled to 4-speed constant mesh gearboxes, and Newport went with the exposed radiator version. 146 (with one less seat) had an unladen weight of 8tons 3cwt, while the other three were slightly lighter at 7tons 19cwt. Like the Dennis saloons, these buses also featured route number displays to the left of the front destination display.

Davies-bodied Guy Arab IV 149 (LDW 512) has just crossed Newport Bridge over the River Usk and is now crossing the Old Green heading for the pull-in in Dock Street.

(John Jones collection)

Eighteen buses were withdrawn from service in 1954/55 as follows:

Leyland TS8	61/4/5, 84/6
Leyland TD5	66-9, 72/3/5/6/8/9
Leyland TD7	87, 92/6 (last of this type)

61, 65, 72 and 84 became driver training vehicles in the ancillary fleet for a short period. The Leyland TD5s had put in good service at Newport with most of them having achieved between 586,000 and 663,000 miles at withdrawal.

Longer motor buses?

In mid-1956 the law changed allowing 30ft double-deckers to be built on two axles, and soon afterwards a number of manufacturers announced a 30ft version of their existing chassis. However Newport was not tempted to go for a bigger bus and did not operate any 30ft long half-cab double-deckers.

A national fuel shortage caused by the Suez crisis had an impact on Newport Corporation which from December 1956 had to reduce service levels after 6.30pm and after 2.30pm on Sundays. They were able to maintain a normal weekday service from 5am to 6.30pm by adding creosote to the diesel to make it go further. As fuel prices had also risen, all fares were increased by 1d. Fuel rationing was discontinued on 1 April 1957, and three weeks later fares were returned to their earlier levels.

More Daimler CVG6s and the delivery saga

To accommodate the Gardner 6LW engine, the CVG6 required a bonnet six inches longer than other Daimler models. In 1950 the Birmingham City Transport "new look" front started to appear and eventually this became the standard configuration for the CVG6 chassis in 1956. From 1957 the electro-pneumatic operated Daimler Daimatic direct selection epicyclic gearbox became available. During July and August 1955 Transport Vehicles (Daimler) Ltd of Coventry lent Newport Corporation Daimler CVG6 demonstrator PHP 220. This bus had a sixty-one-seat NCME body and was painted in a maroon and cream livery and featured a "new look" bonnet. In June 1956 SDU 711 arrived on loan from the same source. This was the prototype low-height CVG6 demonstrator that was fitted with a 66-seat Willowbrook body and also featured platform doors. This bus was in a green and cream livery, and was used on the Cardiff service 30.

Newport went ahead and ordered a dozen Daimler CVG6 models with Daimler centrifugal clutches, for delivery in 1957 to be numbered 150-61. They had fifty-eight-seat bodies from D J Davies constructed as before with Metal Sections parts. The chassis for numbers 150/1 were delivered to D J Davies on 30 July 1956 with that

Here is the Willowbrook-bodied (CVG6 SDU) 711 in Cardiff bus station in 1956, while working the 30 service. This bus had platform doors fitted, something Newport never adopted for its front-engined double-deckers.

(G H Truran courtesy of The Omnibus Society)

for 152 following on 14 September. Davies had by now indicated that they would not be able to complete this order and so the balance of eleven bodies was switched to Longwell Green of Bristol. Davies constructed just one (150), which had a four-bay body completed by D J Davies staff in Newport Corporation's workshops. It featured seats from withdrawn Leyland TD5s and entered service in May 1957 with an unladen weight of 8tons 2cwt. The chassis for 151/2 were soon moved to Longwell Green at Bristol. During this period of uncertainty, the chassis for 153-6/8/60 were all delivered to NCT's depot by 22 October while the chassis for 157/9/61 went direct to Longwell Green on 3 December.

Longwell Green was a coachbuilder which can be traced back to the early part of the twentieth century, being founded by the Bence family. They were based at Longwell Green near Bristol and following World War Two, business really picked up with involvement in the rebuilding of existing buses as well as the construction of new bus bodies. They were also involved with lorries and vans and became masters in the use of fibreglass mouldings. Apart from Caerphilly UDC, all of the South Wales municipal fleets took Longwell Green bodies on either double or single-deck chassis. They also built bus shelters for Newport Corporation.

The Longwell Green buses (151-61) entered service between May and July 1957. These had sixty-one-seat five-bay bodies and all twelve had "new-look" fronts. Somewhat lighter than 150, they had an unladen weight of 7tons 17cwt, and each completed bus had cost £4,555. The Daimler CVG6s appeared on the Cardiff route when new, but after a while settled down to work on route 9 from Corporation Road to the docks. It was reported that these buses were rather slow, not being able to exceed 29mph.

An article in *Bus and Coach* dated January 1958 stated that Newport Corporation was suffering serious delays caused by congestion at Newport Bridge over the River Usk, which was now heavily used by lorries during the day and the Transporter Bridge further downstream offered little extra capacity. The Transport department was also suffering from staff recruitment and retention problems with a deficit of around fifty drivers at this time.

150 (NDW 601) the Davies-bodied Daimler CVG6 is seen in Cardiff bus station when quite new. The new look bonnet boasts an impressive Daimler scroll.

(R H G Simpson from the Cardiff Transport Preservation Group collection)

153 (NDW 604) is one of the Longwell Green-bodied Daimler CVG6s and is seen on Corporation Road in the summer of 1967.

(Cliff Essex)

Two services commenced in 1958 to serve new housing estates that were now being built on the outskirts of Newport. On 16 February route 12 began operating between the docks and Gainsborough Drive on the St. Julian's estate. It ran out via St. Julian's Avenue and Firbank Avenue, returning to the docks via Hove Avenue. This was followed on 1 June by a change to some route 8 journeys which previously only ran as far as Hawthorn Avenue, but now all journeys extended into the new Ringland estate, terminating at the junction of Ringland Circle and Hendre Farm Drive.

Twenty-one buses were withdrawn from service in period 1956/57.

Leyland TS8	54/5/9, 62, 82/5 (last of type)
Leyland TD5	70/4/7, 81/8, 90
Guy Arab I	99
Guy Arab II	107/9, 114/7/8
Daimler CWG5	100
Daimler CWA6	120
Daimler CWD6	122

Numbers 59, 85, 90 and 118 briefly spent periods as driver training vehicles in the ancillary fleet.

More PD2s and standardisation

By 1957 fleet renewal at Newport Corporation was well in hand, and there were around eighty-six post-war buses now in service. However, there had been very little effort to standardise on any one manufacturer which must have been something of a nightmare for the Engineering Department. That was all set to change in 1958 when Newport began receiving the first of what would become a fleet of forty Leyland Titan PD2/40 models, of which thirty-nine had virtually identical bodywork. They entered service between February 1958 and March 1961, and bodywork was supplied by Longwell Green.

The PD2 was one of the most successful front-engine bus chassis of all time until production finally ceased in 1969. It was initially produced with an exposed radiator and traditional bonnet. However, a full-width bonnet arrangement known as the "tin front" was introduced

The first of the Leyland PD2/40s was 162 (ODW 298), the odd one out with its Park Royal-style Longwell Green body. It is seen at the Hove Avenue terminus in the St. Julian's area of Newport.

(Cardiff Transport Preservation Group collection)

as an option in the early 1950s, and in 1960 a stylish glass-fibre bonnet assembly known as the "St. Helens bonnet" appeared, which could be found in the Cardiff Corporation fleet. Newport adopted the exposed radiator variant which had featured on its earlier PD2/3s.

The first PD2/40s were numbered 162-83 and all entered service between February and December 1958. 162 was the odd one out as its sixty-one-seat Longwell Green four-bay body was constructed on Park Royal frames, and was quite different in appearance to the thirty-nine that followed. These had 5-bay bodies and had a lower seating capacity of 58. 162 had an unladen weight of 7tons 16cwt while the remainder were 7tons 19cwt. The rear route number display on these buses was just above the rear platform window to allow for more advertising space. It was positioned much higher up on the Longwell Green-bodied Daimlers of 1957.

Some novel bus shelters were introduced during 1958. They were constructed from glass-fibre mouldings and manufactured by Longwell Green. This material offers the advantage of being corrosion-free, light and can be colour-impregnated. The 10ft long shelters were constructed from two 5ft panels, and each panel incorporated four glazed windows.

The 1959 intake of Leyland PD2/40s was represented by 184/5, 51-61, and all entered service between January 1959 and January 1960. They were identical to the 162-83 of 1958.

Twenty-five buses were withdrawn from service in period 1958-60.

Leyland TD5	91 (the last TD5)
Guy Arab II	101-6/8/10-13/5/6
Daimler CWA6	119
Daimler CWD6	126
Daimler CVG6	129-36 (entire 1947 batch)
Leyland PD1A	138

169 (PDW 14) in the later 50:50 livery is seen in Griffin Street with 184 for company. The buses are parked alongside Newport's Victorian indoor market on the right of the picture. The staff canteen is just out of sight on the left.

(Cardiff Transport Preservation Group collection)

181 (PDW 779) is another of the PD2/40s. It was one of four that entered service in December 1958, and is seen at the bus station on a very wet day in June 1970 with a Bristol RESL behind.

(David Beilby)

Leyland PD2s 57/8 and 61 (SDW 133/4/7) are having an outing to Porthcawl, probably in 1962.

(Cardiff Transport Preservation Group collection)

101/3/5, 110-2 and 138 became driver training vehicles in the ancillary fleet. 138 continued in this role for nearly four years. Daimler 119 on the other hand was accident damaged in 1957.

In the late 1950s a special service to St. Illtyd's College at Splott in Cardiff commenced. This was needed as there was no Catholic Grammar school for boys in Newport or Monmouthshire, and 40-50 pupils required transport. The school moved to a new building on Newport Road, Rumney in 1964 and the service continued until 1968 when it was promptly withdrawn.

On 29 February 1960 a new works service numbered 12 commenced running from Clarence Place via Corporation Road and Nash Road to the new Spencer steelworks out at Llanwern. On 9 April 1961 a second service 12 commenced to Llanwern, running via Chepstow Road.

Other works services in operation at this time included:
i) Town Centre to Westgate Ironworks in the Old Town Dock area.
ii) Alway Estate to Channel Dry Dock via Chepstow Road. The docks service now extended to the South Quay/ main lock.

The Corporation Road service 9 was extended at certain times to the British Aluminium Company (service 9B) at the southern end of Corporation Road, and also to Monsanto Chemicals (Traston Road).

From 4 December 1960 there was a major revision of services. They were intended to cater for the continuing development of new housing estates and to overcome the increasing traffic congestion in Newport. Three routes were split into separate east and west components. In 1960 some thought was given to converting the rear-entrance Dennis Lancet UFs to forward entrance but this idea was never progressed.

Summary of services in December 1960	
Route	Area served
1	Town Centre-Christchurch Road-Christchurch
2	Newport to Caerleon (The Common or Lodge)
3	Maesglas-Cardiff Road-Town Centre-Malpas
3A	Town Centre-Malpas Road-Brynglas Estate
4	Western Avenue-Risca Road-Stow Hill-Town Centre-Caerleon Road-St. Julian's Road-Gibbs Road
4A	Bassaleg Road-Stow Hill-Town Centre-Caerleon Road-Beaufort Road-St. Julian's Estate (Hove Avenue)
5	Newport-Nash-Goldcliff Newport-Nash-New House
6	Town Centre-Chepstow Road-Aberthaw Road-Alway Estate
6A	Town Centre-Nash Road (Traston Rd)
7	Newport-Caerleon-Ponthir-Llanfrechfa
8	Town Centre-Chepstow Road-Royal Oak-Ringland Estate (Llanwern Road)
9	Pill (Docks)-Town Centre-Corporation Road
10	Newport-West Nash Camp (Uskmouth)
11	Town Centre-Caerau Road-Masefield Avenue
12	Town Centre-Richard, Thomas & Baldwins Ltd. Llanwern
13	Town Centre-Ridgeway
14	Town Centre-Barracks
15	Town Centre-Lliswerry Road-Moorland Avenue
16	Town Centre-Chepstow Road-Ringwood Avenue-Ringland Estate (Hendre Farm Drive)
17	Town Centre-Caerleon Road-St. Julian's Estate (Merlin Crescent)
30	Newport-Castleton-Cardiff Newport-Castleton-Marshfield

Looking rather smart in the livery in which it entered service, 62 (UDW 835) is laying over in the bus station. Although not the original intention, Leyland PD2s 62-6 were the last new half-cabs for Newport.

(The late John Wiltshire collection)

The balance of the order for forty Leyland PD2/40 double-deckers was received in the first quarter of 1961. These were numbered 62-6 (UDW 835-9) and were identical to the earlier buses. They would be Newport's last front-engine double-deckers and no further new buses were received until 1966.

Four Daimler CWD6s (123-5/7) were withdrawn from service in 1961, together with Leyland PD1A number 140. The latter became a driver training vehicle in the ancillary fleet. The Passenger Transport Yearbook for 1961 stated that Newport Corporation Transport had 121 buses consisting of 106 double-deckers and fifteen saloons. The chassis comprised sixty Leyland, twenty-six Guy, twenty-one Daimler and fourteen Dennis.

In November 1962 an advert was placed in several transport publications plus the *Western Mail* inviting tenders for the supply of twelve all-metal omnibus bodies with sixty seats and suitable for mounting on 27ft x 8ft Leyland chassis. Delivery was for six in July/ August 1963 followed by six in July/August 1964 and the chassis was of course the Leyland PD2/40. Following on from this tender, omnibus body specification details were forwarded to Messrs M H Coachworks, Belfast; Duple Coachworks, London; East Lancs Coachbuilders, Blackburn; MCW, London; Park Royal-Roe, London; Strachan Coachbuilders, London; Longwell Green Coachbuilders, Bristol; Massey Brothers, Wigan and Atlas Contractors Ltd, Newport. From the above, five tenders shown in the table below were considered by Newport, these being from Massey, Longwell Green, Park Royal, M C W and Strachan.

Coachbuilder	Price per body
Massey	£2,655
Longwell Green	£2,950
Park Royal	£2,950
Metro-Cammell	£2,895
Strachan	£3,383

From these Massey gave the best quote and best delivery times and this tender was recommended. In January 1963 the Town Clerk wrote to the South Wales office of Leyland Motors in North Road, Cardiff, asking for the PD2 chassis order to be deferred because the General Manager, Mr Reg Hawkins, was at that time on sick leave pending early retirement on the grounds of ill health, and the council was in the process of appointing a new General Manager. He asked if the first six chassis could now be delivered to the bodybuilder at the end of July 1963 with the remaining six following in the middle part of 1964, or even later. These points were discussed at a Council Transport Committee meeting on 12 February 1963. Looking ahead, a further ten new double-deckers were also envisaged for 1966/67 delivery. However, by June 1963, it was thought that the outstanding order for twelve PD2s had been cancelled.

The new Bettws housing estate to the north of the town was built in the 1960s and the roads are named after rivers. An hourly service to this new estate which was outside the Borough boundary commenced on 1 April 1962, and was numbered 18. Dennis saloons 37 and 38 were frequently used on this service, but the frequency was soon increased and it became popular, and was converted to double-deck operation by late 1962. In 1965 it was split into anticlockwise and clockwise circulars 18A and 18C. An additional route to the expanding Ringland estate was the 19 which started in September 1963, and this terminated at the Llanwern Road roundabout. On the same date service 16 was extended along the full length of Hendre Farm Drive to the same terminus.

Around 1962 Bruce-bodied Leyland PD2s 29, 30, 33 and 34 plus Weymann-bodied PD1As 140/2 had an illuminated advertisement above the front destination indicator. They normally carried adverts for Newport County FC home game fixtures, the Monmouthshire Building Society or the Civil Defence Corps.

29 (GDW 96), one of the 1950 Leyland PD2/3s, arriving at Cardiff bus station. The top-lit advert panel on the front of the bus should be noted.

(R H G Simpson from the John Jones collection)

In 1963 seven of them, (137/9, 141-5), had their rear destination apertures painted over, leaving just the route number in use. By January 1963 the use of rear destination boxes on double-deckers had been eliminated and all had either been panelled over or painted out. Rear route number boxes were however retained. Leyland PD1As 142 and 144 were rebuilt with rubber-mounted windows at around this time. The last of the Daimler CWD6s (128) was withdrawn from service in May 1962 and became a uniform store at the garage until it was sold in 1965. In January 1963 two buses were withdrawn with accident damage. Leyland PD2/3 number 29 with a cracked chassis, and Dennis Lancet UF number 45 of 1956. The Lancet had been badly damaged in January 1963 after an accident with a coach at Goldcliff.

In February 1963, the General Manager and Engineer Mr Reg Hawkins retired due to ill health. His place was taken by Mr Frank Thorp who had previously been General Manager at Bury Corporation Transport. The

new George Street Bridge over the River Usk opened on 9 April 1964 but no bus services took advantage of this crossing for some years.

Demonstrators

Four demonstrator double-deckers were taken on loan between 1963 and 1965. Leyland's revolutionary new rear-engine double-deck chassis the Atlantean went into production in 1958 and soon attracted many orders. From 10 June 1963 Leyland Motors Ltd supplied Newport with SGD 669, which had an attractive seventy-eight-seat Alexander body. The bus had been built for Glasgow City Transport in January 1963 but was re-acquired by Leyland two months later for use as a demonstrator. It was used on routes 3, 4, 4A, 8 and 9.

Daimler introduced a rear engine double-deck chassis in 1960 which was christened the Fleetline. It initially featured a Daimler engine, and its drop-centre rear axle made it suitable for low-height bodywork with a

7000 HP was the prototype Daimler Fleetline that was on loan to Newport in June 1963. It is seen in a rather damp Cardiff bus station on service 30.

(Cardiff Transport Preservation Group collection)

normal seating layout. Transport Vehicles (Coventry) Ltd supplied the prototype on loan in June 1963. Registered 7000 HP it had a Weymann seventy-seven-seat body and was used on service 30. Production Fleetlines were fitted with Gardner engines and 565 CRW was loaned to Newport by Transport Vehicles (Coventry) Ltd in April and May 1965. Finally, in November 1965 Newport tried another Atlantean, Park Royal-bodied KTD 551C fitted with the more powerful 153bhp Leyland 0.680 engine. Both vehicles were used on a number of services.

In 1963/64 front-entrance Dennis Lancet UFs 39-42 lost their cream fronts and side waistbands upon overhaul. The condition of the Davies bodies on all the Dennis UF saloons was poor, and this was not helped by the excessive vibration from their engines when idling. Meanwhile the remaining rear-entrance examples 43, 46-50 now saw very little use. Commencing in 1964 the buses with Longwell Green bodies began to receive major body overhauls. This included fitting new 2-piece lower panels, new interior floors and new rear mudguards. PD2/40 166 was the prototype for this work and received brown Treadmaster flooring, while all other vehicles had green flooring. The Daimler CVG6s had a relatively easy life on the Docks services compared to the PD2/40s, and did not require such extensive rebuilds.

A new livery layout was proposed subject to council approval on 14 January 1964. It comprised the lower half

of the bus in green and the upper half in cream. Approval granted, early recipients were Daimler CVG6 159 and Leyland PD2/3 number 32. It was soon referred to as the 50:50 livery. However, a number of PD2s subsequently had partial repaints into the 1954 livery (with the 1959 coat of arms) in 1964/65, just to tidy them up until they were overhauled.

Six buses were taken out of service during 1964. These were Leyland PD1As (137/9/41/3/5). 137 and 143 went on to become driver training vehicles in the ancillary fleet. A surprising withdrawal was Dennis Lancet UF 44 in April 1964, which was only eight years old. It was converted into a mobile cash office, and fitted out with racks for the conductors' boxes. It was parked in Dock Street daily from 20 July 1964 for the benefit of platform staff whose duty did not commence at the depot. It had a revised unladen weight of 7tons 3cwt and continued in this role until December 1968. At some point it received the engine from withdrawn 45.

In 1965 the General Manager was quoted as saying that the average life of a bus in the Newport fleet was around seventeen years. It was also announced that the garage in Corporation Road would be rebuilt which took place in 1966/67. The last of the 1948 Leyland PD1As (142 and 144) were withdrawn in 1965, together with the first of the 1949 Guy Arab III double-deckers (14 and 16).

Positively gleaming, 6 (FDW 56) an all-Leyland PD2/3 of 1949 shows off its new 50:50 livery. It is seen at Malpas, having just turned left into Whittle Drive from Malpas Road.

(The late Dave B Thomas)

CHAPTER FIVE
REAR ENGINES AND ONE-MAN OPERATION

Enter the Atlanteans

Having trialled both Leyland Atlanteans and Daimler Fleetlines, Newport remained loyal to Leyland and consideration was given to the purchase of ten Atlanteans in February 1965. The Atlantean chassis were then ordered at a cost of £3,047 4s 10d each, five for December 1965 delivery with the remainder for delivery by July 1967, later amended to December 1967. The body chosen for the first five was Massey Bros who tendered a price of £3,675 each. However, in April 1965 Massey indicated that they could not meet the delivery date, and were relieved of the contract. The bodies for all ten would now be supplied by Walter Alexander of Falkirk at £3,885 each. These buses had sixteen more seats than a PD2/40 and therefore offered much needed extra capacity on the busy routes serving the new post war estates at Bettws, Ringland and St. Julians.

The first Atlantean 67 was delivered on 13 March 1966 with the remainder taking fleet numbers 68-71. They were the first new vehicles in the 50:50 cream and green livery, and were PDR1/1 MkII models with 4-speed, semi-automatic gearboxes. The MkII was introduced

from 1963 and featured an improved 9.6-litre Leyland 0.600 engine, a Self Changing Gears (SCG) fluid friction clutch and a three-piece rear engine bonnet. Their seventy-four-seat Alexander A-type bodies featured split windscreens, a stepped entrance and were similar in appearance to the demonstrator SGD 669 inspected in 1963. A new destination aperture layout was specified by the General Manager Mr Frank Thorp and was similar to that used at Bury Corporation where he had been Transport Manager since 1956. These buses were suitable for one-man operation should that be a requirement at a future date. They had an unladen weight of 8tons 9cwt.

These new buses entered service on 17 March, with 68-71 put to work on Bettws services 18A/C, while 67 spent the day working the 30 to Cardiff. However, the 30 did not see regular Atlantean operation until 1969.

By August 1966 around sixty-one buses were in the 50:50 green and cream livery, and it would appear that all the half-cabs delivered from 1949 onwards went on to gain the new livery at some stage with the exception of Leyland PD2 number 29 and many of the second

69 (EDW 69D) one of Newport's first Leyland Atlanteans in Upper Dock Street laying over on the Bettws 18A service.

(Roy Marshall collection courtesy of The Omnibus Society)

batch of Guy Arab IIIs (17-26). Towards the latter part of 1966 it was established that there were still forty-three buses that did not have flashing indicator lights. Of these, twenty-one were due for early disposal, but it was decided to install this feature on twenty-two buses. In the event it is thought that only seven vehicles were so treated.

One-man operation is back on the agenda

In 1965 Newport was still not in a position to contemplate the introduction of one-man operated buses, and legislation to permit the use of double-deckers in this mode had yet to be passed. There were still thirteen saloons on the fleet strength, although from a practical point of view, only four of these could be adapted for one-man operation.

At a Transport Committee meeting held on 26 May 1966, Mr Thorp reported that the fleet of Dennis single-deck buses was in very poor condition and that five should be scrapped immediately and a sixth reconditioned. Eight new single-deckers suitable for one-man operation should be ordered, to allow the remaining eight buses to be withdrawn. Three rear engine saloons were then demonstrated to the Transport Department in 1966 prior to an order being placed including, as might be expected, a Leyland Panther. Despite having never previously operated an AEC, a Willowbrook-bodied AEC Swift was put to service on route 17 to Merlin Crescent. The third vehicle was a fifty-seat Marshall-bodied Daimler Roadliner which featured a Cummins V6 engine.

Eight new single-deckers were ordered for delivery before April 1968 at a cost of £44,000 and this was approved by the Transport Committee on 23 June 1966. The tender specified a 30-33ft long chassis, 8ft wide with a front entrance body to seat a minimum of forty-four. Bizarrely Newport went ahead and ordered eight Bristol RESL6L saloons with forty-two-seat ECW bodywork at a cost of £6,460 each. The Bristol chassis was the third lowest tender at £3,130 each. Alexander bodywork was considered, but ECW was accepted with the lowest tender price of £3,330 each. Mr Thorp specified a modification to the chassis which incurred an additional cost of £53 per bus.

In March 1967 the remaining five Leyland Atlanteans from the original order for ten were delivered as 72-6, and were virtually identical to the first five. The only noticeable differences were a decorative aluminium strip between the wheel arches on each side of the bus, and the dividing line between the green and cream was slightly lower on the latest and all subsequent Atlanteans. In addition to the Bettws services 18A/C, they were regular performers on the 16 (Ringland Estate via Ringwood Avenue).

On 13 August 1967, the route network was considerably revised and there was some reduction in frequencies. This affected services to the Gaer and Ringland Estates for which some new circular routes were created. Spytty Road was opened which joined up Nash Road and Corporation Road. The 6A and 9 service then became circular services 9A/9C. There was also some consolidation of older routes and renumbering. Some changes in the Caerleon area occurred in February 1968.

It is worth mentioning at this point that in May 1967 the M4 motorway was opened, and from the east it followed an undulating route to the north of the town centre terminating at Tredegar Park. A major engineering project, this involved excavating a number of cuttings and constructing the twin-bore Brynglas tunnels. One positive outcome of this was to divert passing traffic from the centre of Newport and therefore helping to reduce congestion at peak times.

On a rather wet day, new Atlantean 74 (HDW 774E) waits at the pull-in bus station. There is an alloy decorative strip between the wheel arches.

(Cardiff Transport Preservation Group collection)

Newport's first Bristols

With the reliability of the Dennis saloons becoming even worse, the new single-deck Bristols were eagerly awaited. It is reported that on a number of occasions, no saloons were available for service. The new forty-two-seat Bristol RESLs were delivered in October and November 1967 as 101-8. They were fitted with Leyland 0.600 engines and had semi-automatic gearboxes and an unladen weight of 7tons. Their ECW bodies featured flat two-piece windscreens and had a large luggage rack over the nearside wheel arch. They had a wide front entrance/exit 4-piece door with two front and rear sections that could be opened and closed independently.

This was to a design submitted by General Manager Mr Thorp, and so impressed were ECW by this feature that they added it to their catalogue of optional extras. Their livery featured the 1959 coat of arms.

These were actually the first and last Bristol buses for Newport, and were the first Bristols for a Welsh municipal operator after this marque was made available on the open market once again in 1965. 102 was in service by 7 October and was noted heading for Marshfield. Once in service this batch of buses could be found on a wide variety of routes.

A further eight Leyland Atlanteans were received in February 1968 as 77-84, and as with earlier deliveries they had seventy-four-seat Alexander bodywork. However, these and all subsequent Atlanteans featured the larger Leyland 0.680 engine. This batch did not have the decorative alloy strip on the lower panels, but did have twin headlights from new. Due to late delivery their booked registrations JDW 877-84F had to be surrendered. When new this batch tended to operate the hilly routes 4, 4A and 4C to Gibbs Road/St. Julian's which took advantage of their more powerful engine.

108 (JDW 308F), one of the Bristol RESL saloons, is seen in original livery on Corporation Road. The bus garage is out of the picture to the right.

(Peter Keating)

81 (KDW 81F) is one of the eight Leyland Atlanteans delivered in early 1968 and is in original condition.

(Cardiff Transport Preservation Group collection)

New Bus Grant

The 25% New Bus Grant was introduced with the Transport Act of 1968 and came into effect from the autumn of that year. It is interesting to note that it was introduced by the Labour government at that time, and its main aim was to do away with conductors' jobs. Not too long before this Act, double-deckers without conductors were not permitted. To qualify for the grant, buses had to be built to very specific dimensions and configurations, and overnight, this spelt the end for the traditional front-engine double-deck designs.

Possibly even more curious politically was that from November 1971, the Bus Grant was increased to 50% by the then Conservative government and continued as such until 31 August 1980. To conclude, the Bus Grant was then reduced as follows:

40%	from 1 September 1980
30%	from 1 April 1981
20%	from 1 April 1982
10%	from 1 April 1983
nil	from 1 April 1984

A proposed fleet replacement programme announced in 1968 makes for interesting reading. What eventually happened in reality was very different from this.

New vehicles			For disposal		
Date	Quantity	Type	Quantity	Fleet numbers	Type
Jan 1969	9	Leyland Atlantean	15	1-6, 27/8/30-6	Leyland PD2
Jan 1970	7	Leyland Atlantean	7	152/3/5/8-61	Daimler CVG6
Jan 1971	9	Double-deckers	9	146-9	Guy Arab IV
				150/1/4/6/7	Daimler CVG6
Jan 1972	5	Double-deckers	5	181-5	Leyland PD2
Jan 1973	7	Double-deckers	7	162-8	Leyland PD2
Jan 1974	6	Double-deckers	6	169-74	Leyland PD2
Jan 1975	6	Double-deckers	6	175-80	Leyland PD2
Jan 1976	6	Double-deckers	6	51-6	Leyland PD2
Jan 1977	6	Double-deckers	6	57-62	Leyland PD2
Jan 1978	4	Double-deckers	4	63-6	Leyland PD2

36 (GDW 103) was one of the Bruce-bodied Leyland PD2/3 of 1951 and scheduled for disposal. In this photograph it had just crossed Newport Bridge late on a summer afternoon in 1967.

(Cliff Essex)

In 1966 a trial was carried out with a radio system that provided a link between the Chief Inspector, town centre inspectors and the Depot Traffic Office. It consisted of a base station and four mobile units all linked by a phone line which was quite novel for its time. The trial proved successful and a further four mobile units were purchased in December 1968. Upon repaint in October 1968, it is thought that Daimler CVG6 158 was the last bus in the old livery.

The following buses were withdrawn in the years 1966 to 1968.

	1966	1967	1968
Daimler CWA6	121		
Guy Arab III	12 15	7 19 20 21-3 25	8-11 13 17 18 24 26
Dennis saloons	40 42 43 46-8 50	37-9 41 49	
Leyland PD2			2 4 27 28 30 31 33 35 36

In the table above 121 was the wartime Daimler re-bodied as a saloon in 1954. It had seen little use after June 1966 but did manage the odd trip to Marshfield on the 30. It was delicensed in December and sold for scrap. Lancets 42, 43, 46-8 went straight for scrap. Guy Arab III 26 was an accident victim, while Leyland PD2 number 2 became a driver training vehicle in the ancillary fleet.

The next batch of Leyland Atlanteans, nine in total, arrived in January and February 1969 numbered 85-93. This time they were PDR1A/1 models which featured the rationalised pneumocyclic gearbox. The chassis were £3,317 each while the bodies cost £3,990 each. They were originally allocated registrations NDW 85-93G, but these were cancelled. Their nearside destination screens were fitted within the front nearside lower deck window, and this featured on all subsequent Atlantean deliveries. In addition to existing Atlantean duties these buses also worked routes 3, 6 and 9.

Atlanteans on the 30

The withdrawal of the St. Illtyd's Catholic school service in Cardiff from the summer of 1968 caused additional loading issues on the Cardiff service 30, which was still worked by fifty-eight-seat Leyland PD2/40s. The transport department was eventually persuaded that higher capacity buses should be used, and the route was duly converted to Leyland Atlantean operation by early 1969.

One-man operation returns to Newport

Newport had been forced to abandon its early attempts at one-man operation in 1930 due to new legislation at that time. Finally, on 27 April 1969, after 39 years, and by agreement with the TGWU, one-man operation commenced on some of Newport's quieter services. This was initially with two crew for both staff and public to get accustomed. The eight Bristol RESLs were put to work as such on routes 1, 3A, 11, 13, 14, 15 and 17. They had their nearside destination blinds set to PAY AS YOU ENTER and their rear route number display fell out of use. Their cab doors were fitted with a mounting for an Ultimate ticket machine together with a cash storage facility.

In early 1969 Bruce-bodied Leyland PD2 31 became the new cash office in the bus station, replacing Lancet UF number 44. Its lower deck was racked out as per Dennis 44, but its upper deck became a crew rest room. In January 1970 a further seven Leyland Atlanteans entered service numbered 94-100 and were identical to the nine delivered the previous year. They cost £7,665 each.

In very wet conditions, 86 (MDW 386G) is at the Dock Street pull-in in June 1970. This view gives the reader a chance to compare the detail differences between 86 and earlier Atlantean 67 behind it.

(David Beilby)

Interesting demonstrators

In 1969 Metro-Cammell-Weymann (MCW) announced that they had entered into an agreement with Swedish vehicle builder Scania to build a rear-engine single-deck citybus for the British market. It was christened the Metro-Scania and was a fairly modern looking vehicle of integral construction. The running units were shipped over from Sweden and the complete bus was assembled in Birmingham. It was particularly noted for its impressive acceleration and innovative safety features.

During June and July 1970 Newport took a demonstrator on loan which was evaluated on a number of routes in the town including the 1 to Christchurch and 3 to Brynglas. It made quite an impression during its visit, and was equipped for one-man operation with a similar set up for the Ultimate ticket machine as found on the eight Bristol saloons. Later in the year another rear engine single-deck vehicle was inspected, this time a Seddon RU model featuring a Gardner engine and fitted with a forty-five-seat dual-door Pennine body.

Also on that very wet day in June 1970, the Metro-Scania demonstrator VWD 452H is seen in Cambrian Road in the town centre. It is on its way to Brynglas.

(David Beilby)

Mr Thorp, the General Manager, had proposed that a one-man operated flat-fare system be introduced across the entire network at Newport; and this was accepted by the council at a meeting in October 1970. The scheme would be introduced as soon as possible and there would also be a significant investment in new vehicles. Atlantean 100 was fitted with an Autofare system in November 1970. Manufactured by Bellpunch, this incorporated a cash vault for fare collection. This proved successful and the decision was made to use this method with the roll-out of the flat-fare system. To bring them in line with the rest of the one-man fleet, the eight Bristol RESLs were fitted with this system, which involved the removal of the cab doors which were never re-instated.

In November 1970 it was reported that there had been a 20% increase in the cost of the sixteen Leyland Atlantean chassis on order. The chassis of the nine buses due for delivery in 1970 would therefore rise in price from £3,650 to £4,363 and would also be delayed. At this point the seven outstanding chassis were cancelled. The batch of nine Alexander-bodied Atlanteans eventually arrived and entered service in April and May 1971 as 10-8. They featured reversing lights and upper-deck periscopes from new. This brought the total number of Leyland Atlanteans in the fleet to forty-three. The price of each body had also risen from £4,714.83 to £5,710 due to the dramatic increase in the cost of certain materials like steel and hardwood. 10-8 featured a new style of front dash panel with a revised fibreglass moulding which was retrospectively fitted to all earlier Atlanteans in due course.

Decimalisation

On 15 February 1971, the pound sterling was decimalised and the whole country switched from using pounds, shillings and pence to a new system of pounds and pence with 100 pence to the pound. All businesses would have to adjust including Newport Corporation Transport and its customers. However, this was not too much upheaval as on 28 February Newport introduced its flat-fare system to most crew-operated routes, and the fares charged were 2p, 3p or 4p. Services 7, 12, 30 and 31 were not included at this stage. On 30 June 1971 twenty-five buses had been fitted with Autofare equipment which enabled routes 2, 6, 8, 16, 18, 19 and 30 to be converted to one-man operation.

All the earlier Atlanteans (67-100) were converted to one-man operation and had Autofare ticket and fare collection equipment fitted, as well as upper-deck

16 (TDW 316J) is one of the final batch of Atlanteans that entered service in May 1971. It is seen on the perimeter of Cardiff bus station on bright and sunny 8 December 1973.

(John Jones)

periscopes and reversing lights. When they operated in one-man mode, they would have their nearside destination blinds set to PAY AS YOU ENTER. In February 1971 it cost 9p to travel by service 30 from Cardiff to Newport, while a return would set you back 16p. The Transport Department was in the news for a good reason this time, as they appointed their first female bus driver which in 1971 was still quite unusual in the UK. By the end of the year, all the Leyland Atlanteans had their rear route number boxes painted over.

Largest order for new buses

The largest single order for new buses ever to be placed by Newport Corporation Transport was for forty-four MCW Metro-Scania single-deckers, to be delivered by the end of 1971. This order created a great deal of interest in the bus industry as the Metro-Scania was a new model incorporating a large number of non-British components. This order was quite controversial locally, and five manufacturers tendered for it, three of them being British. Two of these were unable to meet the required delivery date while the third was not considered capable of producing a vehicle to the required standards. The Metro-Scania cost more to purchase, but it was hoped this would soon be offset by an increase in reliability and reduction in maintenance costs.

The new Metro Scanias would be numbered 19-62, with 19-46 obtained in the 1971/72 financial year, and 47-62 now falling into the 1972/73 financial year. Their MCW dual-door bodies had forty seats with standing for twenty-two passengers. They were BR111MH models powered by the Scania D11 CO1 diesel of 11 litres coupled to a Scania HR501 2-speed fully automatic gearbox installed in a specially designed sound insulated engine compartment. They also featured power steering and air suspension and were thought to be the first examples of the shorter 32ft 10in model. They also introduced a new livery of cream with a green roof and skirt. Mechanically the bus was well engineered, but spare parts were expensive and often not easy to obtain, and it was heavy on fuel. Only eight of the new Metro-Scanias had arrived by the end of 1971 and 19 and 20 were used for driver familiarisation in December. Numbers 19-31 entered service in January 1972 and could initially be found on routes 2, 3, 4A, 4C, 6 and 11, and all forty-four buses were in service by July. 19-46 ended up costing £10,377.82 each while the remainder were £10,403.42 each. The Metro-Scanias were very popular with drivers and must have made most of the existing fleet seem quite basic by comparison. It was reported that the General Manager Mr Thorp had nothing but praise for these new vehicles, and also for the service that the Transport Department received from Metro-Cammell Weymann Ltd.

Metro-Scania 57 (YDW 757K) is seen on the High Street in June 1974. It is about to depart for Ringland on service 16. Just visible on the right of the picture is the Greyhound public house which was still in existence in 2021.

(Andrew Wiltshire collection)

The following buses were withdrawn in the years 1969 to 1971.

	1969	1970	1971
Leyland PD2	1 3 5 6 32 34		
Guy Arab IV	146	147	148 149
Daimler CVG6	159	150-3 155-8 160	154 161

Leyland PD2/3 number 5 became a driver training vehicle in the ancillary fleet and had an orange band added below the lower deck windows. Twenty-four Leyland PD2/40s were offered for sale in December 1971 and would be available from January 1972, once they had been released from service by the new Metro-Scania saloons.

More service revisions

On 26 March 1972 one-man operation was extended to all other services apart from the 7 to Llanfrechfa and 31 to Marshfield. There were also major alterations to routes 4, 5, 5A, 9A, 9C and 19 while routes 1, 3A, 4A, 4C and 11 were discontinued. Following its revision, the 19 was the first service to run over the George Street Bridge which had been open for eight years. Parts of 4A and 4C were renumbered 11A and 11C. Routes 4 and 11 would be the last routes regularly operated by the handful of remaining PD2s. However, these new routes were created:
i) 1A via Summerhill Avenue to Gibbs Road or Christchurch.
ii) 1C via St. Julians Road to Gibbs Road or Christchurch.

What was thought to be the first renumbering ever of vehicles in the Newport fleet took place in June 1972 when four of the Longwell Green bodied Leyland PD2s were renumbered to make way for the new Metro-Scania saloons as follows:

From	To
57 (SDW 133)	7
61 (SDW 137)	1
62 (UDW 835)	2
63 (UDW 836)	3

The arrival of the Metro-Scanias resulted in the withdrawal of thirty-three of the forty Leyland PD2/40s that were new between 1958 and 1961. See below.

Year	Vehicles withdrawn
1971	60 171/2/9 180-3/5
1972	1-3/7 51-6/8/9 64-6 162/5-8 170/3/4/6 184
1973	169

In March 1970 local Newport coach operator A B Smith acquired the Newport-St. Brides-Cardiff service from Red & White followed on 4 November 1972 by service 31 to Marshfield surrendered by Newport.

Smith then combined this with their Newport-St. Brides service to form a circular route, travelling out via Marshfield and returning via St. Brides, or vice versa and abandoning the Cardiff portion at the same time.

In January 1972 Atlantean 84 received the revised style of front dash as found on the final batch 10-8. Others would soon follow while by March Bristol RESL 101 had received the Metro-Scania style of livery. Four Atlanteans (72-4/7) were occasionally used as driver-training buses during 1972.

Nine Leyland PD2s were offered for sale by tender in September 1972 and the table below gives details of the vehicles and the condition they were in which makes interesting reading.

Vehicles	Certificate of fitness	Remarks
FDW 52/5	None	Driveable, some body damage
56 (PDW 997)	None	Runner
7 (SDW 133)	None	Engine fault
58 (SDW 134)	None	No engine, faulty differential
1 (SDW 137)	Until 3/73	Runner
2 (UDW 835)	Until 11/72	Runner
3 (UDW 836)	Until 4/74	Runner
165 (ODW 301)	Until 12/74	Runner

All passed to dealer Lister, Bolton for £1,075. FDW 52/5 were latterly driver-training buses. PD2s 2, 3 and 165 were sold for further service.

Another controversial order

Following the initial success of the Metro-Scania saloon Metro-Cammell-Weymann (MCW) announced that they would be building a double-deck version which created considerable interest in the UK bus industry. Christened the Metropolitan, even before a vehicle was completed MCW received a number of orders. In April 1973 Newport ordered ten Metropolitans for delivery in 1974 at a cost of £17,805 each.

As had happened before, the Transport Department came in for some criticism, as it was thought that Newport should have gone for the lowest tender which also happened to be a 100% British product.

To counter this, the General Manager argued that the Metro-Scania had been an impressive vehicle and that the Metropolitans would contribute towards fleet standardisation.

In the summer of 1973 service 14 was discontinued and some journeys on service 19 were diverted up Barrack Hill. Meanwhile service 13 and 17 were combined to form a new cross-town service 13 which ran between Ridgeway and Merlin Crescent. The service to South Quay was given number 14 at this time.

Big changes in the town centre

On Sunday 26 August 1973 there were major changes to traffic flows in the town centre which saw the reversal of a number of one-way streets, junction modifications and the introduction of two dedicated bus lanes. The bus station (or pull-in as it was known) in Dock Street was closed and most Newport buses began using the new purpose-built bus station on Kingsway the same day. The exceptions at this time were services 1A, 1C, 3, 13, 19 and 19B.

Towards the end of the year the last crew-operated service, the 7 to Llanfrechfa via Ponthir was converted to one-man operation. On 12 November 1973 it was extended to Cwmbran bus station, and was now run jointly with Western Welsh and Red & White. A new circular "shoppers service" numbered 17 also commenced. This ran from the bus station via Stow Hill and Bassaleg Road to the New Pastures estate and returned to town via Gaer Road and Cardiff Road. To round things off, in November 1973 a flat fare of 6p was introduced on all services except 7, 12 and 30.

Local Government reorganisation

The Local Government Act of 1972 resulted in major boundary changes to the County Borough of Newport with effect from 1 April 1974. A new district was created and named the Borough of Newport which took in Caerleon Rural District Council and parts of Magor and St. Mellons Rural District Councils (Magor and St. Mellons was a single RDC created in 1935, albeit in two distinct parts). Statistically this saw Newport increase in size dramatically from 11,675 acres to 49,534 acres. Its population grew too, but only from 110,000 to 130,000 which reflected the rural nature of the territory gained. The title of the transport department thus changed from Newport Corporation Transport to Borough of Newport Transport.

From 1 April 1974 the bus services operated were still largely the same as those running before the local government changes, being constrained by the 1925 Newport Corporation Act. Several attempts were made by residents in the outlying parts of the new Borough of Newport to secure council-run bus services, but with little success.

A summary of vehicles transferred to Borough of Newport Transport on 1 April 1974					
Fleet no.	Registration	Chassis type	Bodywork	Year new	
163/4/6	ODW 299, 300/2	Leyland PD2/40	Longwell Green	1958	
169	PDW 14	"	"	"	
175/7/8	PDW 481/3/4	"	"	"	
67-71	EDW 67-71D	Leyland PDR1/1	Alexander	1966	
72-6	HDW 772-6E	"	"	1967	
101-8	JDW 301-8F	Bristol RESL6L	ECW	"	
77-84	KDW 77-84F	Leyland PDR1/1	Alexander	1968	
85-93	MDW 385-93G	Leyland PDR1A/1	"	1969	
94-100	PDW 94-100H	"	"	1970	
10-8	TDW 310-8J	"	"	1971	
19/20	VDW 419/20K	Metro-Scania BR111MH	MCW	"	
21-46	VDW 421-46K	"	"	1972	
47-62	YDW 747-62K	"	"	"	

NB: 169 was actually withdrawn at the time of transfer.

Leyland Atlantean 76 (HDW 776E) is seen in the top shed in June 1974. It still sports its original front dash panel, but has lost the alloy decorative strip between its wheel arches.

(Andrew Wiltshire collection)

Bedford coaches

Having surrendered the Marshfield service 31 to A B Smith in November 1972, Newport Transport took over Smith's St. Brides and Marshfield service on 8 July 1974. Smith had acquired a pair of new Bedford coaches to grant specification for this route and they passed to Newport for £7,500+VAT as part of the deal. They were Newport's first coaches and details are given below.

109	XDW 741K	Bedford YRQ	Duple Viceroy	C45F	1972
110	ADW 178K	"	Willowbrook 002	"	"

They were numbered 45/46 in the Smith fleet. Prior to purchase they were inspected by Newport Transport engineering staff and were found to be in poor shape for their age with numerous faults. 110 was the worst of the pair. They were re-seated to C43F with luggage pens and Autofare equipment before entering service with Newport.

The Bedfords were mainly used on services to Marshfield and Whitson but in theory could be used anywhere. However, having a manual gearbox, not many drivers were licensed to drive them.

In the summer of 1974 Lancaster City Transport was experiencing a vehicle shortage, and so Newport sent five buses on loan from 5 to 30 August. They were Leyland PD2/40s 163/4/6/78 and Metro-Scania 46. Shortly before heading off on loan to Lancaster, Leyland PD2 166 was used on an enthusiasts' tour of Newport to commemorate 100 years since Newport's transport system was inaugurated as the Newport (Mon) Tramways Company and 50 years since Newport Corporation Transport introduced its first motor buses. It also provided the opportunity to use one of the six remaining Leyland PD2/40s before they were replaced by the forthcoming Metropolitan double-deckers.

The flat fare of 6p made a substantial rise to 10p on 5 January 1975, but there was a reduced 5p fare for travel in the am and pm off-peak periods.

The two former Smith's Bedford YRQs are nicely posed in the depot yard. 109 (XDW 741K) has the Duple Viceroy body, while 110 (ADW 178K) has a Willowbrook 002 body.

(The late Dave B Thomas)

Leyland PD2 166 (ODW 302) was used on an enthusiasts' tour of Newport on 28 July 1974. It is seen at Brynglas terminus alongside what appears to be a Longwell Green grp bus shelter.

(John Jones)

Enter the Metropolitans

The MCW Metropolitan double-decker was similar in many ways to the Metro-Scania single-decker with a stepped windscreen and twin radiators mounted just ahead of the rear axle. However, it had engine compartment air intakes at roof level at the rear. The decorative mouldings seemed a little excessive for a service bus and would no doubt be costly to repair. The model was given Scania chassis designation BR111DH and the engine used was the 200bhp Scania D11 CO6 of 11 litre coupled to a Scania HR501 fully automatic gearbox. They had an overall length of 31ft 10in, a wheelbase of 16ft 10in and an overall height of 14ft 5½in.

The ten new Metropolitan double-deckers began to arrive in December 1974 with the delivery of 111/4/5/7 on the 22nd. The batch 111-20 was completed with the arrival of 116 on 8 February 1975. Unfortunately, their registration numbers did not relate to the fleet numbers in any sense. They carried a new double-deck version of the Metro-Scania livery which was cream with a green roof and green lower panels. It looked very smart compared to the 50:50 livery. These buses had single-door bodies and seating for seventy-three passengers.

With the arrival of the Metropolitans, the last Leyland PD2s and of course the last half-cabs in the fleet were disposed of. These were 163/4/6/9 and 175/7/8 five of which were sold for scrap, while 177 and 178 were sold for further use. Interestingly 177 passed to Reverend David Green of Weymouth who eventually exported the bus to the United States. Meanwhile, 178 stayed in Newport passing to Father A Hanson of St. Mary's Church, Stow Hill, for use by their youth club. The church paid the princely sum of £5 for the bus.

In June 1975 Bristol RESLs 103 and 107 were hired to Rhymney Valley District Council. No new vehicles were received in the years 1975/76 but there were a number of significant service changes in order to address financial losses at this time. Areas affected by these changes included Caerleon, Western Avenue, Merlin Crescent, Barracks and Alway.

In February 1976 neighbouring fleet City of Cardiff Transport was experiencing a vehicle shortage due to problems with some four-year-old Daimler Fleetlines, which needed urgent rectification. Newport Transport was able to supply a number of buses on hire from 1 March 1976, but were not all present at the same time.

113 (GKG 34N) at Tredegar Park when new. It is on service 3 from Maesglas to Malpas. Only certain journeys were extended from Old Cardiff Road to the park gates where this view was taken.

(The late Dave B Thomas)

The vehicles are detailed below and retained their Newport fleet numbers as shown:

101-4, 107	JDW 301-4/7F	Bristol RESL6L	ECW	B42F
89	MDW 389G	Leyland PDR1A/1	Alexander	H43/31F
98, 100	PDW 98/100H	"	"	"

These buses returned to Newport for servicing, often as a one way trip on the 30. The Bristol REs were used on a variety of routes, but the Atlanteans were confined to the Tredegar service 36. All had returned by the end of March.

On 17 March 1976 Bedford YRQ 109 caught fire while on the M4, but was not too badly damaged. The passengers were brought home to Newport in AEC Reliance service bus CRD 154C, which Newport had hired from Reading Transport. It was returned to Reading the following day.

Newport's first Leyland Atlantean 67 was withdrawn from service in March 1976 after suffering a fire in its engine bay. It was gradually stripped for spares and sold to a dealer in July 1978, who resold it for scrap.

General Manager departs

In December 1976 Mr Frank Thorp retired from the Transport Department after nearly fourteen years in post as General Manager and Engineer. He achieved a great deal in this time notably the conversion of all services to one-man operation and the introduction of the flat fare system. The fleet of buses had become very standardised and he reduced staffing levels from 611 in 1963 down to 289 in 1976. His post was filled by Mr George Cottham who came from Merseyside PTE where he had been manager of the St. Helens district.

1977 brings more innovative developments

Newport Borough Transport was one of the UK's first operators to cease issuing bus tickets on most of its services in May 1977. It was found that the use of the Autofare machines in conjunction with the flat fare system had made conventional paper tickets obsolete and many passengers simply did not bother to take them, which created other problems. They were however still issued on services 7, 30 and 31. A new section of road named Queensway was opened in August 1977 which linked Station Approach and The Old Green with Bridge Street. This resulted in the re-routing of a number of services. In August 1977 some journeys on service 3 were extended from Maesglas to the new housing estate at Duffryn, which had been built on land belonging to Tredegar House. Then in May 1978 service 15 was extended from the docks via Docks Way to Duffryn.

In October 1977 Atlantean 69 was withdrawn and by July 1978 had become a towing vehicle in the ancillary fleet, later numbered B1 and then 169. Bristol RESL number 106 was also withdrawn after sustaining accident damage in a head-on collision at Nash on 9 November 1977 while operating service 5. After being cannibalised it was sold for scrap on 2 August 1978.

New coaches for the fleet

The arrival of the two second-hand Bedford coaches from Smiths in 1974 had resulted in an increase in the demand for private hire work, and encouraged by this Newport Borough Transport decided to purchase two new Leyland Leopards, both of which would qualify for a 50% bus grant as they could also be used in normal service. The first of these arrived in April 1978 as 63 and had a fifty-one-seat Duple Dominant II Express body finished in a white and green livery. This new coach was acquired through the dealer Arlington, Bristol, and replaced Bedford YRQ 109 which was withdrawn and sold to Prior Park College, Bath in June 1978.

Wearing the Metro-Scania style livery, Bristol RESL 107 (JDW 307F) is seen in Cardiff on Llanrumney Avenue, Llanrumney, on 6 March 1976 while on loan to City of Cardiff Transport.

(Cardiff Transport Preservation Group collection)

On 11 March 1982 Leyland Leopard 63 (UTX 463S) calls at the last stop on Llan-yr-avon Way. It will then turn right and head for Cwmbran bus station.

(Geoff Gould)

The second Leyland Leopard 64 (WTG 64T) with a Duple Dominant Express body that featured a roof-mounted destination box.

(Cardiff Transport Preservation Group collection)

On loan for evaluation Dennis Dominator SHE 722S is being put through its paces on the Ringland service. It is seen in Skinner Street on the approach to the bus station on 29 July 1978.

(The late Dave B Thomas)

The second coach entered service in August 1978 as 64. It was basically similar to number 63 except that it had a roof-mounted destination box and was obtained from the dealer W S Yeates of Loughborough. The arrival of 64 resulted in the withdrawal and sale of the last Bedford YRQ 110 in June 1979. That coach passed to Atlantic Marquees, Barry by February 1980. The new Leopards could often be found working services such as the 7 to Cwmbran, the 30 to Cardiff and 31 to Marshfield.

Newport inspected another demonstrator in the summer of 1978, the East Lancs-bodied Dennis Dominator double decker SHE 722S that arrived on loan from Hestair-Dennis Ltd of Guildford. This new model featured a Gardner 6LXB engine and was initially aimed at customers who were finding it difficult to obtain the Leyland Fleetline. It wore a light blue and white livery and was used on most town services from 18 July to 2 August.

Leyland Atlanteans 68, 70 and 71 were withdrawn between February and May 1978. 68 and 70 were sold for further service while 71 became driver training vehicle T1.

Demise of the Bristol REs

After the Metro-Scania saloons had settled down in service at Newport, the eight Bristol RESLs led a fairly quiet life. By the mid-1970s they were mostly confined to the rural routes like Whitson, Uskmouth and Marshfield as well as being chosen for schools and works services. As mentioned earlier 106 was written off in late 1977 and scrapped. 105 did not work after February 1976 having suffered a major mechanical breakdown, and 108 was also out of use by September 1977. The remaining Bristol RESLs were officially withdrawn between October 1978 and January 1979. Silcox Motor Coach Co Ltd of Pembroke Dock initially offered £12,000 for all seven, although 105 was actually described as being fit only for scrap with no real value. Silcox only took 101-5/7, and not surprisingly 105 was used as a source of spare parts. This left 108 which was eventually sold by Newport to Cynon Valley Borough Council in January 1980 to be cannibalised for spare parts.

More Metro-Scanias

London Transport had evaluated six Metro-Scanias and six Leyland Nationals from 1973, while looking for a replacement for its troublesome AEC Merlins and Swifts. It subsequently opted for the Leyland National. When the trial ended in 1976, the Metro-Scanias were put into store, although PGC 201L had not worked since early 1975. Newport was initially interested in these dual-door buses as a source of spares, but after inspection they were found to be in very good condition. On 16 October 1978 Newport Transport purchased five of them (PGC 201/3-6L) for £8,500 plus VAT and renumbered them 101, 103-6. PGC 203-6L were runners and were collected

A fine study of Metro-Scania 104 (PGC 204L) at Ringland Circle on 10 May 1980. In addition to mechanical differences, these former London buses did not have a Metro-Scania badge on the front dash and also had fewer opening windows.

(Geoff Gould)

from storage at Clapham at noon on 20 October 1978. 101 was not a runner and was stored at Clapton garage being collected by suspended tow at a later date. They were not totally compatible with Newport's own Metro-Scanias having different engines as well as differing brake and exhaust systems. On the positive side they featured improved soundproofing and rustproofing.

All were repainted into Newport livery and the first into service was 106 in November 1978 followed by 105 in December and 103/4 in January 1979. They were acquired as thirty-seven-seaters, but this was increased to forty-one for service with Newport.

101 needed a lot more mechanical attention than the other four, but was repainted to speed up the process of returning it to service. However, when work did start it was found to be far worse than originally thought and so its rebuild was halted. 101 was then gradually broken up for spares, its remains being sold in 1980.

The town centre stand in Skinner Street for service 3 to Maesglas was moved into the Kingsway bus station from 17 June 1979. The five Atlanteans delivered in 1967 were withdrawn during 1979 and sold in 1980. 72 went for further service while 73-6 were sold to a breaker.

A minibus experiment

A sixteen-seat minibus was hired from Bournemouth Transport for use on an experimental service commencing on 3 December 1979. The service ran between Alway shops and the Home Farm Estate, Caerleon via Hendre Farm Drive, Llanwern Road and Belmont Hill. The vehicle was a Strachan-bodied Ford Transit registered ERU 401L which carried Newport coat of arms during its stay. It took about an hour to complete a full circuit and the fare was 10p. The service was not a success and was terminated on 23 February 1980. Towards the end of its stay with Newport, the vehicle was also used on an experimental service linking the railway station to the bus station during the evening.

Another experiment was Centrebus, a free bus service aimed at shoppers that linked the railway station, High Street and Kingsway bus station on Mondays to Saturdays. It began operating from 6 May 1980 between the hours of 10.00 and 17.30.

Its rebuild having been abandoned, 101 (PGC 201L) was being dismantled for spare parts in 1979 having never entered service with Newport.

(The late Dave B Thomas)

The Bournemouth Ford Transit ERU 401L is seen on Aberthaw Avenue at the next stop to Alway shopping centre. It will now proceed to Ringland Centre and then travel over Christchurch Hill and Belmont to Caerleon (Home Farm Estate).

(The late Dave B Thomas)

Metro-Scania 22 (VDW 422K) is seen in September 1980. It is working the Centrebus service, linking the railway station to the Kingsway bus station.

(Peter Smith)

Leyland Titan B15 was a well-designed and comfortable bus, but technically rather complex. Demonstrator FHG 592S is seen on the Duffryn estate on 31 March 1979.

(Geoff Gould)

Titan demonstrator and another new coach

City of Cardiff Transport received Leyland Titan B15 demonstrator FHG 592S on loan from British Leyland in February 1979. This complex integral bus assembled by Park Royal was powered by a Gardner 6LXB engine and featured a single door. It was lent to Newport from 18 March until 9 April and in exchange Newport sent Leyland Atlantean 99 to Cardiff.

Another new Leyland Leopard coach was received on 7 March 1980 as 65. This, the third new Leopard, was identical in most respects to number 64, with a Duple Dominant II Express body seating fifty-one. It also qualified for a 50% bus grant.

Earning its keep on stage-carriage work, Duple-bodied Leyland Leopard 65 (DTG 365V) is seen in Cardiff bus station on the 30 service in September 1980.

(The late John Wiltshire)

Disruption on High Street

During rebuilding work in April 1980 Ye Olde Murenger House on High Street was found to be in danger of collapse. This Grade II listed public house dated from 1819 having replaced an earlier structure, and was in a poor state of repair when it was bought by brewery owner Sam Smith in 1980. The front of the building had to be shored up which narrowed the roadway and caused major disruption to bus services. Buses were diverted away from the High Street bus lane onto Kingsway until the rebuilding work was completed in 1983.

On a run in from Malpas, Leyland Atlantean 82 (KDW 82F) skirts around an Austin Allegro and enters Kingsway bus station on 3 May 1980. The bus has now gained the later style dash panel. The background in this view makes a fascinating study compared to the scene today.

(John Jones)

Front-engined double-decker

The Ailsa was a double-deck chassis that featured a front-mounted 6.7 litre Volvo TD70H engine. It was introduced in 1973 and built in the UK by Volvo at its Irvine plant in Scotland. Most examples were bodied by Alexander of Falkirk. Newport inspected a MkII model in May 1980 but was obviously not impressed. The bus was in the livery of Tayside Regional Council.

The unusual Volvo Ailsa MkII double-decker CSL 602V, that was inspected by Newport on 6 May 1980, but not used in service.

(Ivor Homfray)

New from Metro-Cammell-Weymann

The MCW Metropolitan double-decker went out of production in early 1978 after a fairly successful production run. The partnership with Scania had ended and MCW were now concentrating on building their own integral double-deck bus. Christened the Metrobus, it offered a Gardner engine and Voith fully-automatic transmission. It was aimed at large operators like London Transport and the PTEs who were experiencing great

difficulties obtaining new double-deckers in sufficient numbers from British Leyland. MCW were on to a winner and a number of municipal fleets also placed orders for the Metrobus early on.

No alternative Scania-based double-decker was available at this time and so Newport Transport ordered seven MCW Metrobus for delivery in 1980. They were delivered as 66-72 and entered service between April and July. They had seventy-seven-seat single-door bodies finished in the 50:50 livery but with a black skirt and window surrounds. They had Gardner 6LXB engines and Voith DWA type D851 fully-automatic gearboxes, and were obtained on a ten-year lease. 68 was notable as being the 500th Metrobus produced by MCW.

Another rather interesting vehicle inspected in 1980 was a fairly new Scania CR112 loaned by Scania (GB) Ltd for six days in March. It was a 3-door, left-hand drive service bus that was actually owned by Swedish operator Kalmar Omnibusförening U.P.A. of Kalmar as their number 40. The General Manager Mr George W Cottham left the undertaking in July 1980 to take up a position as Manager at Cleveland Transit. His position was taken by Mr Colin Thompson who had previously been Deputy Manager with Hull City Transport.

In July 1980 a section of Commercial Street between Charles Street and Corn Street was closed to through traffic except for access which meant that inbound journeys on routes 1, 11 and 11A were diverted down Stow Hill to Westgate Square and took advantage of a new bus lane which ran against the normal flow of traffic. In October 1980 Newport Borough Transport became the sole operator of service 7 to Cwmbran and also took over the Newport to Cefn Mably Hospital via Bassaleg service from National Welsh. This only ran three times a week. Newport numbered this service 32. Buses taken out of service between April and December 1980 comprised Leyland Atlanteans 80/1/3/4, all dating from 1968.

Brand new Metrobus 69 (DTG 369V) is seen at the depot in April 1980 before entering service. The rubble behind the bus was from part of the old power station that was being demolished at this time.

(Ivor Homfray collection)

A further nine MCW Metrobuses were received in March and April 1981. They were numbered 73-81 and were virtually identical to the first batch of 1980. They were also obtained on a ten-year lease.

In early February 1981 Leyland Leopard coach 64 was involved in an accident while running empty at Thame in Oxfordshire. In icy conditions it ran off the road into a ditch and its recovery caused even more damage to the vehicle. It was later returned to Duple for repair.

A new Scania double-deck chassis

In 1981 Scania introduced the BR112DH double-deck chassis onto the UK Market and it created quite a bit of interest. It had many of the features that the Metropolitan had offered with similar impressive performance, but allowed the operator to specify a bodybuilder of its own choice. The BR112DH was available in two lengths, 9.5m and 10.2m, and was powered by the 11-litre Scania DN11 engine (and later the turbocharged DS11 engine), coupled to either a Scania or Voith fully-automatic gearbox. Newport was one of the first fleets to place an order for the competitively priced BR112DH chassis,

specifying eleven with Marshall bodywork. Alas, as was the case in 1974 with the Metropolitan order, this order caused quite a storm locally, with respect to the Transport Department buying foreign buses again.

Newport's new Scanias entered the fleet as 82-92. 84 and 85 were the first into service on 28 June and this was concluded by 92 on 17 August. They had Scania DN11 CO1 engines of 203bhp coupled to Voith D851 3-speed gearboxes. The Scania chassis cost £28,600 while the bodies were £25,730 each and all eleven buses were obtained on a twelve-year lease. They were the first Marshall bodies for Newport and had seating for seventy-four. Marshall was a relatively new builder of double-deck bus bodies having completed only single-deck bodies up until early 1978.

To coincide with the school summer holidays, from 27 July 1981, a thrice daily service 85 was operated to Barry Island on Mondays to Saturdays. It was jointly operated with City of Cardiff Transport and National Welsh and ran from the Bettws Estate picking up in Newport and a number of locations in Cardiff. The adult fare was £1.80 return from Newport.

From the second delivery of MCW Metrobuses, 80 (JBO 80W) is nearly at the end of its run from Newport on the 30. It is heading along Wood Street, Cardiff, on 4 August 1981.

(Geoff Gould)

Scania 91 (JBO 91W) is seen on Newport Road in Cardiff on 12 March 1982, inbound from Newport. The Marshall body was quite a distinctive design and was slightly shorter than the Scania chassis resulting in an untidy rear end elevation.

(Geoff Gould)

Tramcar livery

In July 1981 Metropolitan 116 was repainted into a special maroon and cream livery as carried by the electric tramcars. This was to commemorate the 80th anniversary of the Council taking over the operation of Newport's transport system in 1901. The same month saw a limited night service commence on Fridays and Saturdays.

By 1981 sections 38 and 40 of the 1925 Newport Corporation Act were revoked which opened up the way for Newport Transport to operate services to places like Rogerstone, Penhow and Underwood, which since 1974 had been part of the enlarged Borough. The first evidence as a result of this change came in November 1985 when the Newport buses reached Cefn Wood in Rogerstone. Buses withdrawn during 1981 comprised twenty Atlanteans (77-9, 82, 85-100). This just left the nine J-registration examples of 1971 in service, out of what was once a fleet of forty-three Atlanteans. 100 was briefly used as a driver training vehicle in March 1982 and then as a canteen/rest room at the bus station in May and June, while the staff canteen was upgraded. It was then sold.

A new Tiger

1982 was a quiet year but on 12 May another new coach was delivered and not to grant-specification this time. It was a Leyland Tiger with a fifty-one-seat Plaxton Supreme V body. It was numbered 1 and entered service in the white and green coach livery.

The Leyland Tiger was the new coach chassis from Leyland that was introduced in 1981, and featured the Leyland TL11 engine. The Tiger would soon be the replacement for the Leyland Leopard which was gradually being phased out during 1982.

In 1982 Newport announced a new summer service to Porthcawl from Ringland, Alway and St. Julians with a fare of £3.00 return. The advert gave a start date of 26 July, but it is unsure if this service was actually operated. Newport inspected five single-deckers with a view to ordering a small quantity for 1983. One of these was an interesting Gardner-powered Dennis Falcon H with Duple Dominant bodywork that was owned by Leicester City Transport.

Metropolitan 116 (GKG 37N) looks quite smart in its special livery to celebrate 80 years of the Newport municipal undertaking. It is in the depot yard on the occasion of the 1983 PSV Circle AGM visit on 9 April.

(Andrew Wiltshire)

The Leyland Tiger coach 1 (OBO 631X) in the coach park at Tenby in the later coach livery. The one-piece coach-style door is noteworthy.

(Cardiff Transport Preservation Group collection)

90 (PJU 90W) was the prototype Dennis Falcon H and was on loan from Leicester City Transport. This Gardner-engined single-decker was photographed in the Kingsway bus station on 22 February 1982.

(Ivor Homfray)

Also available as a single-decker

The outcome of all these demonstrators was that Newport played it safe and ordered nine Scania BR112DH double-deck chassis, which would receive Wadham Stringer Vanguard single-deck bodies with seating for forty-two. This was in addition to a follow-up order for nine seventy-six-seat Marshall-bodied Scania double-deckers. The latter began to enter service in December 1982 and were all operating by February 1983. They were numbered 93-101 and were virtually identical to the 1982 delivery. The main difference was that the front upper deck windows were now separated by a thin alloy strip instead of being two separate apertures. The Scania badge was also placed higher up on the front dash grill. Meanwhile numbers 90 and 91 from the previous batch were fitted with Scania DS11 turbocharged engines in 1982/83.

From the second batch of Marshall-bodied Scanias, 101 (PTG 101Y) is seen on Chepstow Road near the junction with Hawthorn Avenue on 30 April 1983.

(Geoff Gould)

On the last day of Leyland Atlantean operation, 30 January 1983, 18 (TDW 318J) picks up in Newport bus station. Atlanteans had served the town for nearly seventeen years.

(Andrew Wiltshire)

Vehicles withdrawn from service during 1982 included Leyland Atlanteans 10-2 and 14-6. The last examples in service were 13/7/8 which were taken out of service in January 1983.

The new Scania saloons aroused quite a bit of interest in the bus industry at a time when Wadham Stringer Coachbuilders Ltd was just establishing itself as a mainstream coachbuilder. Up until the early 1980s they had tended to specialise in building ambulances and bus bodies for the MoD and non-PSV operators such as local authority social services. The new saloons were

delivered and entered service in March and April 1983 as 10-8, and were quite heavy vehicles tipping the scales at 9600kg unladen.

Plaxton was chosen to body a second new Leyland Tiger coach which was supplied by Yeates of Loughborough in June 1983. Coach number 2 was fitted with the new Paramount 3200 style body with seating for fifty-three and costing £59,599.26. It was re-seated to fifty-one in August 1985. The excursions and tours programme for 1983 included destinations such as West Midlands Safari Park, Tenby and the Greenham Common Air Tattoo.

12 (RUH 12Y) is seen leaving Christchurch bound for the town centre on 9 April 1983. The tower of the Holy Trinity Church is in the background.

(Geoff Gould)

Leyland Tiger 2 (STG 2Y) is seen on Park Lane on an outing to London on 27 October 1990. It has a Plaxton Paramount body.

(John Jones)

Return of a Titan

The most interesting purchase in 1983 was the re-acquisition for £5 of Longwell Green-bodied Leyland PD2/40 178 (PDW 484) for restoration. The bus which dated from November 1958, had been sold eight years previously to St. Mary's Youth Club, Newport, for non-PSV use. Some of the seating had been removed and replaced with bunks for intended use on adventure holidays.

In reality it was rarely used and was often parked at Newport's depot in Corporation Road. It was originally planned to restore it in time for the HCVS rally in Cardiff in 1983, but that never happened of course.

In August 1983 Marshall-bodied Scania number 83 returned to Scania (UK) for repairs and in its place Scania loaned BR112DH demonstrator EMJ 560Y to Newport. This bus had a seventy-eight-seat East Lancs body and was new in 1982. It was with Newport from 23 August until 10 October 1983 and was only used for private hire and contract work.

Newport lent Wadham Stringer-bodied Scania saloon number 12 to Chesterfield Transport for evaluation in November 1983. In its place Newport were provided with Chesterfield Leyland Atlantean PNU 122K. This 1972 vintage bus had a Roe dual-door body and was only used for private hire and contract work.

Scania demonstrator EMJ 560Y at the RAF St. Athan open day on 10 September 1983. This bus later entered service with Nottingham City Transport.

(The late John Wiltshire)

MCW Metrobus number 70 (DTG 370V) in High Street and looking smart after a repaint. It no longer features a black skirt and window surrounds.

The Faresfair experiment

From 5 December 1983 as a twelve-month experiment, customers could purchase a Faresfair ticket that gave them one week's unlimited travel in Newport for a mere £2.50. Also available was a four-week ticket for £9.50. This proved to be a major success and became a permanent feature.

As already mentioned, the last Leyland Atlanteans were taken out of service at the beginning of 1983. Also withdrawn that year were the first of the Metro-Scania saloons including 19-27 in February and March, followed by 33, 39 and 106 in July after sustaining fire damage at the depot.

Leyland Leopard coach 63 was withdrawn in September and sold to D Henderson & Sons, Carstairs, in February 1984. Meanwhile, all sixteen Metrobuses lost their black skirts and window surrounds at their first repaint.

1984 was quite an uneventful year. Leopard coach 64 was withdrawn in February and in March 1984 also passed to D Henderson & Sons, Carstairs. It wasn't until the end of the year that the first of eight new Scania double-deckers began to appear when 20 was delivered on 3 December. These were N112DRB models which featured the turbo-charged DS11 CO1 engine of 193bhp and Voith D851.2 3-speed gearboxes, and were fitted with seventy-eight-seat Alexander RH bodywork. The batch was numbered 19-26, with 22 to 26 entering service in January 1985. Their unladen weight was 9,712kg and they were on a ten-year lease. The arrival of these buses enabled Metro-Scanias 29-32/4-6 to be taken out of service.

Newport received another new Plaxton Paramount-bodied Leyland Tiger in May 1984. Numbered 3 it was similar in appearance to number 2, but was a TRCTL11/3R model that featured a 245bhp engine and a ZF 6-speed manual gearbox. It was supplied by a dealer and had seating for fifty-five.

20 (B220 YUH) is seen on Queensway approaching the Old Green on 13 May 1996. Behind the bus is the signal box at Newport station which was later demolished.

(John Jones)

Leyland Tiger 3 (B603 DDW) is seen resting at services on the M1 on 1 October 1990. It was on its way to the National Garden Festival at Gateshead.

(The late John Wiltshire)

30 (C30 ETG) is one of the eight East Lancs-bodied Scanias. It is seen entering the Kingsway bus station on 30 July 1989.

(Cliff Essex)

There were no bus services in Newport on 2 April 1985 due to staff attending a protest march in London against Government plans to privatise all council-owned bus undertakings. This action had full management backing. As a result of vandalism to its upper deck caused by football supporters, MCW Metropolitan 114 was withdrawn in May 1985. It was sold in January 1986 for non-PSV use. In October 1985 the last of the three Leyland Leopards (65) was withdrawn and sold to Merthyr Tydfil Borough Transport in whose fleet it became 242.

The final buses delivered to the Borough of Newport Transport before deregulation in October 1986 were another batch of eight Scania N112DR double-deckers. Although mechanically virtually identical to numbers 19-26, this batch had seventy-six-seat East Lancs bodies that were to a similar design, but by no means identical

to the Alexander RH batch. They entered service in March and April 1986 as 27-34.

The remaining nine MCW Metropolitans (111-3/5-20) were taken out of service in March 1986. They had been well-liked by drivers as they were so easy to drive. However, they had a tendency to bounce up and down when at speed due to their air suspension, and were also light on the front end and prone to skid in wet and greasy conditions if not treated with respect.

Most Metropolitans were prone to corrosion, especially at the rear end, and Newport's examples were no exception, which led to their demise. The last nine passed to dealer London Bus Export Company, Lydney in June 1986 and all found new homes. The standard flat fare on town routes was increased to 30p (25p off peak) on 20 September 1986.

CHAPTER SIX
DEREGULATION AND SMALL BUSES

What is deregulation?

Deregulation of bus services in the United Kingdom took place on 26 October 1986, a very significant event for the bus industry. Newport's municipal fleet was set to become an "arms-length" operation, remaining in Council ownership, and run as a separate business. With effect from this date the title of the fleet would change to Newport Transport Limited.

Newport had made great strides during the 1970s and achieved 100% one-man operation long before some fleets. It also was an early pioneer of the flat-fare system which was later to become ticketless.

Following the introduction of a fleet of forty-four impressive Metro-Scania saloons in early 1972, vehicle standardisation had been a priority with the Scania marque proving to be a reliable choice for the undertaking.

The MCW Metrobuses were an exception, obtained at a time when Scania was not able to offer a double-decker. The private hire side of the business has done well, and six Leyland coaches have been purchased since 1978.

Until now in this book, driver-only operated/pay-as-you-enter vehicles have been referred to as one-man operated vehicles. This was the term generally used by the industry at the time, but from the 1980s it was gradually deemed politically incorrect, and so the term one-person operated was introduced.

Are small buses the way forward?

Deregulation on 26 October 1986 was soon followed by the gradual introduction of midibuses on some services, as Newport cautiously followed the trend across the entire bus industry at this time. The small bus revolution had got underway in certain parts of the United Kingdom during 1985. It was set to spread rapidly across the nation with large fleets of van-derived vehicles being pressed into service in many fleets, and often replacing larger buses. The overall aim was to reduce costs in the industry by using small cheap vehicles and introducing lower rates of pay and to extend bus services along roads unsuitable for big buses. On the positive side frequencies were sometimes increased on busy routes making the service more attractive to the public. However, the passenger experience in these small and uncomfortable vehicles often left a lot to be desired.

The birth of the Newport Nipper

The Dodge 50 series was a light commercial vehicle chassis built in the UK by Chrysler Europe from 1979 and later by Renault. Many of the S56 models completed as midibuses were badged as Renault and production in the UK ceased in 1993. During the early years of deregulation East Lancs concentrated on building bodies for full-size vehicles, and completed only thirty-two midibuses all on Dodge chassis in 1986/87. These were coach-built bodies as opposed to conversions, and utilised some aluminium sections that were also employed in double-deck bodies.

The following vehicles passed to Newport Transport Ltd on 26 October 1986.

Double-deckers				
Fleet nos.	**Chassis type**	**Body**	**Year**	**Comments**
66-72	Metrobus DR102	MCW	1980	
73-81	"	"	1981	
82-92	Scania BR112DH	Marshall	"	
93-101	"	"	1982/3	
19-26	Scania N112DRB	Alexander	1984/5	
27-34	"	East Lancs	1986	
Single-deckers				
37/8, 40-6	Metro-Scania	MCW	1972	
47-62	"	"	"	
103-5	"	"	1973	ex London Transport
10-8	Scania BR112DH	Wadham Stringer	1983	
Coaches				
1	Leyland Tiger	Plaxton	1982	
2	"	"	1983	
3	"	"	1985	
Preserved bus				
178	Leyland PD2/40	Longwell Green	1958	To be restored

The first post-deregulation midibuses for Newport were a batch of eight Dodge S56s with automatic gearboxes. Their rather angular East Lancs bodies had twenty-four high-backed seats and 4-9 entered service in January and February 1987 being followed in May by 63/4. They had a cream livery with green bands and introduced the Newport Nipper branding that was used for the new minibus services which commenced from 17 May 1987.

64 (D64 MTG), one of the rather ugly East Lancs-bodied Dodge S56s, at Glasllwch on 5 September 1988. It is bound for Rogerstone.

(Geoff Gould)

The eight East Lancs-bodied Dodges were particularly disliked by drivers as they had a low driving position, the cabs got very warm in hot weather and they also suffered from braking problems. As a working day progressed these buses would suffer from brake fade, a problem that was eventually rectified by the manufacturer. The build quality of the bodywork eventually became an issue too.

Later in 1987 a further three Dodge S56s entered service but this time with bodywork completed by Reeve Burgess. They were numbered 35/6 and 65 and were fitted with twenty-five traditional bus-type seats. The earlier braking issues had been resolved by the time these buses arrived and their Reeve Burgess bodies were regarded as a superior product.

The initial Newport Nipper network of services is shown in the table below. The buses would stop on a Hail and Ride basis in certain areas.

Route	Area served
1A/C	Town Centre to Rogerstone
1B/D	Town Centre to Gibbs Road/Christchurch
10A/C	Town Centre to St. Julian's (circular via bus station)
13A/C	Town Centre to Brynglas
14A/C	Town Centre to Allt-yr-Yn (circular)

Extra midibuses needed

It soon became apparent that more buses would be needed to help with the introduction of new Nipper services in 1987/88. As a result, Newport took six Dodge midibuses on loan from a number of sources. Nottingham provided three, Ipswich one and Thamesdown supplied a pair, but not at the same time.

36 (E36 RBO) is one of the more attractive Reeve Burgess-bodied Dodge S56s. It is seen on Bassaleg Road on 16 September 1988 also bound for Rogerstone.

(Geoff Gould)

During August and September 1987, Reeve Burgess-bodied Dodge D401 TMW was on loan from Thamesdown in which fleet it was number 401.

(David Donati)

East Lancs-bodied Dodge C200 WGV on loan from Ipswich is seen in the Kingsway bus station. It was in Newport from August to October 1987.

(David Donati)

Returned to Scania

East Lancs-bodied Scania double-decker 29 was loaned to Scania (GB) Ltd from 10 to 26 April 1987 for use by Brighton and Hove Bus and Coach Co Ltd, Brighton, from 13 to 16 April 1987 moving on to Brighton Borough Transport Ltd from 16 to 26. It returned on loan to Scania for a second period in June 1987, and was believed to have been used by Grampian Regional Transport, Aberdeen in July 1987. Meanwhile Newport loaned Scania single-decker 11 to Rossendale Transport for two weeks in September 1987. It is thought this may also have been on behalf of Scania (GB).

Upon deregulation Newport Transport Ltd inherited twenty-eight Metro-Scanias which had put in good service considering some operators had rid themselves of the type by 1980, and these were now due for replacement. During 1987 a total of nine (37/8, 44-6) were withdrawn. On 31 March 1988 the fleet stood at 94 vehicles while there were 174 platform staff and the operation was supported by sixty-nine engineering and thirty-two administration staff.

The Metrorider

Several manufacturers were developing purpose-built minibuses and midibuses which although more expensive, were seen as a more attractive vehicle than a van conversion. MCW launched its Metrorider midibus in 1986. Available in two lengths, 7m or 8.4m, it was of integral construction and came with a choice of either Cummins or Perkins engines. Transmission was either an Allison fully-automatic or a ZF manual gearbox. Its functional-looking body featured a large two-piece windscreen, while the interior was well laid out compared to some of the van-derived vehicles. Newport Transport received a pair of 7m models in June 1988 numbered 37 and 38 and fitted with twenty-five high-backed seats. They featured the Cummins B-Series engine and an Allison fully-automatic gearbox.

MCW Metrorider 38 (E38 UBO) was nearly seven years old when noted in the layover lane in the Kingsway bus station in February 1995. It saw nine years' service with Newport.

(The late John Wiltshire collection)

A Dodge from down south

In September 1988 a second-hand East Lancs-bodied Dodge S56 D474 UHC was acquired from Eastbourne Borough Transport Ltd, in whose fleet it had been number 74. It was one of a batch of four that Eastbourne had purchased new in late 1986, and was very similar to the eight Dodges already owned. It had twenty-four high-back seats and was given Newport fleet number 39.

By September 1988 these additional Newport Nipper routes had been introduced.

Route	Area served
3A	Maesglas
3X	Malpas, Oliphant Circle
32/33	Rhiwderin
20	Ringland, Howe Circle

The former Eastbourne Dodge 39 (D474 UHC) entering the bus station on 8 April 1989. The rear wheels have been faired in.

(The late John Wiltshire)

More double-deckers

Twelve new double-deckers were ordered for delivery in two batches during 1988/89. The Scania N113DRB was a popular chassis which was introduced in 1988, and was a development of the N112 of which Newport had sixteen examples in service. The initial half dozen new double-deckers entered service in November and December 1988 and were numbered 41-6. They had Alexander RH-type bodywork with seating for eighty.

All were fitted with a Scania DS11 11-litre engine of 253bhp and a Voith D863 fully-automatic gearbox. A further addition to the coach fleet in December 1988 was 4 (XFM 203), a forty-nine-seat Duple 340-bodied Leyland Tiger that featured a toilet. It was acquired via bus and coach dealer Stuart Johnson and had been new to Crosville Motor Services as CTL73 in May 1986 and, until September 1986, had been registered C73 KLG.

43 (F43 YHB) is one of the first six Scania N113DRB double-deckers in Cardiff bus station. These buses were outwardly similar to the eight N112 models (19-26) new in 1984.

(The late Dave B Thomas)

Leyland Tiger 4 (XFM 203) has a high-floor Duple 340 body. It is seen at the M4 Membury services on 8 July 1989 and had been new to Crosville in 1986.

(The late John Wiltshire)

Dodge midibus 4 (D804 MNY) was renumbered 40 in December 1988 to make way for the coach mentioned above. At around this time the East Lancs-bodied Dodge midibuses had their seating capacity reduced from twenty-four to twenty-two, while the pair with Reeve Burgess bodies were reduced from twenty-five to twenty-three. Number 5 then had bus type seats fitted in January 1990.

A splendid restoration

Restoration of 178, the Leyland PD2/40 re-acquired in February 1983 first got underway between March and May 1986. Initially this work was done by Work Experience apprentices provided by the Manpower Services Commission, who removed most of the exterior panelling and interior fittings. No further work was carried out due to a shortage of skilled labour. With the National Eisteddfod of Wales due to be held in the grounds of Tredegar House in July and August 1988,

Newport Transport sought financial assistance from Newport Council to complete the restoration of the Leyland PD2. The plan was to use the bus on a special shuttle service between the centre of Newport and Tredegar House for this high profile event. The appeal was successful and restoration resumed in February 1988 when Newport's own skilled staff went on to finish the job, completing it on 23 July 1988. The restoration of 178 included new flooring, window frames, staircase and a set of new seats that matched the originals.

This special shuttle service operated between Newport's rail and bus stations and Tredegar House, from Saturday 30 July until Saturday 7 August. Since that time 178 has been used mainly for private hire, but did see use in normal service on a couple of occasions. It was also used for driver training work which continued until 1991, when new legislation meant that it was no longer suitable as a training bus. It has also attended a large number of vintage vehicle and bus rallies over the years.

Having been stripped down, work has now started on repanelling the body of Leyland PD2/40 number 178.

(The late Dave B Thomas)

The completed bus makes a fine sight out on the road. Here it is at Rhymney Bridge two years later on 31 March 1990 while engaged on an enthusiasts' tour.

(John Jones)

This interesting shot shows a pair of Wadham Stringer-bodied Scania saloons 10 and 13 and was taken at the junction of Skinner Street and High Street on 14 May 1988. Number 10 is on the 2X which served the Ponthir Road, College Glade and Lodge Farm areas of Caerleon.

(The late John Wiltshire)

Scania N113 50 (G50 FKG) is seen at St. Woolos heading out of town to the Gaer estate in the afternoon sun on 10 July 1990.

(Geoff Gould)

Vehicles withdrawn in 1988 were Metro-Scania saloons 47-50, 52/4/7. Amongst the buses received on loan during 1989 was a Leyland National 2 from South Wales Transport which was inspected for assessment of its suspension-lowering "kneeling" facility.

Delivery of the second batch of six Scania N113DRB double-deckers commenced in November 1989. All were in service by the end of December as 47-52. The bodies were the same as the first six, but 47-52 were fitted with Scania GAV771R 4-speed gearboxes which featured an integral retarder. They had an unladen weight of 10,020kg compared to 9,766kg of the previous batch.

Vehicles withdrawn during 1989 were Metro-Scania saloons 51/3/5/6, 59-62, which left just four of this type in service. These were 58 and 103-5. 58 was given a makeover and a repaint. It is worth noting that 61 and 62 had accident damage, having been involved in separate road accidents within a few weeks of each other. This was most unfortunate as both had recently received replacement engines, and one of the pair was earmarked for preservation by the Transport Department. Three different midibuses were evaluated in 1990 with a view to replacing the Dodges. They were Mercedes 811D and 709D models, together with an Optare Metrorider.

Metrorider demonstrator G842 LWR was used for around two weeks to evaluate the Optare product prior to any orders being placed. It is seen in the bus station on 14 April 1990.

(Andrew Wiltshire)

Metroriders from Optare

The MCW Metrorider design was purchased from Metro-Cammell-Weymann by Optare in 1989, and only a small number of modifications were carried out before production resumed in 1990. A one-piece windscreen was offered along with the option of a larger destination box. The Metrorider had previously sold well and Optare were hoping for similar good fortune.

In July 1990 Newport Transport took half a dozen 7m Optare Metroriders numbered 53-8. They had one-piece windscreens, 23 bus seats and were powered by the Cummins B-series engine coupled to an Allison AT545 4-speed automatic gearbox. Consequently, Metro-Scania 58 was renumbered 102. Two of the three surviving former London Transport Metro-Scanias 103 and 105 were used as polling stations in May 1990. Then all three (103-5), were placed into store in July, and officially withdrawn in December 1990. The new Metroriders also resulted in the withdrawal of the first of the Dodge S56 midi-buses with 63, 64 and former Eastbourne example 39 going in 1990. The Dodges were found to be unsuitable to work on Newport's hilly routes.

53 (G53 KTX) is passing the Greyhound pub in High Street on 28 July 1990 having not long entered service. This Metrorider is working the Nipper service 1X to Rogerstone.

(The late John Wiltshire)

59 (H59 PNY) is one of the second batch of Optare Metroriders from 1991, and is seen working service 10C on Chepstow Road, heading into the town centre from St. Julian's.

(Cardiff Transport Preservation Group collection)

In April 1991 a further six twenty-three-seat Optare Metroriders arrived which were numbered 59-64. The same month Newport purchased an Alexander Y-bodied Leyland Leopard with manual gearbox for conversion to a driver-training bus. It was XGM 450L which dated from 1972 and was originally new to Central SMT (T150). It came to Newport from Morris Travel of Pencoed and was later given fleet number 174.

A brand new Leyland Tiger was added to stock in October 1991 numbered 5, and featuring a Cummins L10 engine and ZF 5-speed automatic gearbox. It was renumbered to 1 in January 1993. This replaced Leyland Tiger number 1 which was withdrawn the same month, and passed via a dealer to Summerdale Coaches (J R Davies), Letterston, Pembrokeshire, in May 1992. Withdrawals in 1991 eliminated the last Dodges from the fleet, 5 to 8, 35/6 and 40 (D804 MNY). Five of them passed to Cynon Valley Transport at Aberdare in July 1991.

Newport Transport was involved with providing transport for the National Garden Festival at Ebbw Vale held between May and October 1992 including the provision of a Park & Ride service from Cwm. To round off what was a fairly quiet year, 1992 witnessed the withdrawal of the first MCW Metrobuses when 70-2 passed to the Cowie Group Ltd (Grey Green), Stamford Hill, for use on London Regional Transport (LRT) tendered services in north east London.

Scania saloons

Newport Transport was always eager to take a closer look at what the industry was able to offer, despite having settled on the Scania chassis for its big bus needs so that more demonstration vehicles were inspected in 1991. Scania sold very few saloons in the UK after production of the MCW Metro-Scania ceased in 1974, but this was to change with the introduction of the Scania N113 model.

The Cummins-powered Leyland Tiger 5 (J905 UBO) has just been delivered to Newport Transport in October 1991, and has yet to be given its fleet number and registration plates.

(Ivor Homfray)

On 14 September 2001 we find 6 (K106 YTX), an Alexander Strider-bodied Scania N113CRB inbound on Stow Hill having just passed the entrance to St. Woolos hospital.

(John Jones)

In 1991 Plaxton introduced the alloy framed Verde body which soon appeared on the Scania N113CRB chassis and Newport inspected a demonstrator. Dennis Specialist Vehicles Ltd supplied the Dennis Lance demonstrator on loan between 12 and 18 February 1992. Meanwhile Newport ordered six Scania saloons with Alexander's new Strider body for delivery in 1993.

The six new Alexander Strider-bodied Scania N113CRBs entered service in March 1993 as 4 - 9. The Strider was an attractive body with simple lines and featured a deep curved windscreen and shallow roofline. They had forty-eight seats and were powered by the Scania DS11 CO1 engine of 206bhp @ 2000rpm, while the transmission was the Voith D863 gearbox. The front nearside suspension could be lowered in a kneeling fashion enabling the platform to be more or less level with the kerb. These buses had an unladen weight of 9,620kg.

In February 1993 work started on rebuilding the Kingsway bus station to a new layout. The new bus station came into use from November 1993 and was officially opened on Saturday 30 April 1994. The £700,000 facelift now featured a saw-tooth layout where buses pulled in and reversed out. The last Metro-Scania 102 (YDW 758K) was taken out of service in February 1993, but was quickly pressed back into service for a few months pending delivery of Scania N113s 4-9. Subsequently it was retained by Newport Transport as a preserved vehicle, until sold privately for preservation in July 2006.

Also taken out of service were the last of the 1980 Metrobuses 66-9, which also passed to the Cowie Group Ltd (Grey Green), Stamford Hill for use on LRT tendered services in north east London. Meanwhile Metrobus 73 was condemned in February 1993 after sustaining serious fire damage. This was a result of an arson attack while working a school service. It was subsequently cannibalised for spares and sold for scrap. Scania 23 sustained serious accident damage on Cefn Road, Rogerstone when hit by a car in February 1993 in icy conditions. It was repaired in Newport's workshops and did not re-enter service until August 1994.

In January 1994 Newport borrowed an MCW Metrorider 668 (F668 YOG) from West Midlands Travel Ltd. This twenty-three-seat midibus was trialled from 8 January to 30 April on a new free bus service from the Kingsway bus station to the Royal Gwent Hospital. The trial was a success.

February 1994 saw the entry into service of a repeat order for six Scania N113 single-deckers. They were similar to 4 - 9 of 1993, but featured the Euro1 compliant Scania DSC11 CO2 engine of 230bhp but with the same Voith D863 transmission. They were also the first buses in the fleet with an inter-cooler. They were allocated fleet numbers 68-73.

The last Metro-Scania in service 102 (formerly 58) was taken out of service in 1993. It is seen here at Tredegar House.

(Cardiff Transport Preservation Group collection)

An interesting acquisition in April 1994 from Parfitt's Motor Services Ltd, Rhymney Bridge, was 39 (D478 PON), a twenty-three-seat MCW Metrorider new in June 1987, and had originally operated for London Buses Ltd as MR18. It was not fitted with any fare collection equipment upon entry into service at Newport, and was used exclusively on the new Royal Gwent Hospital free bus service, following the earlier trial of the West Midlands Travel Metrorider.

Withdrawn from service in 1994 were the 1981 Metrobuses numbers 74-81, the last of the type in the fleet. All passed to the dealer Ensign, which resold 74, 76-9 and 81 to Merseyside Transport Ltd, while 75 and 80 passed to County Bus and Coach Ltd, Harlow as M75 and M80.

A third batch of Scania saloons, six in all, were received in February 1995 and numbered 65-7 and 74-6. As before, they had forty-eight-seat Alexander Strider bodywork, but featured for the first time, dot-matrix electronic destination displays. Mechanically they were the same as the 1994 delivery, but incorporated the Scania MAXC1 front-end low floor structure, which enabled shallower front-entrance steps. This gave them the chassis designation N113CRL and an increased unladen weight of 9,800kg.

An Optare Prisma was an interesting single-decker provided by Optare Ltd of Leeds during the summer. The Prisma was based on the Mercedes-Benz 0405 chassis and marketed as a complete vehicle by Optare. The first examples of the Marshall-bodied Scania double-deckers (85, 87-91) were withdrawn in February 1995 having been replaced by the new saloons. They passed to Ensign the following month and were purchased by Redby Coaches Ltd of Sunderland. Also withdrawn and sold in 1995 was Tiger coach number 2, which passed to local operator Croydon Minibus Hire (Boyd and Chick) of Newport. As of 31 March 1995 the fleet strength was down to eighty-nine. This comprised forty-three double-deckers, twenty-eight saloons, fifteen midibuses and three coaches.

Still bearing the Newport Nipper brand, 39 (D478 PON) is dropping off passengers at the Royal Gwent Hospital on free bus service 99.

(Cardiff Transport Preservation Group collection)

Newport had this DAF MB230 coach K536 RJX on loan from a dealer for just over three months in 1995. It has a Van Hool body featuring a toilet, and is seen at the depot.

(Ivor Homfray)

69 (L69 EKG) turns out of Havelock Street onto Stow Hill on 5 August 1998 on Gaer service 11A.

(John Jones)

76 (M76 KTG) was one of the 1995 batch of Scania saloons. It is seen on Caradog Road, Cwmbran, on 17 August 1999 and its electronic destination blind can be clearly seen.

(Geoff Gould)

A Scania coach

A used coach was purchased in January 1996 from a dealer and placed in service in March, and this time it was a Scania. Numbered 2 (J96 NJT) it was a K113CRB model with a Plaxton Premier 320 body seating fifty-three. This coach had a 320bhp Scania 11-litre engine coupled to a Scania CR801/C5 compact shift gearbox and Telma retarder. It had been new in May 1992 to Excelsior of Bournemouth as their 322, registered A15 XEL, and gained the registration J96 NJT upon disposal in December 1995.

As we can see from the image below it introduced a new coach livery of cream with dark green fleet name and NT logos on each side. Upon entry into service, older Leyland Tiger number 3 was withdrawn and sold to local operator Croydon Minibus Hire (Boyd and Chick) of Newport, where it joined STG 2Y. A repeat order for six Scania N113CRLs with Alexander Strider bodies entered service in April 1996. They were numbered 78-83 and were identical to the 1995 order.

Optare Metrorider 54 was destroyed by fire in August 1996 and was subsequently written off. A replacement bus was sought and arrived in the form of another used MCW Metrorider, 36 (D477 PON). This was

coincidentally a sister bus to 39, but was obtained in September 1996 from the recently defunct Cardiff Bluebird (Tellings-Golden Miller Ltd) fleet. It was actually purchased from Cardiff Bus who was disposing of many of the Cardiff Bluebird vehicles at this time. D477 PON had been new to London Buses as MR17 in May 1987, and was initially sold to Darlington Transport Ltd in 1994, passing to Cardiff Bluebird in 1995. To round off 1996, the withdrawals this year also included further Marshall-bodied Scania double-deckers (82-4/6, 92/4 and 101) which all passed to Black Prince of Leeds for use on local services.

Ten new buses were taken into stock during 1997. April would see the fifth and final batch of Scanias with Alexandra Strider bodies numbered 77, 90 to 94 and fitted with 260bhp Scania DSC11 engines to Euro 2 specification. The desire to keep fleet numbers below 100 has meant that in order to fill gaps, 77 stands alone.

Also acquired during April was 3 (J97 NJT) another Scania K113CRB, a sister coach to 2 (J96 NJT) that Newport had purchased the previous year. It was purchased from Smith's Travel (High Wycombe) Ltd, High Wycombe and had originally been A16 XEL in the Excelsior, Bournemouth fleet. Meanwhile Leyland Tiger coach 1 (J905 UBO) was re-registered XFM 203 in April 1997.

Strangely Newport did not buy their first Scania coach until 1996, when this second-hand example 2 (J96 NJT) was obtained from a dealer. The striking new coach livery is noteworthy.

(Cardiff Transport Preservation Group collection)

Brand new Scania 83 (N83 PDW) passes the St. Woolos cemetery on Bassaleg Road in April 1996.

(The late Dave B Thomas)

90 (P190 VDW) is from the final batch of Striders delivered in 1997. It is observed picking up on Beaufort Road, St. Julians.

(Cardiff Transport Preservation Group collection)

Four new twenty-five-seat Optare Metroriders were placed in service during August 1997. They were numbered 86-9 and were the last new step-entrance midibuses acquired. Optare revised the Metrorider model in 1994 and these four vehicles were to the new design with a much more angular and slightly wider body which incorporated a bigger destination display. They had Cummins 6B engines of 115bhp and replaced the four MCW Metroriders 36-9.

Withdrawn from service in March 1997 were Marshall-bodied Scania double-deckers (93, 95-100), the last of the type, and these also passed to Black Prince of Leeds. Leyland Tiger coach 4 (XFM 204) was withdrawn and sold in April 1997 passing to Croydon Minibus Hire (Boyd and Chick), Newport. This operator also took the original pair of MCW Metroriders 37 and 38 two months later. Just before it was sold Metrorider 38 undertook a charity run to Belarus, returning to Newport on 12 September.

Low-floor easy access buses

From 1994 low-floor easy-access single-deck buses began to appear in ever increasing numbers across the UK. The stylish Optare Excel was the first purpose-built low-floor single-decker to be produced by this Leeds-based bus manufacturer. It was a full-size bus launched in 1995, constructed as a fully-integral vehicle with a very striking deep windscreen and was available in four lengths. Newport took the opportunity to test Optare Excel demonstrator P447 SWX in late September 1997. Unfortunately, it had only been in service for four days when it sustained accident damage on 29 September. It was consequently returned to Optare a week later.

Nine low-floor Scania L94UB single-deckers, numbered 10-8, were received in August and September 1998 with bodies built by Wrightbus of Ballymena, a first for Newport. The L94 series chassis was introduced in 1996

The later Optare Metroriders have a more angular appearance as depicted here by 86 (R86 BDW). It has just turned on to North Street and is bound for Rogerstone on 5 August 1998.

(John Jones)

and featured a longitudinally-mounted Scania engine, Newport opting for the 9-litre DSC911 version of 220bhp. The bodies were the Axcess-Floline model and were the first buses to appear in a revised livery of cream and dark green. Number 18 had forty-two seats with extra space for wheelchairs; the remainder had seating for forty-six and their unladen weight was 9,520kg.

Optare of Leeds launched the Solo midibus in 1998, its low-floor replacement for the very successful Metrorider, and Newport tried out the brand new thirty-seat demonstrator V235 LWU in November 1999. This particular Solo had a Mercedes engine, and it was used on the Royal Gwent Hospital free bus service.

Withdrawn from service during 1998 were the nine Wadham Stringer-bodied Scania saloons (10-8). Of these 10, 14-6/8 passed to Black Prince of Leeds. After withdrawal 13 went on loan to Red & White, Cwmbran, from September to 9 November 1998. 17 was sent to Belarus with aid supplies during September 1998 returning to Newport the following month. After a period in store 11-3 were sold for scrap in 2000, while 17 was converted into a training bus.

Testing a Dennis Dart

The Dennis Dart was a rear-engine midibus launched in 1989, and rapidly became very popular with operators large and small across the whole of the United Kingdom. In 1996 a low-floor version the Dart SLF was introduced, which was equally as popular, and now placed Dennis Specialist Vehicles amongst the ranks of the major bus and coach manufacturers. Newport Transport evaluated a Dart SLF fitted with a twenty-nine-seat Plaxton Pointer body in late November 1999.

Scania 79 (N79 PDW) makes a fine sight as it accelerates up Stow Hill in the late afternoon winter sunshine on 2 February 1998. The bus is heading for the Gaer estate on the hillside to the west of the town centre.

(John Jones)

14 (S114 TDW) was one of the first low-floor buses in the Newport fleet. It is seen on 20 August 2000 passing Eastern Leisure Centre playing fields, Rumney, bound for Cardiff. It remained in the fleet as a school bus until 2020.

(Geoff Gould)

Scania N113 50 (G50 FKG) is seen on Queensway on 23 October 2003 in the 50:50 dark green double-deck livery introduced in 1998.

(Andrew Wiltshire)

CHAPTER SEVEN
INTO THE 21ST CENTURY

Newport had continued to invest in new buses during the 1990s and unlike many fleets had returned to full-size buses, only maintaining midibuses for a handful of appropriate routes. Moving into the next century, Newport would continue to move with the times in the new world of low-floor buses, and this would see an eventual return to Scania products once again. Eleven new buses were delivered in 2000 and, surprisingly all were from Dennis Specialist Vehicles. There was a reason for this as Scania were unable to offer a low-floor double-decker or low-floor midibus for the UK market at this time.

The first low-floor double-deckers in South Wales

Dennis launched its Trident low-floor double-decker in 1997 and it soon became very popular with orders coming in from operators both large and small, including a large number for service in London. Newport ordered six with single-door Alexander ALX400 bodywork. The ALX400 body was also introduced in 1997 and replaced Alexander's long-running R-series body. The Newport Tridents were numbered 35-40 and initially had seating for seventy-nine and an unladen weight of 11,360kg. 38 received rear-end damage on delivery and was returned to Alexander for repairs returning to Newport six weeks later. The remaining five entered service in January 2000 and by March the seating capacity of all six had been reduced to seventy-six. Under the bonnet was a 220bhp Cummins C220 8.9-litre Euro2 diesel coupled to a Voith transmission. 35-7 carried overall advert liveries while 38-40 were in the 50:50 livery of cream and dark green. They had Newport Transport in large letters below the upper deck windows and a large impression of Newport's "wave" sculpture in red on each side and the rear of the bus.

These impressive vehicles were the first Dennis buses purchased since 1956, the first new double-deckers for ten years and the first low-floor double-deckers for an operator in south Wales. They were initially placed into service on the Bettws routes, but due to vandalism were soon switched to the Cardiff and Caerleon services.

Midibus required

A second-hand MCW Metrorider was purchased in March 2000 as a stop-gap measure. Numbered 54 (F360 URU), it was a twenty-three-seat bus dating from 1989. It was purchased from Wilts and Dorset (2360) and was required to cover extra contract work that Newport had gained. It was painted in an overall dark green livery and put to work on Royal Gwent Hospital and Sainsbury's free bus services. It did not receive any fare collection or radio equipment, and its stay was brief as it was withdrawn in July 2000. The direct service to the Royal Gwent was numbered 99 while the 98 ran via St. Woolos Hospital. The Sainsbury's service was officially numbered 88 but was rarely displayed as such. As of 31 March 2000 the fleet strength was down to eighty-three. This comprised twenty-five double-deckers, thirty-nine saloons, sixteen midibuses and three coaches.

The former Wilts & Dorset MCW Metrorider 54 (F360 URU) in overall dark green livery at the Royal Gwent Hospital in 2000 having arrived via St. Woolos Hospital.

(The late Dave B Thomas)

Complete with the red "wave sculpture" design, brand new Dennis Trident 40 (V140 HTG) is noted on Monnow Way at the Bettws estate working the clockwise service 18C.

(The late Dave B Thomas)

A very colourful Trident 37 (V37 HTG) enters Newport bus station on 22 September 2000 on a service from Caerleon. It is advertising Darlows estate agents who have many offices throughout south-east Wales.

(Andrew Wiltshire)

Dennis Darts

Newport had also ordered five Alexander ALX200-bodied Dennis Dart SLFs for 2000 delivery, but these were subject to a short delay. As a result, Alexander loaned a Mercedes 0814D minibus to Newport between 28 June and 24 August 2000. The new Darts eventually entered service in July and August as 95-9. They were 8.8m long models and seated twenty-eight. They had Cummins B5.9 Euro2 engines of 130bhp and had an unladen weight of 6,750kg. For about a year the visual identities of 95 and 96 did not match their registration documents with 95 masquerading as 96 and vice versa. This was eventually corrected in July 2001. All six Darts gained Newport Nipper branding during 2001 and would replace some of the Optare Metroriders.

In November 1999 Scania double-deckers 27 and 28 were withdrawn followed by 29-34 in early 2000. This eliminated the East Lancs type from the fleet, all of which passed to Black Prince. This Leeds based operator was a notable Scania user, and was now running thirty-three former Newport examples. Optare Metroriders 55 and 57 were also taken out of service in 2000 and sold to Croydon Minibus Hire (Boyd and Chick) of Newport. 63 was withdrawn and stripped for spare parts.

There was a further revision of services in both March and October 2000. Newport ordered a second batch of Alexander ALX200-bodied Dennis Dart SLFs for 2001, taking half a dozen this time.

They entered service in May 2001 and were numbered to take advantage of gaps in the existing fleet number series. Thus they were 31-4, 84/5 and were identical in most respects to the previous batch. 85 carried an overall advert for Adult Education Classes from new, while the remainder gained Newport Nipper branding by the end of the year.

Seen later in its working life with Newport Bus branding, Dart SLF 97 (W97 VWO) in the grounds of St. Woolos hospital whilst working service 98.

(Cardiff Transport Preservation Group collection)

Dennis Dart SLF 31 (Y131 GBO) is from the second batch. It is noted on Hendre Farm Drive, Ringland, on 12 May 2001. Its next stop will be the timing point at Sterndale Bennett Road.

(Geoff Gould)

A century of service

Newport Transport celebrated its centenary on 30 July 2001 and a 24-page booklet was published by the company giving a brief history of significant events during the 100 years since 1901. A bus rally was held at Tredegar House Country Park on Sunday 5 August and was attended by a number of preserved buses mainly from south east Wales. Newport Transport sent Leyland PD2 178, a selection of buses in overall advert liveries including Tridents 35 to 37, Dart 85 and Scanias 43 and 52 plus Leyland Leopard training bus 174 (XGM 450L). The Centenary-liveried Scania 20 provided a service to and from the bus station. Also on show was X94 USC, a Wright-bodied Scania L94 demonstrator that Newport had on loan at this time.

Both Rogerstone services (Mount Pleasant and Cefn Wood) were extended to the new housing development at Foxgloves in January 2001, while in March Rhiwderin benefitted from two more services. Volvo Bus lent Newport an East Lancs Vyking-bodied B7TL double-decker from 4 December, which was used on the Newport to Cardiff service. In 2001 Edwin Marsh retired as Managing Director and his place was taken by Trevor Roberts.

Scania N112s 19 and 25, of the 1984/85 batch were withdrawn in March 2001, and both passed to local operator Croydon Minibus Hire (Boyd and Chick) of Newport. Optare Metroriders 53 and 58-62, 64 were also withdrawn. 53, 59-62 ended up in Scotland with Coakley Bus Company Ltd of Motherwell while 58 was retained and dismantled for spares. Leyland Tiger coach 1 (XFM 203) which was new in 1991 as 5 (J905 UBO) was also sold.

Two interesting demonstrators were inspected in the first half of 2002. One of these was a brand new Wright Solar Fusion-bodied Scania L94UA bendy-bus, which was road tested for a week. Newport Transport was the first operator in South Wales to trial a bendy-bus. The other visiting bus was a Scania OmniCity saloon, a new model for the UK, which was inspected in March.

A red Mercedes Citaro saloon with a dual-door body was inspected on 25 March 2002, while on 24 May an overall white Mercedes saloon with a single door body was also inspected.

There was just one withdrawal during 2002. Alexander-bodied Scania N113 45 was de-roofed at Mill Street, Risca on 22 May, while returning to the depot light after a school service from St. Joseph's School, Duffryn. It was subsequently withdrawn and sold to dealer Ensign, for conversion to an open-topper. It was put to work at Eastbourne in red City Sightseeing livery, and by 2007 was performing sightseeing duties in Bristol.

Wearing its special Centenary livery, Scania 20 (B220 YUH) is parked in the grounds of Tredegar House, the setting for the Newport Transport Centenary bus rally on 5 August 2001.

(Andrew Wiltshire)

A summary of the Newport fleet in July 2001

Fleet no.	Chassis type	Bodywork	Year new
Coaches			
2, 3	Scania K113CRB	Plaxton	1992
Single-deckers			
4-9	Scania N113CRB	Alexander Strider	1993
68-73	" "	"	1994
65-7, 74-76	" N113CRL	"	1995
79-83	" "	"	1996
77, 90-4	" "	"	1997
10-8	Scania L94UB	Wright	1998
Double-deckers			
178	Leyland PD2/40	Longwell Green	1958
20-4/6	Scania N112DR	Alexander RH	1984
41-6	" N113DRB	"	1988
47-52	" "	"	1989
35-40	Dennis Trident	Alexander ALX400	2000
Midibuses			
56	Optare Metrorider	Optare	1990
64	"	"	1991
86-9	"	"	1997
95-9	Dennis Dart	Alexander ALX200	2000
31-4, 84/5	"	"	2001

Note that coaches 2 and 3 were acquired in 1996/97 respectively. 178 is a special events vehicle.

YP02 AAN was an impressive Scania bendy-bus that was road tested in March 2002. It had a fifty-nine-seat Wright body, and was later purchased by Nottingham City Transport.

(Ivor Homfray)

This unregistered dual-door Mercedes Citaro was inspected and road tested in March 2002. It is thought that this demonstrator became LV02 UUC, and was eventually exported to Ireland.

(Ivor Homfray)

The Scania OmniCity

The Scania OmniCity N94UB single-decker first appeared in right-hand drive layout for the UK market in 2002. It was an integrally-constructed bus using a substantial number of aluminum components. Unlike some low-floor models being offered at the time, the OmniCity featured a low floor extending beyond the rear axle. Newport, not surprisingly was an early customer for the OmniCity and received six in December 2002 which entered service in January 2003. They were numbered 53-8 and were the first buses in the fleet with the new style of registration numbers introduced from September 2001. They had seats for forty-two passengers and were assembled at Scania's bus plant at Slupsk in Poland. The OmniCity was fitted with a Scania DSC9 9-litre transverse engine developing 230bhp, and the transmission consisted of a ZF 4-speed gearbox. They were the first buses in the Newport fleet to meet Euro 3 emission specification.

As a result of the above delivery, Optare Metrorider 56 was renumbered 156 in November 2002. It was then withdrawn in January 2003 and went to work for Jaycrest Ltd of Sittingbourne in Kent.

A further six Scania OmniCitys arrived during the summer of 2003 numbered 59-64. They entered service in August and September, and unlike the first six, had seating for forty-one and were built at the Scania plant in Sweden.

The well-respected bus dealer Ensign of Purfleet loaned Newport two quite interesting vehicles in 2003 including a former Isle of Man Marshall-bodied Dennis Dart SLF registered DMN 20R. This was road-tested for a week in March when Newport Transport were looking to acquire an additional vehicle.

Newport organised a special event at Tredegar House on 6 December 2002 to mark the entry into service of the new Scania OmniCity saloons. 57 is seen next to 54, one of two that entered service in advert liveries.

(The late Dave B Thomas)

From the second batch of Scania OmniCity saloons, 61 (YV03 PZR) is seen on Chepstow Road heading for the town centre on 24 May 2008. The advert across the top of the windscreen is for the £2.50 Day Ticket. It now carries the new style of fleetname, "Newport Bus serving the city".

(Andrew Wiltshire)

This Dennis Dart was on loan from Ensignbus for evaluation. It had a Marshall Capital body and was new to Isle of Man National Transport.

(Ivor Homfray)

Sightseeing Tour for Newport

The other vehicle on loan from Ensign was an open-top Leyland Atlantean dating from 1980 which had been new to Plymouth City Transport and had an East Lancs dual-door body. ATK 154W entered service on 12 August 2003 in Guide Friday livery for a trial period ending 5 September. It was used to launch the Discover Newport Tour and remained on loan until a suitable Newport bus was converted the following year. The hourly "hop-on hop-off" sightseeing tour featured eight stops, and commenced at 10.00 with the last tour departing at 16.00.

Starting in Newport bus station it served the Roman attractions at Caerleon, the Transporter Bridge, Tredegar House/Country Park, Tredegar Park, St. Woolos Cathedral and Newport railway station. The adult fare was £5. The spare bus, which was used on at least two occasions, was Bristol FS6G open-topper 868 NHT, owned by A Smith (Welsh Dragon), Newport.

In July 2003 the coach fleet was disbanded and the two remaining coaches, Scanias K113CRs 2/3 were sold to Phil Anslow Travel of Pontypool. Newport joined a growing list of former municipal fleets to give up coaching activities and concentrate on stage work.

The Discover Newport Tour was launched using this East Lancs-bodied open-top Leyland Atlantean ATK 154W supplied on loan from Ensignbus. It is seen here calling at the Transporter Bridge stop.

(Cardiff Transport Preservation Group collection)

A brand new dedicated school bus

On 24 February 2004 Newport took delivery of a Scania K94 to be used exclusively on school contracts. It was fitted with a Spanish-built Irizar seventy-seat Intercentury coach body and was on a one year extended loan from Scania Bus and Coach. It entered service on 4 May and was initially used on a Duffryn school contract. Numbered 19, it was painted in an all-over yellow livery with "S-KOOL" logos on each side. It featured 3+2 seating and was fitted with seat belts and CCTV throughout. The Scania K94 had a longitudinally-mounted Scania DC09 Euro3 engine at the rear which produced 220bhp @2200rpm.

Scania OmniCity 56 (CA52 JKJ) is on the approach to the Kingsway bus station on a fine 18 March 2003. It is wearing a livery modified to advertise Newenergy, a scheme promoted by Newport Council.

(Andrew Wiltshire)

In its very distinctive yellow livery with S-KOOL branding, number 19 (YN04 AFU) was a new Scania K94 obtained specifically for school transport in Newport.

(Cardiff Transport Preservation Group collection)

Scania 141 (F41 YHB) had been converted for its new sightseeing role on the Newport Sightseeing tour when noted at Tredegar House on 17 August 2005.

(Andrew Wiltshire)

Seen when quite new, OmniCity 45 (YN54 AOE) passes through The Friary, Cardiff, on its way back to Newport on the 30 service.

(Cardiff Transport Preservation Group collection)

In March 2004 Scania N113s 42 and 46 were withdrawn and later passed to Northern Blue of Burnley. At this time another of this batch 41, was converted to partial open-top layout for use on the Discover Newport tour and marketed under the City Sightseeing brand in red livery. The Leyland Atlantean on loan became the back-up vehicle until it eventually returned to Ensign in July 2006. In October 2004, 41 together with 43 and 44 were renumbered 141/3/4 to make way for new buses.

The final withdrawal in 2004 was the first Scania/ Alexander Strider saloon to go. Number 9 was taken out of service in October, and converted into a driver training vehicle to replace Wadham Stringer-bodied Scania 117 (RUH 17Y). Even more new buses were delivered to Newport Transport between October and December 2004 comprising twelve new Scanias. A further six forty-two-seat N94UB OmniCity models were numbered 41-6 and entered service in January 2005. These and all subsequent OmniCity saloons were built at Scania's bus plant at Slupsk in Poland. As with the earlier OmniCity saloons, these had an unladen weight of 11,700kg.

The trial with Scania coach number 19 was deemed a success and a further six identical coaches arrived on 23 December 2004 numbered 20-5. Although taxed in 2004, they eventually entered service between January and March 2005. They had a team of dedicated drivers who were allocated their own coach and did the same school duty every day. The option to purchase similar school coach 19 was then taken up and this would become the spare vehicle covering for any of the other six being off the road. On weekends and in school holidays these coaches were often used on private hire work.

As a result of these new arrivals, quite a few buses were withdrawn. They comprised Scania N113 double-deckers 143/4 (F43/4 YHB) and 47-52. All eight passed to Northern Blue of Burnley. The remaining five Scania/ Strider saloons of 1993 (4-8) were also taken out of service and all but number 5 made their way to Northern Blue to join the double-deckers. Number 5 passed to charity Teen Challenge of Newport as a non-PSV.

Wright-bodied low-floor Scania L94UB 16 was badly damaged by an engine fire in October 2005 and was sold. Finally, three of the 1997 Optare Metroriders, 86/7/9 were taken out of service in August 2005 with 88 following in January 2006. 86-8 passed to Northern Blue while 89 went to R Giles (James Wedding Cars) of Caerphilly.

Scania school bus 21 (YN54 OCC) with 24 behind at Asda, Duffryn having just come off the morning school run.

(Cardiff Transport Preservation Group collection)

The first of several Mercedes Citaro demonstrators was put through its paces with Newport Transport in January and again in April 2006. In between these two visits Scania Bus and Coach (UK) Ltd provided an OmniCity demonstrator for two weeks in February, but this was only used on contract work. In 2006 the Scania OmniCity model was designated N230UB and updated to feature a 5-cylinder Euro 4 engine. In the latter half of 2007 Newport received twelve of this updated model, and the first half dozen took fleet numbers 47-52.

The second batch of buses entered service in November as 1-6. It should be noted that 1/2/4 were initially numbered 65/6/8, but were renumbered before they entered service. All twelve were forty-one-seaters and fitted with air-conditioning. This was disabled after a few years to reduce fuel consumption. OmniCitys 50-2 were branded for the new X30 express service to Cardiff that operated via the M4 and commenced on Monday 19 November 2007. Six Optare Solo midibuses were ordered for delivery in early 2008.

All six of the 1994 Alexander Strider-bodied Scanias (68-73) were taken out of service in August 2007 and were soon sold to dealers eventually finding new owners. Scania saloon 92 was withdrawn with accident damage after being stolen from the garage in December 2007 and driven into a wall. It was stripped for spares and eventually sold locally for scrap.

Midibuses from Optare

The Optare Solo is a very successful low-floor integral midibus that was first introduced in 1998. It is rear-engined and has the front axle ahead of the entrance door. Prior to the arrival of Newport's Solos, two Solos were loaned to Newport by the dealer Mistral. They were required to assist with the launch of the new rail-link service, as part of the re-opening of the passenger train service to Ebbw Vale from Cardiff, which did not call at Newport.

The new Optare Solo midibuses entered service between February and April 2008. They were twenty-seven-seat buses fitted with MAN D0834 engines and were numbered 68-73. 68 and 69 carried a special two-tone green livery with branding for the Rogerstone rail-link service 907, which linked the newly re-opened Ebbw Vale to Cardiff service with Newport town centre. This commenced on 6 February 2008, but was poorly patronised and ceased on 30 May and 68 and 69 duly received fleet livery.

X30-branded Scania OmniCity 52 (YN57 FZR) heads into Cardiff city centre on 13 April 2010. It is seen passing Cardiff University's Bute Building on North Road appropriately on an X30 working.

(Andrew Wiltshire)

Optare Solo 68 (YJ57 YCG) was one of the pair dedicated to the unsuccessful rail-link service. It is seen waiting at the newly opened Rogerstone station in 2008 in its special livery.

(Cardiff Transport Preservation Group collection)

Having left the bus station, 73 (YJ08 PKO) is about to join Kingsway. This Optare Solo is off to Rhiwderin, a village to the west of Newport near Bassaleg on 24 May 2011.

(John Jones)

All six of the 1995 delivery of Alexander Strider-bodied Scanias (65-7, 74-6) were taken out of service in the autumn of 2008 and sold in November. All apart from 74 were exported to the Republic of Ireland by July 2009 for use as school buses.

A brief summary of the Newport fleet in December 2008

	Chassis type	Bodywork	Year new
Single-deckers			
11	Scania N113CRL	Alexander Strider	1996/7
8	Scania L94UB	Wright	1998
30	Scania OmniCity	Scania	2003-7
Double-deckers			
1	Leyland PD2/40	Longwell Green	1958
1	Scania N113DRB	Alexander RH open-top	1988
6	Dennis Trident	Alexander ALX400	2000
Midibuses			
11	Dennis Dart	Alexander ALX200	2000/1
6	Optare Solo	Optare	2008
School coaches			
7	Scania K94	Irizar	2004/5
Total = 81 vehicles			

CHAPTER EIGHT
NEW IMAGES, VARIETY AND EVEN GREENER BUSES

The promise of more variety

It was announced in 2009 that due to the poor service and late delivery dates Newport was receiving from Scania, an order had been placed for six MAN NL273F (A69) single-deckers with Wright Meridian bodywork. They were expected in June/July, and would be the first full-size saloons since the Bristol RESLs in 1967, that were not of Scania manufacture. Meanwhile in March 2009 Optare Solo 69 was involved in a serious accident on Western Valley Road, Rogerstone when it left the road and went down an embankment. Following its repair and re-entry into service in July, it was given fleet number 74.

Managing Director Trevor Roberts left Newport Transport in May 2009 to take up a post at Blackpool Transport. His place was taken in June by Chris Blyth who had previously been Director of Delivery at Newport Transport.

Volvo double-deckers

Having gained additional school contracts for the academic year 2009/2010, extra vehicles would be needed and duly arrived in the form of seven rather impressive former Lothian Volvo Olympians. These twelve-year old buses had attractive eighty-one-seat Alexander Royale dual-door bodywork and entered service as 266/8/72/6/7/9 and 283 (P266 PSX etc), thereby retaining their Lothian fleet numbers. They carried what was described as a trial livery of dark green and white. Not long after the Olympians entered service, Dennis Trident 37 and Scania OmniCity 43 gained this livery too.

As a gesture of thanks to regular customers, and to encourage people to leave their cars at home and come into the centre of Newport, Newport Transport offered free travel to all on Christmas Eve and New Year's Eve 2009. The dark green and white livery was soon adopted and will be referred to as the 2010 livery. Thirty-eight buses were repainted into this scheme during 2010 and included a large number of OmniCity saloons together with a few of the Optare Solos, the seven surviving Wright-bodied Scanias, four Dennis Darts and one of the Scania/Striders (78).

In May 2010 Newport Transport became the first bus operator in the UK outside London to offer its customers a pre-paid Smart Card for travel. Weekly, monthly or annual versions of the card were made available which it was hoped would make paying for travel even more convenient for passengers.

Dart 84 is seen on 4 March 2009 operating the Tesco free bus service at St. Mellons, Cardiff. There is no longer any free bus service to this store.

(Andrew Wiltshire)

Initially the former Lothian Volvo Olympians were regularly used in normal service as depicted here by 276 in Westgate Street, Cardiff, on 13 October 2009.

(Andrew Wiltshire)

A good example of the 2010 livery is seen on low-floor Scania L94 number 10. It is approaching Kingsway on 24 May 2011.

(John Jones)

Trident 37 has carried numerous different liveries during its service with Newport Transport. Here it is in the Lothian style livery introduced by the Volvo Olympians from Edinburgh. It is entering the Kingsway bus station on 12 February 2011 on service 29 from Cwmbran.

(Andrew Wiltshire)

The 3-axle Scania OmniLink is seen in Cardiff bus station on a gloomy 10 November 2009. This massive bus seated fifty-four and was used on the X30 service during its brief stay.

(Andrew Wiltshire)

More demonstrators

In 2009/10 Newport Transport kept up its tradition of inspecting and testing the various types of vehicle currently available and wherever possible placed them in passenger service. In addition to a Mercedes Citaro 0530 saloon, 2009 witnessed on loan a 3-axle Scania OmniLink which was put through its paces on the X30 in November.

In December 2010 Newport Transport's Managing Director Chris Blyth left the company. Consequently, Newport's Director of Delivery Scott Pearson became acting MD until being appointed to the role of Managing Director in April 2011.

Advertising its Euro 5 credentials, the Scania OmniCity double-decker was a model that Newport didn't pursue. YR10 BBO is seen in Cardiff on 22 June 2010.

(Andrew Wiltshire)

The MAN saga

In the latter part of 2009 an attempt was made to cancel the order for the six new MAN saloons, but this was not possible. They were consequently delivered to Commercial Motors (Wales) Ltd, Newport (MAN dealer) in January 2010 for storage pending the outcome of the dispute. At this stage all six buses were in Newport's dark green and cream livery, and from February were put into storage in the Midlands.

After nearly a year in store, the new MAN saloons were redelivered to Newport Transport in December 2010 and registered. They were repainted into the 2010 livery and given fleet numbers in a new series, 101-6. 103 was initially used for driver familiarisation from 21 February 2011. They soon proved to be popular vehicles with drivers at Newport Transport and were quite different from the Scania OmniCitys.

Alexander Strider-bodied Scanias 79-82 were withdrawn in February 2011 and sold by March, passing to RSG Global, an international mining and quarrying company. It is thought they were exported for use as staff transport. During the same month Dennis Trident 40 was repainted in overall mid-green and 39 followed suite in June. By August 39 and 40 had been refurbished and new seats were fitted. White was added to the overall green together with green and yellow swoops. This was then confirmed as the new double-deck livery.

Return to Scania

In 2011 Newport took some of the last Scania OmniCity saloons completed for the UK market. Eight new forty-one-seat examples were received in June numbered 110-7. 110-2 were delivered in overall mid-green and were branded for the X30 service. The remainder, 113-7 entered service in the 2010 livery.

One of the MANs as originally delivered at Commercial Motors, Newport in February 2010. It is unregistered and without a fleet number.

(The late Dave B Thomas)

The MANs 101-6 occasionally made an appearance on the Cardiff services. Here is 105 (CN60 FBL) on service 30 in Wood Street, Cardiff on 22 May 2013.

(Andrew Wiltshire)

Refurbished Dennis Trident 39 (V39 HTG) in the new double-deck livery in High Street on 10 July 2014. High Street was the terminus for a number of services until the new bus station was completed.

(John Jones)

112 is one of the three Scania OmniCitys in overall green with X30 branding. It is passing Cardiff Castle on 27 June 2011 on its return to Newport via Gabalfa interchange and the M4.

(John Jones)

The other five OmniCity saloons were finished in the 2010 livery. Looking immaculate, 117 is seen in Wood Street, Cardiff, when new on 14 June 2011.

(Andrew Wiltshire)

Buses to Monmouth

Following a public consultation exercise, a new commercial service X25 commenced on 5 December 2011 operating between Monmouth and Newport. It was aimed at both commuters and shoppers and called in at Raglan and Usk en route to Newport. It only ran until 17 June 2012 after which customers had to rely on the tendered service 60 between the two towns. Also during 2012 the fast X30 service to Cardiff was diverted into the University Hospital of Wales site at the Heath, Cardiff. Withdrawn between May and August 2011 were Scania saloons 77, 78, 83, 90, 91, 93, 94, and Darts 31, 34, 85, 95-9. However, during November and December Scania 77 and Darts 95-7 and 99 were back in service. Dennis Trident 35 received a Christmas overall advert livery for the duration of December 2011.

During 2012 the remaining four Dennis Tridents were refurbished, with 38 completed in November, 37 in December followed by 35 in February 2012 and 36 in March. All received the new double-deck livery and at this point the new seating capacity of all six was confirmed as H47/25F.

A new standard single-decker

The first of a new fleet of Alexander Dennis Enviro200 saloons was also received during June 2011. The Enviro200 in its revised form was launched by Alexander Dennis in 2008 as a direct replacement for the Dart from which it was developed. It featured a Cummins engine with a choice of transmission and was available in a number of lengths. It was revised again from 2009 and remained in production until 2018 by which time it complied with Euro5 emission legislation. It would soon become a very popular lightweight bus in the UK. Newport's first examples were numbered 301 and 302 and were followed in July by similar 303-6 and in the autumn by 307-9. All nine buses had seating for twenty-nine and entered service in overall white with Newport Transport logos.

This is how the first nine Enviro200s looked when they entered service in 2011. 304 (YX11 AGY) is seen on 4 July leaving the terminus of Brynglas Road, shortly after entering service.

(The late Dave B Thomas)

From Risca to Cardiff

The X16 was a service that was subsidised by Caerphilly and Newport Councils. The X16 initially ran from St. Mary Street, Risca to Cardiff serving Rogerstone, Cleppa Park, Castleton, Marshfield and St. Mellons Business Park along the way. Newport Transport won the tender for the X16 service (Monday to Saturday) from 5 January 2009 when it was relinquished by Stagecoach in South Wales. The Risca terminus was later moved to Crosskeys College from 6 April 2009. Veolia Transport Cymru took on the service from 27 July 2009. The service then passed back to Newport Transport on 26 September 2011 with Stagecoach operating a number of early and late trips. By this time the normal starting point was Tredegar Gardens in Risca, and the route now took in the Tesco superstore in Risca. The X16 finally passed to Stagecoach on 25 January 2014, and all Sunday journeys were withdrawn from 31 July 2016. Due to continued poor patronage it was completely withdrawn on 21 January 2018.

More Enviro200s both large and small

Two further twenty-nine-seat Enviro200s were added to the fleet in 2012. They were numbered 310 and 311 and were obtained to operate the Monmouth town services

contract which had recently been won by Newport. These services W3-W5 commenced on 2 April and were manned by drivers local to Monmouth. The vehicles were garaged overnight and at weekends at a yard in Symonds Yat, but were regularly exchanged for another vehicle from Newport to enable routine maintenance.

Ultimately any available Enviro200 was used at Monmouth until the contract ended on 25 March 2016. Enviro200s 310 and 311 were immediately followed by six longer thirty-nine-seat models, numbered 312-7, in April/May. Newport Transport was awarded a contract to operate a Park and Ride service from Cardiff East Park and Ride site to the University Hospital of Wales (UHW). This began on 14 May 2012 using new Enviro200 number 317 which carried appropriate branding for this service, which lasted less than a year due to poor patronage.

In a surprise move, Optare Solos 68, 70-4 were withdrawn in April and May 2012. Besides being non-standard, these buses had proved to be unreliable on Newport's hilly terrain and regularly overheated. They were however popular with drivers. All six were sold to the Plaxton Coach Sales Centre in April/ May as part exchange for two Volvo coaches.

During the first period of X16 operation Newport's Optare Solo 68 (YJ57 YCG) is heading for Cardiff along St. Mellons Road, Marshfield, on 2 June 2009.

(Andrew Wiltshire)

Enviro200 317 was dedicated to the UHW Park and Ride. It is seen at the Heath Hospital, Cardiff, on 27 June 2012 and was destined to have a very short life as it was destroyed by fire five months later.

(Andrew Wiltshire)

Return to coaching

Having disposed of its last coaches in 2003 (excluding the dedicated Scania school coaches 19-25), a decision was made to acquire a pair of used Volvos. They were B12B models with Plaxton Panther bodywork that were new in 2006. Numbered 26 and 27, they came from Woottens (Opperman) of Chesham in April/May 2012, and had seating for forty-nine plus a toilet facility. By July they were in service in a white livery with green swoops, and were later named Sophie and Olivia respectively.

Volvo B12B 27 (YN06 MXV) "Olivia" is seen at Rhossili on the Gower Peninsular on 16 August 2012.

(The late Dave B Thomas)

Unfortunately, Scania OmniCity 113 was badly damaged by fire on 19 May on the M4 when working the X30 service but it was deemed not beyond repair. While 113 was away for attention, a former Nottingham Scania OmniCity was supplied on loan from Scania, and this was later substituted for an OmniCity double-decker.

By June 2012 Newport Transport had been appointed as an Alexander Dennis agent, and it would be fairly common to see vehicles from other local operators receiving attention at Newport Transport's garage in Corporation Road. A Mercedes Sprinter 515CDI minibus dating from 2009 was acquired from White, St. Albans in September 2012. Numbered 207 it had an eighteen-seat Ferqui Soroco body and entered service in a silver livery, but was later painted white in a similar fashion to coaches 26 and 27.

Image upgrade

During the summer of 2012 Dennis Darts 96 and 99 were some of the last buses repainted into the 2010 dark green and white livery. The dark green used was replaced by mid-green, and Scania OmniCity 48 was repainted thus in October. This would become what will be referred to as the 2012 livery. By the end of the year Enviro200s 301 and 302 had gained this livery in place of overall white. It was however some time before all the white Enviro200s received fleet livery. In November and for one month only, Scania OmniCity saloons 45/6, 57 and 62 were given artwork to promote a prostate cancer campaign. Enviro200 number 304 carried a Christmas livery for much of December, gaining the 2012 livery in January 2013.

Scania OmniCity 49 shows off the 2012 livery that uses mid-green in place of dark green. It is seen on 14 May 2019 passing the Newport Cenotaph at the junction of Clarence Place and Chepstow Road.

(Andrew Wiltshire)

To end 2012 on a rather positive note, five new Alexander Dennis Enviro400 E40D double-deckers entered service in November. They were numbered 400-4 and featured seventy-six coach-type seats finished in e-leather. 404 had the honour of being exhibited at Expo 2012 at the NEC in Birmingham. It differed from 400-3 in that it had some back-to- back seating with tables on the upper deck.

The Enviro400 double-decker first appeared in 2005 and was available as an integral vehicle, but could also be bodied separately if the customer so wished. It was intended as a replacement for the Trident 2 and was powered by a Cummins engine coupled to either a Voith or ZF transmission.

Following repair, fire-damaged OmniCity 113 returned to service in December in the new 2012 livery. However, on a more unfortunate note three buses were destroyed by fire in an arson attack at the depot on 3 December. They were Dennis Trident 38, Dennis Dart 84 and Enviro200 317. The latter was less than one-year-old. Alexander Dennis Enviro200 demonstrator 320 (YX61 DOU) which had been on loan on a number of previous occasions

in 2012 returned on loan in December having received chassis modifications at ADL.

Three twenty-nine-seat Enviro200s arrived on loan from Alexander Dennis in January 2013 with temporary fleet numbers 444, 555 and 666 (YX59 BZM/L/N). They had been new to Mid Wales, Penrhyncoch in January 2010. In the event 666 was not used and returned to ADL, with 444 and 555 following in June 2013.

Tridents from London

The double-deck fleet was further enhanced in April 2013 when a small batch of Plaxton President-bodied Transbus Tridents were acquired from the dealer Ensignbus which had rebuilt their 10.5m long bodies to single-door seventy-four seat layout. 420 and 421 (LN51 KXR/W) arrived in April 2013 having been repainted into fleet livery by Ensign.

In August another four were acquired becoming 422 (LN51 KXV) and 423-5 (LR02 BAO/U, BBF). All six had been new in 2002 to Metroline. 420/1 were similarly modified at a later date.

Alexander Dennis Enviro400 number 402 has just worked into Newport from Cwmbran on 25 March 2017.

(Andrew Wiltshire)

Newport's double-deck livery is well-suited to the Plaxton President body, despite the unusual window arrangement for the nearside lower saloon. This view of Transbus Trident 422 (LN51 KXV) was taken on 23 July 2018.

(Andrew Wiltshire)

The seven Scania K94s with Irizar bodies (19-25) that were purchased in 2004/5 purely for school contracts were all withdrawn and sold between March and August 2013.

Having given just under four years' service, the seven former Lothian Volvo Olympians were also sold off between April and August. They had been confined to school duties in their latter days at Newport, and all went for further service.

New for Chepstow

In May another pair of Alexander Dennis Enviro200 saloons were acquired as 318 and 319. They were twenty-nine-seaters with leather seats and seatbelts. It is thought that they were acquired from dealer stock which may explain why they featured tinted glass for the saloon windows. They entered service in the 2012 livery, and were initially dedicated to Chepstow town services with appropriate branding.

318 is seen at the bus pull-in at Chepstow town centre while working town service C1 on 13 September 2013. Note the tinted glass saloon windows.

(Andrew Wiltshire)

In July another of the Wright-bodied Scania L94UB saloons, 15, succumbed to fire damage and was later scrapped. On 19 June 2013 Enviro200s 222, 333 (MX09 MHY/Z) which had been on loan were acquired and given fleet numbers 321/2 in the main fleet series. The pair had been new to Solutions SK, Cheadle Heath, near Stockport. As of September 2013, except for the coaches and minibuses, the normal service fleet was 100% low-floor. Some rather interesting saloons were received on loan for evaluation during 2013 including an ADL Enviro300-bodied Scania K230, an MCV-bodied Volvo B7RLE, and two CNG-powered gas buses. These were Caetano-bodied MAN Ecocity and a Scania K270 chassis with Alexander Dennis Enviro300 body.

The Kingsway bus station was finally closed on 26 October 2013 and some services moved to the Market Square bus station from the next day while many terminated at bus stands on Queensway opposite the railway station. Construction of the new shopping centre began in April 2014 which incorporated a new but somewhat smaller bus station.

In the first three months of 2014 Scania OmniCity saloons 53-7 and Dennis Dart 95 were withdrawn from service though the Scanias were reinstated during August. At this point Enviro200 320 returned to Alexander Dennis off loan. In July Enviro200 number 307 received a special World War One commemorative livery. Meanwhile all buses in the fleet received a poppy vinyl on the front dash panel. Also five OmniCitys (shown in the table below) had World War One poppy vinyls added to their whole rear elevation. They were named after Newport Corporation Transport employees who died in action. These names were located on the front dash panel between two poppy vinyls.

Fleet no.	Named in memory of
49	Rifleman W J Williams
59	Rifleman E J Bailey
62	Lance Corporal C Jones
64	Private J N Murray
117	Private A E Passmore

Demand Responsive Transport

Demand Responsive Transport (DRT) schemes usually operate in areas where there are few or no viable conventional bus services. The exact route and stopping points are normally flexible, and in all cases journeys must be booked in advance by the customer. DRT services come with the benefit of commercial bus ticketing and with the customer in control. Customers can use this service at the cost of a bus fare rather than a more expensive taxi and are ideally suited for use by minibuses. At Newport Bus the service began on 3 November 2014 using an eight-seat second-hand Mercedes minibus WM57 GZG, taken on hire from Dawson Rentals and given fleet number 210. It was put to work on service 62 from the centre of Newport to Bishton, Magor and Caerwent. Further services followed.

As part of its low-emissions trials Newport Transport operated this CNG-powered Scania K270UB. It has an Alexander Dennis Enviro300 body and is seen on 3 September 2013 in Cardiff on an X30 duty.

(Andrew Wiltshire)

210 was the Mercedes that was used on the first DRT service 62 that ran out to the east of the city.

(The late Dave B Thomas)

London Dart invasion

In order to meet forthcoming Public Service Vehicle Accessibility Regulations (PSVAR), it was decided to purchase a batch of used Transbus Dart SLFs to replace existing vehicles that failed to meet this standard. Fourteen former London examples were obtained and allocated fleet numbers 323-36. Twelve of them were acquired between October and December 2014. The final pair (331/6) did not appear until May 2015. All were 10.1m long and were supplied by the Yorkshire-based dealer Dawson Rentals, Hellaby.

They were acquired as dual-door buses, and all but one were new in 2002. Ten of them were rebuilt to B27F, but 325/7/8/30 remained two-door vehicles, and entered service as such in overall white livery with Newport fleet names. The first three into service were 323/5/7 in December 2014 and by the end of May 2015 324/6/8-30 were all available for service.

It is believed that the Newport CitySightseeing Tour ended in 2013 and the open-top Scania 141 was then used on the occasional private hire during 2014 and also as a tree-lopper by Newport's engineering staff. The bus eventually passed to the Cardiff Transport Preservation Group at Barry in April 2016. February 2015 saw the withdrawal from service of Scania/Wright saloons 12 and 17 and Dennis Darts 96 and 99.

DRT expansion

In early 2015 a pair of used Mercedes Sprinter 511CDi minibuses arrived on long term loan from Dawson Rentals. New in 2008, KX08 HOJ was an eleven-seater, one seat fewer than KX08 HOH. From 30 March KX08 HOJ was put to work as 211 on DRT service 63 from the centre of Newport to Whitson and Goldcliff which replaced normal route 5. The other Mercedes entered service as 212 in late spring on service 31 which ran out to Marshfield and St. Brides. These services all had dedicated drivers, with replacements to cover for holidays and sickness. These minibuses were joined in July 2015 by 213 (KY15 RBX) and 214 (KY15 PNX) which were longer sixteen-seat 516CDI models and also on extended loan from Dawson Rentals.

In May 2015 Dennis Dart 97 was withdrawn, while similar 32 and 33 followed in July together with the remaining Wright-bodied Scania L94s (10/1/3/4/8). Having left the fleet in 2011, Alexander Strider-bodied Scania 77 was purchased by the Cardiff Transport Preservation Group for preservation in July 2015, having latterly served with Harrogate Coach Travel since 2011. Subsequently Scanias 10/3/4 were due to be sold but, instead, they were fitted with wheelchair ramps to make them DDA compliant and were repainted white. On 5/6 August 2015 the five Enviro400s (400-4) and five MANs (101-4/6) were loaned to Transport for London to assist during a tube strike in London. There were no demonstrators on loan at Newport Transport in 2015.

330 was one of the Darts that was not initially rebuilt and saw some service in white with its centre exit still in situ. This view was taken on 4 September 2015.

(John Jones)

324 (KU52 YKG) had been neatly rebuilt to single-door layout and was in the 2012 livery when caught on Queensway on 5 September 2015.

(Andrew Wiltshire)

The new bus station opens

The new Friars Walk shopping centre in Newport opened on 12 November 2015 and the new adjacent bus station was commissioned on 12 December. The bus station had a saw-tooth layout design which was small and cramped. It had fifteen active bays, a small layover area for buses and incorporated Newport Transport's travel centre. A number of operators refused to use it claiming it was unsafe, preferring the Market Square bus station. Cardiff Bus indicated that they would only use bay 15.

Scania OmniCity 61 was taken out of normal service in February 2016 for conversion to a driver training bus and received a white, green and yellow livery. Mercedes Sprinter 214 was returned off loan to Dawson Rentals in January 2016. By May 2016, the four overall white former London Darts (325/7/8/30) which retained their centre doors were placed into store pending refurbishment and conversion to single-door layout.

Work soon began on 327 and 330 which had been stripped to bare shells and 330 had its centre door removed, before work was halted. Due to a vehicle shortage the three remaining Wright-bodied Scanias 10/3/4 were returned to service having had Newport fleet names added to their overall white livery. The intention was to use them solely on school contracts, but as they were now part of the operational fleet, it wasn't long before they were being used in normal service.

Sprinters for DRT service

In June 2016 Newport took delivery of three new thirteen-seat Mercedes Benz Sprinter minibuses for use on DRT services. They were numbered 216-8 and were on loan from Dawson Rentals replacing three older Mercedes minibuses 210 (WM57 GZG) and 211/2 (KX08 HOJ/H), which were returned the same month.

Mercedes 217 is working DRT service 63 which serves Goldcliff and the Wetlands. This photograph was taken on 17 September 2016.

(Andrew Wiltshire)

Loss of school contracts

Due to the loss of a substantial number of school contracts to operator New Adventure Travel (NAT), a large number of buses were placed into reserve by the autumn of 2016. These were Dennis Tridents 35/6/9, Scania Omnicitys 5, 54/6/7 and 114, plus Enviro200s 306/9/11/21 and rebuilt former London Darts 323 and 336. A rather surprising move was the sale of Scania OmniCity saloons 53/5/8 in December 2016 to Harrogate Coach Travel of Tockworth in North Yorkshire. Here they were soon re-registered XTN 421, JSU 721 and UUG 384 respectively.

Another new image

Whilst both the 2010 and 2012 liveries made a bold statement, they would have been quite expensive to apply and time has shown that they were not easy to maintain. A decision was made in 2017 to paint the bus fleet into an overall mid-green scheme with white fleet names and fleet numbers. The continued use of the attractive mid-green shade resulted in a livery that actually looked fine on most types of bus, and of course more importantly would be cheaper to apply and much simpler to maintain. Scania OmniCity saloons 4 and 115 were early recipients of the 2017 livery in July, followed by Enviro200 number 319 in August.

Schools are back

It was announced that due to regaining all of the school contracts from NAT, a dozen used and refurbished Transbus Trident double-deckers would be obtained from Dawson Rentals. However, only four (426-9) were refurbished and ready in time for the start of the school term. They were all new to Connex, but had subsequently worked for Travel London and Abellio London. Finished in the new 2017 livery, they were also available for normal service with Newport Bus. Details in the following tables:

The Euro6 compliant Volvo B8RLE demonstrator BN64 CNY was with Newport in early 2016. It has an Egyptian-built MCV body and is seen heading for Bettws on 26 March 2016.

(Andrew Wiltshire)

Fleet no	Registration	Chassis	Body	Seating	Year new
426	KV02 USM	Transbus Trident	Alexander	H43/22F	2002
427	KV02 URS	"	"	"	"
428	KV02 URL	"	"	"	"
429	KV02 USB	"	"	"	"

A number of vehicles would have to be hired in on a short-term basis and several of these were ultimately refurbished and taken into stock. Those hired were all numbered in a series commencing with 1001. Details are given in the table below and vehicles on loan were returned as refurbished buses were taken into stock.

Fleet no	Registration	Chassis	Body	Seating	Year new
1001	KN52 NEO	Transbus Trident	Alexander	H43/20D	2003
1002	KN52 NEU	"	"	"	"
1003	LT02 ZZU	"	Plaxton	H45/28F	2002
1004	LR52 LWF	"	East Lancs	H45/17D	2003
1005	KV02 USS	"	Alexander	H43/27F	2002
1006	LR52 LYC	"	East Lancs	H45/17D	2003
1007	KN52 NFA	"	Alexander	H43/20D	"
1008	KN52 NEY	"	"	"	"
1009	KN52 NDY	"	"	"	"
1010	PJ02 PZK	Volvo B7TL	East Lancs	H45/23D	2002
1011	V336 LGC	"	Plaxton	H41/21D	2000
1012	PJ02 PZE	"	East Lancs	H45/23D	2002
1013	LR52 BMO	"	Plaxton	H39/21D	"
1014	LR52 BNK	"	"	"	"
9734	Y133 HWB	Transbus Trident	Alexander	H43/22F	2001
9733	Y134 HWB	"	"	"	"
9736	Y136 HWB	"	"	"	"

1001-9 were initially on loan from Dawson Rentals (dealer).
1010-4, 9733/4/6 were all on loan from Ensignbus (dealer), and most had returned by October/November 2017, with some remaining until the spring of 2018.

Three more Tridents were acquired and entered service in October/November 2018 as 430-2. 430/2 were new to Armchair, Brentford while 431 was new to Connex and all three had latterly worked for Abellio London.

Fleet no	Registration	Chassis	Body	Seating	Year new
430	KN52 NDJ	Transbus Trident	Alexander	H43/22F	2003
431	KV02 USH	"	"	"	2002
432	KN52 NDG	"	"	"	2003

In addition, Plaxton-bodied Transbus Trident PN03 UMK arrived in September 2017 and was used for spare parts. It was latterly with CT Plus but had been new to GoAhead London. From the table above, the following buses were rebuilt to single-door layout, refurbished and joined the main fleet. 438/9 were additional vehicles to the original dozen specified, and were a little more unusual in having East Lancs bodies.

New fleet no	Registration	Old fleet no	Revised seating layout
433	KN52 NFA	1007	H43/22F
434	KN52 NDY	1009	"
435	KN52 NEU	1002	"
436	KN52 NEY	1008	"
437	KN52 NEO	1001	"
438	LR52 LYC	1006	H45/21F
439	LR52 LWF	1004	"

433-7 were previously with Abellio London (9843/37/41/42/40) ex Metroline, but new to Armchair, Brentford. 438 and 439 were ex CT Plus London (HTL12, 7).

Alexander ALX400-bodied Trident 429 is working Ringland service 7 at Alway on 13 May 2019.

(Andrew Wiltshire)

East Lancs-bodied Trident 439 was working a service from Caerleon on 23 July 2018. This former London bus had by then been rebuilt to single-door layout.

(Andrew Wiltshire)

Jumbo coaches

With the demand for private hire starting to increase once again it was found that the two Volvo coaches 26 and 27 were not always available for this work, and so extra vehicles were needed. The first 3-axle passenger vehicles for Newport Transport joined the fleet in October 2017 in the form of SV59 CHL and KX59 DLU,

a pair of Volvo B12BT coaches with Plaxton Panther sixty-five-seat bodywork incorporating toilets. They dated from 2009 and came from Stagecoach Western Buses (54071/61). These massive vehicles were repainted into overall mid-green and were eventually numbered 28 and 29 respectively. Interestingly KX59 DLU had been new to Stagecoach Red & White for Megabus services.

Volvo B12BT number 28 is seen at Porthcawl on 27 May 2019.

(Simon Nicholas)

Further comings and goings

Dennis Trident 39 and Transbus Darts 323-5 and 335 were pressed back into service by September 2017, but 325 was later placed back in store. Former London Dart 328 had by this time been stripped for spares and was sold for scrap. Three buses were donated to the Cardiff Transport Preservation Group for preservation in November 2017. They were 40 (Dennis Trident), 10 (Scania L94/Wright) and TV10, the East Lancs-bodied Dennis Dart training bus. All were later found to be in poor condition and were scrapped. As 2017 drew to a close Scania OmniCity 111 received an overall advert livery for driver recruitment at Newport Bus in November, while sister bus 112 received similar treatment in December. Both buses had previously carried mid-green X30 branded livery from new.

The year of the minibus

A new silver-liveried nineteen-seat Mercedes Benz Sprinter 516CDI minibus arrived from Dawson Rentals, Hellaby, in March 2018. Numbered 219, it enabled 213 to be returned off lease the following month. During the summer months twenty sixteen-seat Ford Transit minibuses were obtained on long term hire from Dawson Rentals for use on school contracts starting in September.

In the event seven of them were returned to the dealer by 1 September. The remaining thirteen were eventually numbered 220-32 which meant some renumbering. All the Ford Transits operate in a plain white livery without fleet names except for 220/6/7 which are silver.

On 10 June 2019, nineteen-seat Ford Transit 232 heads out along Corporation Road on the afternoon school run, having just left the Newport Transport yard beyond their garage, which is the white and green building in the background.

(Andrew Wiltshire)

Recovery mishap

In September 2018 former London Trident 430 was being recovered by a private contractor and on suspended tow. While travelling along Somerton Road it received considerable upper deck damage after striking a railway bridge with just 14ft 6in clearance. Plaxton President-bodied Dennis Trident LR52 KVV was hired from Dawson Rentals as temporary replacement for 430, but was returned in October 2018 after an engine failure. In exchange Dawson sent an Alexander ALX400-bodied Dennis Trident KV02 URM, which entered service in overall white as HV04. This bus had latterly been with McLure, Elderslie but was another example that had been new to Connex, London. Subsequently 430 was written off and KV02 URM was acquired. It entered service in February 2019 as 440.

Cutting emissions

Newport Transport had looked at two Compressed Natural Gas (CNG) powered buses in 2013 and subsequently trialled a number of Euro6 diesel models. However, by 2018 the industry was changing and low-emission vehicles were no longer high on the agenda as zero-emission buses were seen as the way forward for urban use. For three weeks during October and November 2018 Newport Transport was the first operator in Wales to trial the Yutong E12 full-electric bus. This thirty-eight-seat vehicle was on loan from Pelican Engineering, Castleford, the UK's Yutong dealership, and was used on Bettws services 15 and 16. It received positive feedback from passengers who commented on how smooth, quiet and comfortable the bus was to travel on. Drivers reported how easy it was to drive. In January 2019 Evobus the Mercedes-Benz franchise loaned Newport a new Citaro hybrid saloon to test. This smart silver-liveried bus was used on services 8/8A to Ringland.

Electric buses for Newport

It was announced on 6 February 2019 that Newport Transport would receive £1.342m of funding from the Ultra-Low Emission Bus Scheme, which would be put towards new vehicles and infrastructure. During May it was announced that Newport Transport had ordered a fleet of fourteen Yutong E12 12m electric single-deckers.

In addition, the former demonstrator YK66 CBC was acquired and officially handed over to Newport Bus on 19 August. It had been re-upholstered and was placed into service as fleet number Z01. The fourteen similar vehicles were expected in April 2020, but were delayed.

Livery variations

In May 2019, Scania OmniCitys 59 and 110 were given overall advert liveries for the Welsh Government's Mytravelpass. 110 was previously in X30 mid-green livery. Meanwhile the refurbishment of former London Dart 330 re-commenced and the finished bus was placed back in service in the latest livery in June.

During the summer Enviro400 number 403 received an overall advert livery for Coleg Gwent while, while Scania OmniCitys 2-4, 115 and Enviro200 314 received embellishments to promote the Pride Big Weekend celebrations in Cardiff on 24 August, an event Newport Transport attended.

It is worth mentioning that following repaint into the new 2017 livery, OmniCitys 1 and 2 actually carried fleet numbers 01 and 02 on the vehicle exterior. After around three years in store, Enviro200 number 306 was given a new livery and was the second bus to receive a livery to promote Newport Rugby Club. By the end of 2019 around thirty-seven vehicles were in the 2017 livery.

Newport Z01 (YK66 CBC) is the former Yutong E12 demonstrator that joined the fleet in 2019. It is seen here on 12 September 2019 while working the Bettws circular.

(Andrew Wiltshire)

2020 and pandemic chaos

The year 2020 started relatively quietly but within two months the whole world was falling victim to a major health crisis. At Newport Bus from 1 March 2020 a new enhanced ticketing system was launched. The Ticketer ETM system was introduced to enable passengers to use their contactless-enabled bank card or NFC device to purchase tickets or top-up their Passport and Bamboo smartcards. The Ticketer ETM system also recognises QR codes on paper day/week tickets.

As a result of the COVID-19 coronavirus pandemic, there was a substantial reduction in people using public transport across the whole country from mid-March 2020 onwards. Government advice was to avoid public transport and only use it if you were a key worker with no alternative transport. Following the UK wide lockdown from 23 March, bus services in Newport were drastically cut back from 26 March and further revised from 6 April. In addition, Newport provided free transport on its network of bus services to NHS, ambulance, fire and police services personnel upon production of an ID card. They also offered alternative transportation to NHS Staff and Emergency services workers when the revised timetable was not suitable. This included picking up residents from Cwmbran and Newport (from their closest bus stop or safe place) and dropping off at the following points in Newport: Royal Gwent, St Woolos and St Cadocs Hospitals, as well as police and fire stations.

In April Pelican Engineering lent Newport Transport a Yutong demonstrator to work alongside Z01 pending the arrival of the new electric buses. The bus concerned was YG18 CVS, the shorter E10 model with a dual-door layout that had spent much of its time working as a demonstrator in London which explains its red livery.

The fourteen new Yutong E12 electric buses eventually arrived during September 2020 and entered service in October numbered Z02-15. They are fitted with 324kWh batteries and are capable of achieving 281km on a single charge. The buses are equipped with air conditioning, LED lighting and USB charge points. It was later announced that an additional pair would join the fleet and would be the shorter E10 model.

Newport Transport was awarded the Welsh Government funded Traws Cymru T7 service from Chepstow to Bristol which would commence operating on 4 January 2021. Part of the contract was the provision of two vehicles, and so a pair of MCV-bodied Volvo B8RLEs new in 2019 were transferred to Newport Transport from Stagecoach Red & White where they had previously been used on the T4 service. To help with social distancing capacity issues on certain routes including the 30, Newport Bus obtained three brand new eighty-six seat Alexander Dennis Enviro400 MMC double-deckers. They entered service in February 2021 as 405-7 and were the first Euro6 compliant double decker buses in the fleet.

Z10 (YD70 CHH) is one of the fourteen new Yutong E12 electric buses that entered service with Newport in the latter part of 2020. It is seen in Caerleon in October 2020 having been in service for only a week or so.

(Tony Warrener)

CHAPTER NINE
SOME OTHER ASPECTS OF THE UNDERTAKING

There are many other aspects and activities that contribute to the efficient day to day running of a large fleet of buses. These include the people (management and clerical, platform and engineering staff), the commercial activities (revenue collection and advertising) and of course the infrastructure and engineering facilities.

The Who's Who in charge at Newport

There have been just thirteen periods of leadership in the Newport fleet since municipal operations began back in 1901. As can be seen from the table below a number of managers remained in post for very long periods of time. The title General Manager was used up until deregulation, after which Managing Director was used to describe the senior post at the undertaking.

From	Until	Manager
1901	1903	George H Winsor
1903	1912	Henry Collings Bishop
1912	1944	N J Young
1944	1946	Charles W Baroth
1946	1950	Lee Wilkes
1950	1963	Reginald A Hawkins
1963	1976	Frank Thorp
1976	1980	George W Cottham
1980	1989	Colin Thompson
1989	2001	Edwin Marsh (previously Deputy Manager 1971 to 1989)
2001	2009	Trevor Roberts
2009	2010	Chris Blyth
2011	Present	Scott Pearson (acting Managing Director December 2010 to April 2011)

Official titles for the undertaking

The title of the operator and the legend or fleet name that actually appears on the vehicles have changed on a number of occasions over the years. This has in part been due to local political changes, but can also be attributed to the desire to create new bold images for the fleet.

Period	Official title	Fleet-name carried
1901 to 1924	Newport Corporation Tramways	Newport Corporation Tramways then NCT
1924 to 1937	Newport Corporation Tramways and Omnibuses	NCT
1937 to 1974	Newport Corporation Transport Department	None
1974 to 1986	Borough of Newport Transport	None
1986 to date	Newport Transport Limited	Newport Transport then Newport Bus

The official addresses

Year	Address	Telephone number
1948	Newport Corporation Transport, 191/2 Dock Street, Newport	5275/6
2021	Newport Transport, 160 Corporation Road, Newport NP19 0WF	01633 670563

The 2021 official address has been in use for many years. Nowadays contact with Newport Transport can also be made electronically by means of an online form.

The liveries

Tram liveries

The original livery from 1903 was cherry red (described as vermilion) and primrose which was lined out in gold. The tram underframe and truck were black, and from 1912 the underside of the staircase was changed from red to cream. The Newport coat of arms was located on the panel below the centre saloon window, while the legend Newport Corporation Tramways in large gold letters was applied to the primrose painted rocker board on each side of the tram. From 1908 the size of the letters used was reduced for a period of time before reverting to large letters once again. After World War One the title Newport Corporation Tramways was gradually changed to the initials NCT. All passenger trams up to number 44 carried this livery, and 30 was withdrawn in this livery.

During the First World War tram numbers 4-6, 14, 22, 41, 42 and 44 were repainted grey and tram number 6 was withdrawn in this livery. The final tram livery from about 1917 was dark maroon and primrose/cream with lettering in gold. Number 7 was the first repaint while trams 45-58 entered service in this livery. The bogie cars 51-4 had straw lining around their waist and platform panels and 15, 18, 34, 44 and 48 went on to gain this feature.

Motor bus liveries

The buses were painted in the same colours as the trams. Dark maroon formed the main colour and cream was used for the roof and window surrounds. In June 1931 one bus was repainted in an experimental blue and cream livery which was not repeated.

However, the entry into service of Leyland Titan TD5s 66-81 and Tiger TS8s 52-65 from the summer of 1937 introduced a new green and cream livery. Originally there were three cream bands and cream roofs, but during World War Two the bands and roofs were painted grey. Many new vehicles were delivered in all-over grey during 1942/43 but, beginning with Guy Arab 110 in 1944, buses were green with two cream bands, but the cream roofs were reintroduced again by 1950 as buses were repainted. From 1954 the livery applied to rebuilt double-deckers was modified to include cream around the lower saloon windows and the band below these windows was discontinued. This gained approval and was adopted as standard for new double-deckers too.

A new livery layout was proposed subject to council approval on 14 January 1964. It comprised the lower half of the bus in green and the upper half in cream, the so-called 50:50 livery. Approval was forthcoming and this livery continued in use for most double-deckers until 2000. The Metro-Scanias had their own livery of cream with a green roof and skirt and the Bristol RESLs soon received these colours too.

Wearing the 50:50 livery, Leyland PD2 172 (PDW 17) has a Longwell Green body and advertises the Rhymney Brewery as it heads past the castle during the summer of 1967.

(Cliff Essex)

Representing the single-deck livery of the 1970s and 1980s is former London Metro-Scania 105 (PGC 205L) seen on 2 March 1985 in High Street.

(John Jones)

In a move away from the 50:50 livery, the ten Metropolitans (111-20) were painted cream with a green roof and skirt panels. The coach fleet had its own white livery with a dark green band from 1978 changing to overall cream in 1992. The midibuses from 1987 until 2006 were cream and green but with their own Newport Nipper branding. The shade of green used from 1937 until 1998 was sometimes referred to as leaf green and was specially mixed for Newport's paint shop though the shade did vary a little over the years.

Dark green was introduced in August 1998 on the new low-floor Scania L94 saloons 10-8 and gradually replaced the lighter shade. In 2000 three of the new Dennis Trident double-deckers featured a large red swoop design based on the town's wave sculpture that is situated between Kingsway and the River Usk. The Scania school buses 19-25 were in an overall yellow livery with appropriate branding during their time at Newport.

In 2009, the former Lothian Olympians entered service with their previous maroon paint replaced by dark green thus introducing another livery variation which was also applied to Dennis Trident 37. In 2010 these colours were developed into a new livery for the single-deck fleet, which incorporated a new full-height logo at the rear of the bus and the headlamp surrounds picked out in lime green. In 2012 the dark green was replaced by a lighter shade and all the double-deckers received their own version of this which differed considerably from the saloons. In 2017 in an effort to reduce costs, vehicles started to appear in all-over green with a small white fleet name. Exceptions to this were the hired minibuses and the electric bus fleet which had their own livery.

The paint shop at Corporation Road has always brush-painted its vehicles, although there may have been one or two experiments with spray painting. In 2010 when the new image was introduced, some vehicles were repainted by an outside contractor but most subsequent work has been undertaken by Newport's own paint shop.

The coats of arms

Although it had been in use for some time, Newport Council was granted use of the armorial bearings which are a form of heraldry incorporating a design laid onto a shield. For Newport this was a gold shield featuring a red chevron, set below wings and a cherub. This design was carried by all the trams and motor buses up to and including Leyland PD2 173 of July 1958.

In 1958 the College of Arms granted permission for the Borough of Newport to introduce "supporters" to the earlier design. Supporters are usually figures that are placed to either side of the heraldic shield. The Borough of Newport featured a winged sea dragon and a winged sea lion in their new coat of arms design, which was to signify land, sea and air. Below this on a ribbon was the motto Terra Marique which is Latin for land and sea.

78 (N78 PDW) was the only Alexander Strider-bodied Scania to receive the 2010 livery, albeit without any of the extra embellishments. It is seen entering the Kingsway bus station on 30 April 2011.

(Andrew Wiltshire)

The attractive new double-deck livery introduced in 2011 uses a shade of mid-green. Here former Metroline Transbus Trident 421 (LN51 KXW) passes the railway station "out of service" on 4 September 2015.

(John Jones)

The original coat of arms.

(Ivor Homfray)

The coat of arms as used on buses from late 1959 onwards.

Leyland PD2s 174-85 and 51-6 did not carry any emblem when new. The new coat of arms first appeared on PD2s 57-61. It was subsequently applied to all new and existing vehicles as they became due for a repaint. Scanias 27-34 of 1986 were the last double-deckers featuring the traditional coat of arms.

After deregulation in 1986 the new Dodge midibuses and MCW Metroriders 37/8 were delivered without a coat of arms, but all later received them. For larger vehicles a new fleetname Newport Transport came into use that incorporated a small coat of arms in the top left hand corner. From 1990 all full-size saloons and midibuses displayed the coat of arms from new. In 1998 the low-floor Scania L94s 10-8 carried both the coat of arms and Newport Transport fleetname mentioned above. When the fleetname "Newport Bus serving the city" came into use the coat of arms was omitted and has not been used since.

The fleet numbering system

Trams

The electric trams introduced from 1903 were simply numbered from 1 upwards reaching 58 in 1922.

Motor buses

The motor bus fleet commenced at fleet number 1 in 1924 which clashed with the tram fleet. With the end of the trams in 1937 duplication of fleet numbers ceased, and the motor bus series went on to reach 145 by 1948. New deliveries from 1949 commenced from number 1 once again and continued through to 50 with the delivery of the last Dennis Lancet UFs in 1956. However, the new Guy Arab IVs delivered in 1955 were numbered 146-9, thus carrying on from where things ended in 1948. Double-deck deliveries continued with this series until reaching 185 in 1958. From 1959 the remaining Leyland PD2s picked up from where things ended in 1956, commencing at 51 and running through to 66.

The next new buses were the Leyland Atlanteans which continued by taking this series from 67 up to 100 by 1970, with the final nine in 1971 being numbered 10-8. However, the eight Bristol RESL saloons of 1967 took fleet number 101-8. The 44 Metro-Scanias followed the Atlanteans as 19-62, while the second-hand Bedford coaches and the Metropolitan double-deckers were numbered 109-20. Three new coaches were numbered 63-5 in 1978/80 and new double-deckers delivered up to 1983 took the series from 66 up to 101. The former London Metro-Scanias neatly took the numbers vacated by the Bristol RESLs. From 1982 all new coaches commenced from number 1, while the bus series reverted to 10 once again reaching 34 in 1986.

Then things start to follow a more complicated pattern. While generally continuing to ascend from 35, some of the new midibuses took random numbers to fill gaps

namely 4-9 and 63-65. The main series reaches 64 by 1991. From here on new and used vehicles tend to fill gaps in the number series below 100, and some batches are split up which can only be described as a bit messy. This continues until 2011 when a new more logical series was introduced for additions to the fleet, but not existing vehicles.

101>	Full-size single-deckers
207>	Minibuses
301>	Smaller single-deckers
400>	Double-deckers
26>	Coaches
Z01>	Electric zero-emission vehicles

Depots and garages

Newport is quite unusual in that it is still based at the same depot that was built to operate the trams from 1901. There have been a number of modifications to the layout over the years and the power station has long gone, but there is a strong visual reminder of the depot's origins in the number of tram tracks that are still visible.

Tram sheds

The accommodation to house the trams and stables was built in a corner of Friars Field which was just off Commercial Street and accessed via a short spur along Friar Street. In 1886 the original tramcar shed in Friars Field was closed having been replaced by a new facility in Mountjoy Street which could house ten tramcars. A second much larger shed in Clarence Place could hold twenty-eight trams. The horse tram sheds in Mountjoy Street were eventually sold in July 1904 for £520.

In 1901 construction of the new power station and tram sheds on Corporation Road commenced. The tram sheds would be capable of housing approximately fifty tramcars, plus a further twelve in the workshops. By January 1903 the tram shed, at the top of the depot yard, still referred to in 2021 as the "top garage", was completed. This consisted of a twelve-road shed made up of nine roads for stabling tramcars, a repair shop, a motor repair shop and a paint shop. The offices were housed in the two storey building which still stands at the depot entrance. The East Usk power station was nearing completion at this time too.

Motor bus garage

During 1923 plans were discussed with respect to constructing a twelve vehicle garage plus offices for the motor buses at an estimated cost of £6,000. These were not proceeded with and motor buses were therefore housed at Corporation Road from their introduction in 1924. With increasing numbers of motor buses being added to the fleet, the garage that opens onto Corporation Road was constructed between 1928 and 1930 and is always referred to as the "bottom garage". After the tramway closed four new inspection pits were constructed in the main garage for motor buses.

The depot yard on 15 April 1934 during the final years of the tram era. The top shed is at the far end of the yard while the power station is on the right hand side.

(H B Priestley)

A general view of the depot yard taken in April 1960, clearly showing the old tram tracks which were never removed. This makes an interesting comparison with the image above.

(Ivor Homfray collection)

A second depot

In 1948 there was a plan to open a sub-depot on Malpas Road/Kimberly Terrace where the fire station now stands. A converted aircraft hangar was purchased from the Air Ministry for £2,500 in 1949. In January 1950 the tender from Messrs. Hinkins and Frewin Ltd of £8,282 for the erection of the hangar was accepted. Although erected and equipped for servicing and cleaning buses, with paying-in facilities for conductors, the building was never used as a depot. Mr Reg Hawkins, who replaced Mr Lee Wilkes as General Manager in March 1950, was not in favour of the idea preferring to have the open depot yard roofed over to provide the extra accommodation, but, as we know, this did not happen either. In January 1952 the former hangar was hired to H Lotery Ltd, for use as a clothing warehouse and later to British Road Services as a parcels and storage depot. It was later used for the storage of withdrawn Longwell Green-bodied Leyland PD2s buses in 1972.

Extensions to Corporation Road

In 1954/55 it was proposed to extend the garage and offices, but this plan was abandoned by 1956. A new Dawson bus washing machine was installed in 1955/56, while a new office block was completed in about 1959 and a single storey office block at the side of the depot yard was added by 1962. Major depot reconstruction took place in 1966/67, and more inspection pits were added. The paint shop was another addition in the 1970s. Originally this had been behind the line of pits in the workshop where there are still many reminders of the tram days, with tram lines still set into the cobbled floor.

The depot yard with a Dennis Lancet UF saloon 41 and a number of double-deckers including Guy Arabs 23 and 25. The building to the left is bottom garage.

(Newport Borough Transport from the Ivor Homfray collection)

In this view Guy Arab IIIs 9/13 (FDW 43/7) and Atlantean 69 stand in the main (top) shed in about 1967.

(Newport Borough Transport from the Ivor Homfray collection)

There have been other additions and alterations over the years. The refuelling bay has had two locations on the yard before it was moved to the rear of the site in the 1980s. The bus wash which was originally at the side of the depot was moved to a position at the end of the office block on the yard, before it was moved again to the rear of the yard along with the fuelling point.

The power station on the depot site was demolished in the early 1980s and an extension was built on that side of the depot to provide new maintenance facilities for the Council's other vehicles, which were transferred here along with the engineering staff, from Dudley Street depot. When the tramway was abandoned the original fully-tiled tram pits in the top shed were covered over, but never filled in and remained in remarkably clean condition in 2020.

The depot site is currently owned by Newport City Council and about fifteen years ago it was rumoured that it might be sold for development by a leading supermarket. The site of the former Pirelli Cables (formerly Standard Telephones & Cables) works in Wednesbury Street, off Corporation Road was identified as suitable location for a new depot, but nothing happened and houses were eventually built on the proposed site.

In partnership with Zenobe Energy, charging points were installed on site from 2020 to facilitate the introduction of electric buses.

The services

As already described in Chapter One, the electric tramway evolved from the earlier horse tramway, but no major extensions were ever planned as Newport grew in size. The trolleybus proposals failed to get off the ground and so any new services were operated by motor buses. Like many other municipal fleets Newport decided to get rid of its tramway in the 1930s rather than spend money upgrading it, and succeeded in closing it down well before the outbreak of war in 1939. From 1937 the network was operated by motor buses, and during the 1950s and 1960s new services were introduced to serve the new housing developments on the outskirts of the town.

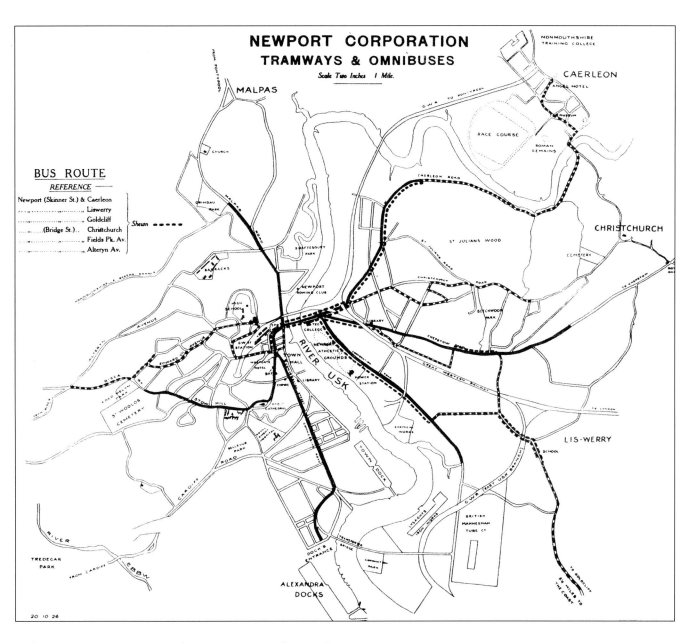

NEWPORT CORPORATION
TRAMWAYS & OMNIBUSES
Scale Two Inches I Mile.

BUS ROUTE
REFERENCE

Newport (Skinner St.) & Caerleon
..........,,..........,,......... ,, Liswerry
..........,,..........,,......... ,, Goldcliff
..........,, (Bridge St.).. Christchurch   *Shewn* ----
..........,,..........,,......... ,, Fields Pk. Av.
..........,,..........,,......... ,, Alteryn Av.

Official route map from October 1926. Heavy lines indicate tram routes.

Many services cross Newport Bridge which is where we see 57 (SDW 133) a Longwell Green-bodied Leyland PD2/40 in 1967. Clearly visible on this fine afternoon are the power station on Corporation Road and the George Street bridge.

(Peter Keating)

The City of Newport had a population of 148,700 in 2020, compared to 67,270 in 1901 when the Corporation first took over operation of the horse tramway. For many years' services were largely confined to operate within the town boundary, but in more recent times Newport Transport has developed new routes to towns like Chepstow and Monmouth, as other operators reduced their network. In 2021 most services operated out of the new Friars Walk bus station, and many of the main arteries in and out of the city centre benefit from bus-priority measures such as bus lanes, which can greatly reduce journey times for Newport Bus's customers.

The 30 service

In July 2020 the Newport to Cardiff service celebrated its 75th anniversary as a joint operation with neighbouring Cardiff Bus. Sadly, due to the Covid-19 pandemic there was no event to mark this. The 30 service is rather significant as it is the last remaining service in the UK jointly operated by two former municipal fleets.

The service itself goes back almost a hundred years as it was acquired by Cardiff Corporation on 15 April 1924 with the business of G. Vernon Jones of Castleton, and by 1929 the service number 30 was being used. This became a joint service with Newport Corporation Transport with effect from 1 July 1945, and it is thought a twenty-minute frequency (Monday to Saturday) was in operation from the start. It was an immediate success and by August 1945 was carrying 35,000 passengers a week. In 1950 the Newport terminus was in Bridge Street, but by 1956 it was running from Dock Street bus station. The 30 moved to the new Kingsway bus station in August 1973 and, when it closed for redevelopment in late 2013, the 30 was transferred to the nearby Market Square bus station, until the new Friars Walk bus station opened in December 2015.

From the beginning both operators normally used their newest double-deckers on this service. However, Newport did not replace the PD2s with Atlanteans, as capacity issues meant the newer and larger buses were needed on other routes until 1969. By the late 1990s single-deckers had become more common. By 2000 an hourly variation was introduced with the service diverting via the Duffryn estate at near Tredegar Park and numbered 30D. It was worked alternately by both Cardiff Bus and Newport Transport, but Cardiff withdrew from this arrangement in June 2003 leaving Newport to work a two-hourly 30D which ceased in October 2008.

The mutual working arrangement between the two fleets was briefly disrupted between 2 August and 14 November 2010 due to a disagreement by Newport Transport over fares. This resulted in Newport running all timings and thus duplicating those of Cardiff Bus until things returned to normal. The Director of Delivery at Newport Transport, Chris Blyth, renumbered most routes into geographical blocks according to the areas of the city they served, the changes taking place in March 2008 and January 2009.

The MCW Metropolitans became regular performers on the Cardiff service when new. In March 1975 brand new 115 (GKG 36N) is seen in Cardiff bus station with a badly set route number blind.

(The late John Wiltshire)

Summary of services in July 1974

Route	Area served	Comments
1A	Christchurch or Gibbs Road-Summerhill Ave-Western Ave	
1C	Christchurch or Gibbs Road-St. Julian's Road-Western Ave	
2	Newport-Caerleon	
3	Maesglas-Malpas (3A with Rowan Way diversion)	Certain journeys extend to Tredegar Park gates
4	Town Centre-St. Julian's (Hove Avenue)	
5	Newport-Whitson circular (clockwise)	
5A	Newport-Whitson circular (ant-clockwise)	
6	Town Centre-Alway	
7	Newport-Cwmbran	
8	Town Centre-Ringland circular (clockwise)	
16	Town Centre-Ringland circular (anti-clockwise)	
9A	Town Centre-Nash Road circular (anti-clockwise)	
9C	Town Centre-Nash Road circular (clockwise)	
9B	Dock-Channel dry dock	
10	Town Centre-Uskmouth (West Nash)	
11A	Town Centre-Gaer circular (anti-clockwise)	
11C	Town Centre-Gaer circular (clockwise)	
12	Town Centre-BSC Llanwern (via Chepstow Rd or Corporation Rd)	
13	Merlin Cresdent-Ridgeway	
14	Town Centre-South Quay (docks)	
15	Docks-Liswerry (Moorland Avenue)	
17	Town Centre-Melfort Road (St. Woolos) circular	
18A	Town Centre-Bettws circular (anti-clockwise)	
18C	Town Centre-Bettws circular (clockwise)	
19	Brynglas or Barracks-Ringland	
30	Newport-Cardiff	
31	Newport-St Brides-Marshfield-Castleton	

11 (RUH 11Y), one of the nine Wadham Stringer-bodied Scania BR112s, had been in service for eleven years when seen leaving Cwmbran on 27 October 1994.

(John Jones)

Summary of services in February 2020

Route	Area served	Comments
1	Ridgeway-Rogerstone-Foxgloves (Morrisons)	Mon-Sat only
1B	Ridgeway-Rogerstone (St. Johns Cres-Ruskin Ave)	Mon-Sat only
2A	Gaer (via Handpost & Drinkwater Gardens)	7 days a week
2C	Gaer (via Drinkwater Gardens & Handpost)	7 days a week
6	Maindee-Alway shops-Ringland Centre-Ladyhill Centre	7 days a week
6E	Maindee-Alway shops-Ringland Centre-Alway shops	7 days a week
7	Ladyhill ctr-Ringland ctr-Alway shops-Royal Gwent	Mon-Sat only
8A	Ringland (via Chepstow Road & Ringland Ave)	7 days a week
8C	Ringland (via Chepstow Road & Llanwern Road)	7 days a week
9	Coldra Court Hotel (via Railway station, Chepstow Road and I.C.C. Wales)	Mon-Sat only
11A	Allt-Yr-Yn (out via Brynglas and Wickes DIY)	Mon-Sat only
11C	Brynglas (out via Allt-Yr-Yn and Wickes DIY)	Mon-Sat only
15	Bettws (via Monnow Way anticlockwise)	7 days a week
16	Bettws (via Monnow Way clockwise)	7 days a week
17	Malpas (Westfield Drive, Llewellyn Grove and Pillmawr Road clockwise)	Mon-Fri only
18	Malpas (Malpas Road and Pillmawr Road anticlockwise)	Mon-Fri only
19	Malpas Court (via Blaen-y-Pant Crescent, Westfield Drive & Edison Ridge)	7 days a week
19E	Malpas Court (via Malpas Court and Pilton Vale)	7 days a week
20A	Spytty Rtl Pk (out Gibbs Rd & return via Christchurch)	Mon-Sat only
20C	Spytty Rtl Pk (out Christchurch return via Gibbs Road)	Mon-Sat only
26A	St. Julians (via St. Julians Road)	7 days a week
26C	St. Julians (via Beaufort Road)	7 days a week
27	Caerleon (Home Farm and Lodge Road)	7 days a week
28	Caerleon (Eastfield Road and Lodge Road)	7 days a week
29B	Cwmbran (via Caerleon and Ponthir)	Mon-Sat only
30	Newport to Cardiff via Castleton	7 days a week
X30	Cardiff Express (via UHW & M4)	Mon-Sat only
34	Duffryn/Celtic Springs direct	Mon-Fri peak
35	Duffryn (Celtic Springs Mon-Fri only) clockwise	7 days a week
36	Duffryn (Celtic Springs Mon-Fri only) anticlockwise	7 days a week
37	Rhiwderin village (via Tredegar Park & Bassaleg)	Mon-Sat only
40	Pillgwenlly (clockwise)	Mon-Sat only
41	Pillgwenlly (anticlockwise)	Mon-Sat only
42	Moorland Park/Spytty Retail Park/Nash College	7 days a week
43	Nash College/Spytty Retail Park/Moorland Park	7 days a week
44	Nash College direct (2 journeys only)	Mon-Fri only
60	Newport to Monmouth (via Caerleon, Usk & Raglan)	Mon-Sat only
63	Whitson/RSPB Wetlands (1x am 1x pm)	Mon-Fri only
73	Newport to Chepstow (via Penhow & Caerwent)	Mon-Sat only
74	Newport to Chepstow (via Magor & Caldicot)	Mon-Sat eve only
X74	Newport to Chepstow (direct via SDR and EDR)	Mon-Sat daytime
74A	EDR/Underwood/Langstone	Mon-Sat only
74C	Langstone/Underwood/EDR	Mon-Sat only
C1	Chepstow BS to Mariners Reach and Bulwark	Mon-Sat daytime
C2	Chepstow Bus station to Fryth Wood	Mon-Sat daytime
C3	Chepstow Bus station to Garden City	Mon-Sat daytime
R1	Risca (via Handpost, High Cross, Ty-Sign)	Mon-Fri (even/s)

EDR is Eastern Distributor Road. SDR is Southern Distributor Road.

Demand Responsive Transport (DRT) February 2019		
DRT31	St. Brides/Marshfield/Castleton	Book, pay and ride
DRT62	Bishton/Redwick/Llanwern village	Book, pay and ride
DRT63	Goldcliff/Whitson/Nash	Book, pay and ride

School services (open to the general public) February 2019		
B1	Bassaleg High School (via Mount Pleasant)	School days only
B2	Bassaleg High School (via Tregwilym Road)	School days only
JF1	Newport Bus Station to John Frost School	School days only
JF2	Pillgwenlly to John Frost School	School days only
JF3	Queens Hill to John Frost School	School days only
JF4	Handpost to John Frost School	School days only
SJ1-13	St. Joseph's High School	School days only
YGl1	Ysgol Gyfun Gwent Iscoed	School days only

SJ1-13 a single AM and PM journey only on each service.

Chepstow Racecourse shuttles operate to coincide with race meetings/events.

Facts and figures

The Passenger Transport Yearbook for 1948 stated that Newport Corporation Transport had 91 buses consisting of 77 double-deckers and 14 saloons. The chassis comprised 51 Leyland, 21 Guy and 19 Daimler. On 11 June 1949, the *South Wales Argus* reported that for April that year, 4,682,000 passengers paid a record total of £29,553 to travel on Newport's buses. It also mentioned that the most crowded services were those to the Caerleon Road and Stow Hill areas, closely followed by Malpas and Corporation Road services. Some interesting statistics are given in the table below.

Year	Net profit/loss	Miles operated
1946	+£49,084	2,518,530
1958	+£629	3,440,253
1962	-£1,282	3,186,037
1970	+£11,687	2,616,930
1980	-£49,063	2,870,763

Destination and route number blinds

Over the years the destination displays on Newport's buses have incorporated a number of different layouts and positions depending on the type of vehicle. Newport has always kept the route number separate from the destination information resulting in two displays. The main destination blind was for many years single line and only showing the ultimate destination. Possibly the neatest arrangement was that used on most vehicles delivered from 1937 to 1961, but did not offer a great deal of flexibility.

The arrival of the Leyland Atlanteans saw the introduction of Bury Corporation style destination layout with two-track route numbers blinds. The real benefits came in the 1990s with the electronic displays, which allowed customised information which could be updated with relative ease and no material cost.

2 (FDW 52) is an all-Leyland PD2 seen at Oliphant Circle, Malpas. It carries the pre-1954 livery and the destination box layout was that of new buses delivered between 1937 and 1961.

(Andrew Wiltshire collection)

Trams		
Era	Design	Comments
1902	Open-top trams. Single-line blind in destination box. Later moved to a lower position on upper deck.	Black blind, white upper case letters
1923	Closed-top trams. Integral destination blind box above cab.	Black blind, white upper case letters
Removable destination boards often in use in lower saloon windows.		

Motor buses		
Era	Design	Comments
1924 to 1937	Many variations including roof-mounted route number boxes with destination blinds at top of windscreen or under canopy. Removable destination boards often in use at waistrail level but replaced by a destination box near to the entrance. Double-deckers introduced had a small route-number box above a single-line destination between decks.	Black blind, white upper case letters 47, 48 and 51 had a destination display above the platform
1937 to 1954	On double-deckers, offside destination box with route number box alongside between decks. Saloons had similar arrangement in roof dome. Many variations in size. Side destinations usually above or just forward of entrance.	Black blind, white upper case letters
From 1955	The layout was reversed with the route number now being positioned on the offside of the vehicle with the destination box alongside. On the nearside of the bus, the blind was usually above the last window before the entrance.	Black blind, white upper case letters
From 1966	Atlanteans had a single-line destination box above a 2-track route number box and were the last buses with a rear route number box. Bristol RESLs had a large screen with a 3-track route number layout on the offside and a rear route number box which was later painted over. The Metro-Scanias had a similar but smaller arrangement, and no rear blinds.	Black blind, white upper case letters
1975	The Metropolitans had two displays side by side with a 3-track route number being on the offside.	Black blind, white upper case letters
1981 to 1989	Single screens of varying size with 3-track route numbers on the offside.	Black blind, white lower case letters introduced in 1981
1990 to 1995	Optare Metroriders re-introduce route numbers on the nearside.	Black blind, white lower case letters
1995 to 2002	Electronic digital displays first appeared on the Scania saloons delivered in 1995. Route number is on the nearside.	Letters were an amber colour (later pale green), and being digital could appear in both upper and lower case format
2002 to date	LED displays first appeared on the new Scania OmniCity saloons in 2002. Some ex dealer stock Enviro200s have the route number on the offside.	Letters were an amber colour

Ticket machines and fare collection

Below is a description as far as is known of the various equipment used over time. The dates are only a guide and at times there was often more than one system in use.

Mechanical machines		
Era	Ticket issuing system	Comments
1903 to 1948	Bell Punch	Tickets issued from a rack
1947 to 1950?	TIM machines	On Cardiff service only
1948 to 1975	Bell Punch Co Ltd Ultimate	Used until crew operation ceased
1971 to 1992	Bell Punch Co Ltd Autofare	Used cash vaults on one-man operated services

A scheme to install "Honesty" boxes on the platforms of twenty-four buses was launched in January 1949. This initially proved successful and all the fleet was equipped with these by 1950. They were discontinued in 1953.

Enviro200 310 is seen helping out on town service C5 in Chepstow on 10 July 2014. This is a good clear example of an LED destination screen in use.

(John Jones)

Electronic machines

Era	Ticket issuing system	Comments
1982 to 1984	Almex Microfare One	Trialled from 1983 on a few vehicles
1984 to 1998	Control Systems Ltd Farespeed	Trialled on 29 buses and then gradually adopted
1998 to 2005	Almex A90	
2005 to 2020	Wayfarer TGX150	
2020	Ticketer ETM	Contactless enabled with built-in GPS

All the above used in conjunction with cash vaults.

Tickets

Below is a selection of tickets from the tramway era through to 2007. It must also be remembered that with the exception of three routes (7, 30 and 31), Newport stopped issuing tickets from May 1977, and did not resume doing so for about 25 years.

Tickets from the tramway era.

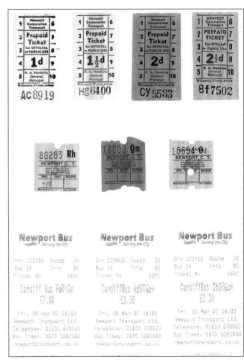

Tickets from the motor bus era (1950s, 1960s and 2000s).

The service vehicle fleet

The service vehicle fleet dates back to the opening of the electric tramway and originally consisted of the water car and rail-grinding tram number 41 and a tower wagon for overhead line repairs. A new tower wagon entered service in 1911, a Walker Bros 25/26hp four-wheel petrol-driven lorry with a wooden-lattice tower mounted behind the cab. In 1920 a Ransomes lorry was purchased for use as a tower wagon which replaced DW 311 and is thought to have continued in use until the end of the tramway in 1937.

Leyland Lion 20 (DW 5637) of 1927 was transferred to the service fleet at the end of World War Two for use as a towing vehicle and fulfilled this role for a number of years. Having been replaced by an AEC Matador, it was sold in July 1952.

Approval was granted in March 1947 for the Transport Department to purchase an AEC Matador tractor for use as a breakdown lorry. These former Ministry of Supply vehicles were being supplied by AEC of Southall for £600 at this time, and were proving to be popular acquisitions by transport undertakings for use as breakdown tenders. They were four-wheel drive vehicles with air brakes, an overall length of 20ft 9in and were powered by a 7.7-litre AEC diesel engine. The vehicle was not received until May 1948, and was registered EDW 351 in June, but was later operated on trade plates 211 DW. It had an unladen weight of 7tons 15cwt.

As mentioned earlier in the book Dennis Lancet UF 44 (LDW 502) was transferred to the service vehicle fleet in July 1964 for use as a mobile cash office, a role which it carried out until the end of 1968.

The Walker Bros tower wagon DW 311 that supported the tramway operation from 1911.

(The late Dave B Thomas collection)

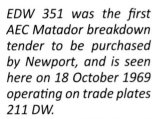

EDW 351 was the first AEC Matador breakdown tender to be purchased by Newport, and is seen here on 18 October 1969 operating on trade plates 211 DW.

(Mike Street)

Dennis Lancet UF LDW 502, formerly number 44, in use as a mobile cash office at the Dock Street bus station.

(RHG Simpson from the Cardiff Transport Preservation Group collection)

SXF 433 a Ford Thames 500E 2-ton lorry of 1957 at a bus rally in Cardiff on 26 June 1988 after being sold for preservation.

(Mike Street)

SXF 433 was a Ford Thames 500E 2-ton lorry dating from 1957 and was obtained from the Civil Defence at Newport in 1968 as a box van, and given fleet number 166. It was converted into a lorry in 1974 and was used very rarely, primarily by the stores department. Withdrawn in 1982, it was purchased for preservation by D G Bowen of Merthyr Tydfil in April 1983. After a number of subsequent owners, it appeared on an online auction site in 2020, albeit in very poor shape.

The Dennis Lancet mobile office LDW 502 was replaced in January 1969 by Bruce-bodied Leyland PD2/3 GDW 98 which was formerly 31 in the main bus fleet. GDW 98 carried out this role as a mobile cash office and rest room at the Dock Street bus station until December 1972, and was eventually sold for scrap in 1975. Between February 1972 and March 1978 Leyland Atlanteans 73 (HDW 773E) and 77 (KDW 77F) were available for use as training vehicles when required.

FDW 55 is a good example of a Leyland PD2/3 that transferred to the training fleet in July 1969. It was previously number 5 in the main fleet and was one of two similar buses to fill this role between 1969 and 1972. It is seen in Cardiff bus station and has an orange band below the lower saloon windows.

(Cardiff Transport Preservation Group collection)

Sandwiched between two Bristol RESLs, AEC Matador 285 DW is captured in the yard at Corporation Road on 4 April 1978.

(John Jones)

Meanwhile a second AEC Matador was purchased in 1970 from dealer Watts of Lydney. This vehicle had a coach-built cab in place of its original AEC cab and only ever operated on trade plates as 285 DW. Little is known about its origin or when it was built. It did however replace the existing AEC Matador 211 DW, which was withdrawn in 1970 and cannibalised. 285 DW served the Newport fleet until late 1977, and was eventually sold to neighbouring City of Cardiff Transport for £500. Here it would be used to provide spare parts for Cardiff's own AEC Matador DKG 601.

Leyland Atlantean 69 (EDW 69D) was converted for use as a tow bus, entering service as such in July 1978. It was renumbered B1 in October 1979 and finally 169 in April 1981. It performed this role quite well for a rear-engine bus, but apparently descending a hill in wet conditions whilst towing could be quite hair-raising. It was sold for further service in June 1983. The replacement for the Atlantean tow bus was AEC Mandator (ELL 518J) which was a tractor unit new in 1971 and obtained from the Texaco Oil Company in December 1982. It arrived already converted to a towing wagon and was withdrawn in August 1991.

The next towing vehicle in the Newport fleet was 182 (DNM 975Y), a Ford Cargo 2817 of 1982 which was acquired from a dealer in Bristol in August 1991. This 3-axle vehicle was painted red and had low profile towing gear. It was sold locally in 2000.

AEC Mandator 171 (ELL 518J), a former tractor unit, is seen at the depot on 19 March 1983 not long after entering service. It began life hauling articulated tanker trailers for Texaco.

(John Jones)

182 (DNM 975Y) a Ford Cargo, complete with Michelin Man figure on its roof, at the depot on 12 October 1991.

(Ivor Homfray)

From 2000 all towing and recovery was undertaken by a specialist contractor. Initially this was carried out by Walls Recovery which still served Newport Bus in 2020, but other contractors like Spiteri of Caerleon have been used.

From 1982, Newport did not have any dedicated driver training buses, choosing to use vehicles from the main fleet when necessary. Then in 1988 they were able to use the restored Leyland PD2 number 178 which also brought in outside work as a private hire vehicle. In 1991 a change in legislation meant that 178 could no longer be used, and so in April that year Newport purchased an Alexander-bodied Leyland Leopard from Morris Travel Ltd of Pencoed. This former Scottish vehicle dating from 1972 was a 36ft version with fifty-three bus type seats.

This bus had a fully-synchromesh manual gearbox, as opposed to a half and half, whereby 1st and 2nd gears were actually constant mesh. It worked in the driver training fleet as 174 until 2002 when it was sold for preservation.

The Leopard was replaced in 2002 by E881 YKY, a Leyland Tiger with a fifty-three seat Plaxton Paramount coach body dating from 1988 and fitted with a manual gearbox. This vehicle had been new to Luton & District and was also used for commercial training at Newport. It was sold in 2007. It was replaced by J232 NNC, a 1992 Volvo B10M-61 with a 12m Van Hool coach body seating forty-nine. This coach had been new to Shearings Ltd of Wigan and also had a manual gearbox.

Leyland Leopard driver training bus 174 (XGM 450L) in the original green and cream livery.

(The late Dave B Thomas)

Wadham Stringer-bodied Scania BR112 RUH 17Y became 117 in the training fleet from February 2000 until October 2004. Its place was taken by K109 KTX, a Scania N113CRB with Alexander Strider bodywork which was itself replaced in 2007 by P136 LNF, a Dennis Dart SLF with an East Lancs body that had been new in 1996 to Stuart's Coaches, Hyde.

While this bus was being prepared for its new role, Scania OmniCity 55 was temporarily used as a training bus. In early 2016 Scania OmniCity 61 (YV03 PZR) was transferred to the training fleet and the Dart was sold by the end of 2017.

A full list of all former buses converted for use as driver training vehicles is in Appendix Three at the back of this book. Newport's driving school instructor also held a Class 1 HGV licence and so Newport Transport decided to branch out into this type of training as well in 1991 on a commercial basis. A 2-axle flat-bed lorry as well as two articulated lorries have been purchased for this purpose over the years. In 1997 a Ford Cargo box van was acquired to provide HGV Class 3 training which provided work for two instructors. Minibus training has also been undertaken and these vehicles appear in Appendix Three.

176 (E881 YKY) was the Plaxton-bodied Leyland Tiger training vehicle. It is seen leaving the bus station on 11 July 2005.

(Andrew Wiltshire)

CHAPTER TEN
LIFE AFTER NEWPORT AND PRESERVATION

Further use

It would seem that the fate of many Newport's buses up to and including the last Leyland PD2/40s of 1961 would be a one-way trip to the scrapyard. But there were many exceptions, and some of the more interesting examples are described below.

Karrier CY 5 (DW 3493) passed to a showman in 1933, most probably for use as a caravan, but only lasted a year. Both Karrier JKLs 17/8 (DW 5586/7) were sold for further use as lorries in 1940, while a similar fate befell Leyland Lions 25/6 (DW 5804/5) in 1941. Leyland Lion 19 (DW 5636) became a First Aid unit for the Health Department in 1940 and eventually ended up with a showman in 1948. Leyland Lion 22 (DW 5801) initially went to Grindle of Cinderford in the Forest of Dean in 1940 and ended its days in Essex as a mobile workshop in Maldon.

Six of Newport's first double-deckers Leyland TD1s 31-6 (DW 6941-4, 7118/9) of 1930 passed to Red & White Services Ltd, Chepstow for further service in 1945, but had all moved on by 1950. The Griffin Motor Company Ltd, Brynmawr took Leyland Lions 49/50 (DW 7756/7) and Tigers 52/3 (BDW 5/6) in 1945. Jones Omnibus Services Ltd of Aberbeeg took Leyland Tigers 56/8 (BDW 9/11) in 1945 and went on to re-body BDW 9 in 1948. The first oil-engined bus in the fleet and former demonstrator Leyland TD2 51 (TJ 1514) passed to David Jones & Sons, Port Talbot in 1947. It later ran for Doolan's Coaches, Neath, for six months, until early 1952.

Leyland TD5 81 (BDW 34) and TD7 92 (CDW 959) passed to D J Davies of Merthyr Tydfil in 1956 and 1955 respectively, but both had been sold by 1957. 98 (DDW 34) was one of the two Guy Arabs with the streamlined Weymann bodies and passed to Doncaster area independent Blue Line (Morgan) of Armthorpe in 1953 for further service. It was withdrawn in 1957 and remained parked in their yard until 1975.

It is thought that in around 1956 a number of former Newport Leyland Titans and utility Guy Arab double-deckers were sold via South Wales Motor Traders, Chepstow, for further service in Iran, probably exported through one of the south Wales ports. It is likely that the Leylands were TD5 models selected from 66-8, 70-3/5/6/8. The Guys may have included 97 and 107.

Very few of the wartime utility buses saw any further use despite some having been heavily rebuilt or re-bodied in the post-war period. A few ended up being converted into lorries while Guy Arab II 110 (DDW 110) lost its engine in 1961, and became a static mess room at nearby Llanwern during the construction of the steel works. Two of the Daimler CWD6s of 1945 (124/7) that

Originally Newport 81, Leyland TD5 BDW 34 saw service with D J Davies of Merthyr Tydfil during 1956, being sold for use as a static store the following year.

(Ivor Homfray collection)

Daimler CWD6 DDW 127 is former Newport 127. It is seen in 1964 with Wessex Coaches, Bristol.

(Ivor Homfray collection)

were given new D J Davies bodies in 1954 passed to Wessex Coaches of Bristol in 1962. 127 was initially for spares but was eventually placed in service as shown above.

Longwell Green-bodied Daimler CVG6s 153/5/8 all found new owners in 1970, but the first two had been scrapped by the end of the year. 158 (NDW 609) on the other hand passed to Suntrekkers, Sutton Coldfield in 1970 and was converted to an open-top caravan. It later made trips to Spain and Morocco and by 1977 Suntrekkers had based the bus in Newport, and it was not scrapped until the late 1980s.

A few of the Longwell Green-bodied Leyland PD2/40s had further roles after Newport had dispensed with them. It seems that in most cases this was simply an owner taking advantage of what was left on the vehicles Certificate of Fitness (CoF) and so the reprieve was usually brief. 174 (PDW 480) and 64 (UDW 837) spent a short spell in Essex with Riverway Enterprises (Harlow) Ltd while 165 (ODW 301) and 63 (UDW 836) spent two years in the London area with Margo, Upper Norwood. Much closer to Newport was 66 (UDW 839) which in May 1972 was in use with contractor Sydney Green & Sons. It was used as a site rest room on the construction of the new A449 trunk road between Newport and Usk.

Far more interesting was 167 (ODW 303), which like Daimler 158 went to Suntrekkers Sutton Coldfield. By 1974 it was in Switzerland with Conti Geneva as a

UDW 839 ends its days with contractor Green of Henley as a site rest room at Coldra near Newport in 1972.

(The late Dave B Thomas)

mobile showroom and in 1979 it was noted with a band of touring musicians at Dunkirk in northern France and registered 8374 LF 59. This may have been the bus that was noted at a caravan site in Spain in 1980. In 1975 St. Mary's Youth Club, Newport took 178 (PDW 484) but it was out of use by 1983. This allowed Newport Transport to re-acquire it that year for restoration as a special events bus.

Finally the furthest travelled Newport PD2 was probably 177 (PDW 483) which was sold to Green (dealer), Weymouth, in 1975 and exported to Oregon, USA. It was last noted in a village on the Columbia River in June 1976, thirty miles west of Portland, painted red and in use by Ye Olde London Bus Christian Bookshop and Boutique.

Of the forty-three Leyland Atlanteans that Newport operated, thirty-five went on to see some form of further use. It is interesting to note that 71, 78 and 96 were exported and may therefore still exist. Many initially found homes in the South Wales area including seven that were purchased by Taff-Ely Borough Council in 1982/3.

Llynfi Motors of Maesteg obtained five former Newport Atlanteans including MDW 389G which came via an operator in the north of Scotland. PDW 98H was still a non-PSV with the London Bus Export Company at Lydney in 2019.

The Metropolitans also fared well after Newport with 111/3/6/8/20 passing to G & G Coaches, Leamington Spa, while 112 and 119 went to Brittain's Coaches Ltd, Northampton where 119 was used for spares. 115 passed to Brixham Coaches Ltd, Brixham and later became a caravan as did 118. 117 went on to become a playbus in Enfield while 114 became a mobile exhibition unit and may still exist in the yard of London Bus Export Company at Lydney.

Deep in Cornwall, Atlantean EDW 70D is with R&M Motors, Par, when seen at St. Austell in October 1980. It was scrapped in 1984.

(Cliff Essex)

Former Newport 81 (KDW 81F) was purchased by Llynfi Motors in August 1981 along with 79 and 84. It is seen here in their yard at Maesteg on 16 February 1983.

(The late John Wiltshire)

When is a bus not a bus?

When Leyland Atlantean 93 (MDW 393G) was withdrawn from service in July 1981 it passed to Newport Borough Housing Department and by December that year had been converted into a mobile workshop/rest room and given fleet number 326. It was garaged and maintained at Corporation Road and a driver would be instructed to take the bus to a designated location, with another collecting it at the end of the working day and returning it to the depot. This arrangement worked well until it was pointed out that MDW 393G was now a Class 3 HGV and no longer a bus, and so there would be fewer staff that could legally drive it. The vehicle was eventually sold in May 1985 to Coastal Continental, Barry, as a source of spare parts.

Parked for the weekend on Saturday 27 November 1982, MDW 393G is seen in the depot yard.

(John Jones)

115 (GKG 36N) passed to Burton Coaches, Brixham in 1986 and by 1990 was a mobile caravan. It is seen here at Wincanton Steam Fair on 11 July 1993.

(Ivor Homfray)

The Metro-Scanias did surprisingly well too after withdrawals began, and nine withdrawn in the years 1983-5 saw some further use. Deregulation in October 1986 witnessed an increased demand for used buses and so most subsequent Newport disposals would be for continued use. A further eighteen Metro-Scanias withdrawn after this date found new homes. Perhaps the most interesting examples were the seven that passed to Drakesmere Developments, Cardiff in December 1989. Numbers 48/9, 51/2/4/9 and 60 were used to convey aid supplies to Poland in time for Christmas. The plan was to leave the buses in Poland for use as mobile business units. All did not go to plan, and it is known that at least two vehicles (51 and 52) never actually made it out of the UK.

Ivy Coaches and Taxis (Linthwaite) Ltd, based near Huddersfield, purchased six former Newport Metro-Scanias in April 1987 for use on local services in West Yorkshire. This was a short-lived venture, as they were sold for use at Gatwick Airport by the end of 1988.

Crowther (Black Prince) of Morley

This Leeds-based fleet operated thirty-three former Newport Scanias from 1996. Six Marshall-bodied Scanias (85/7-91) were sold to Redby Coaches Ltd, Sunderland in June 1995, while 82-4/6, 92/4, 101 passed to Black Prince in April 1996. The Redby examples then passed to Black Prince in July 1996 followed by 93/5-100 in April 1997.

Purchased for local service bus work, Ivy Coaches VDW 445K is seen in Leeds bus station on a dismal 19 July 1987.

(Andrew Wiltshire)

Marshall-bodied Scania JBO 90W was one of six that briefly worked for Redby Coaches of Sunderland in 1995/96 before joining the rest of this batch with Black Prince Buses in Leeds.

(Andrew Wiltshire collection)

Black Prince 85 (JBO 85W) in its owner's very distinctive livery. This Scania has acquired Leyland-style front wheels.

(Ivor Homfray collection)

Five of the eight Wadham Stringer-bodied saloons also passed to Black Prince in August 1998 followed by all eight East Lancs-bodied double-deckers (27-34) in November 1999. Metrobuses 66-72 passed to Grey Green (Cowie) in 1992 for use on London Regional Transport (LRT) tendered service in the Walthamstow area of London. The surviving eight Metrobuses from the second batch also saw further service in 1994. 75 and 80 passed to County Bus and Coach, Harlow, while 74, 76-9, 81 passed to Merseyside Transport Ltd, Liverpool where they put in up to three years' service.

Wadham Stringer-bodied RUH 15Y with Black Prince in Leeds Suburban livery and seen at the Corn Exchange, Leeds, in September 1999.

(John Jones collection)

JBO 78W as Merseyside 3078. It is seen in the Paradise Street bus station in Liverpool in March 1994.

(John Jones collection)

The open-top Metrobuses

After service with Grey Green, four Metrobuses DTG 368-71V were converted to open-top by Ensignbus and used in London by London Pride Sightseeing by 1997. 68/9/71 were later exported to Copenhagen by 2001 for use by City-Sightseeing and an offside entrance door was added to all three buses. 68 later went to work for City-Sightseeing in Oslo, Norway by 2002.

Meanwhile 69 returned to the UK, and was exported to San Diego in California by 2003 for use by City-Sightseeing and fitted with a sliding roof. 71 also went to San Diego but by 2005 was with Starline Tours, Hollywood, and was in the process of being converted to left-hand drive in 2014. 70 continued as an open-top bus in the UK, but had reached the Netherlands by 2017.

Following its de-roofing accident in May 2002, Scania 45 was sold to Ensign bus who converted it to open-top and put it to work at Eastbourne in City Sightseeing livery. It was later with the Bath Bus Company on Bristol sightseeing tours, before passing to J.S.C. Elit Electronics, Tbilisi, Georgia, by October 2012, as a promotional vehicle. After withdrawal in 2008, Alexander Strider-bodied Scania saloons 65-7, 75/6 were all sold to Lough Swilly in 2009 for use as school buses in Northern Ireland and Eire.

Northern Blue

In October 2003 Alexander-bodied Scania double-deckers 22/4 (B222/4 YUH) passed to Travelspeed Ltd (Northern Blue) of Burnley. They were joined in early 2005 by 42, 143/4, 46 (F42-4/6 YHB) and 47/9, 51/2 (G47/9/51/2 FKG). Later that year Scania saloons in the form of Alexander Strider-bodied 4/6-8 (K104/6-8 KTX) joined the Northern Blue fleet. The final additions were three Optare Metroriders 86-8 (R86/7/188 BDW) in early 2006. This brought the total number of former Newport vehicles acquired to seventeen in just over two years.

Newport Buses in North Yorkshire

In November 2008 a pair of Alexander Strider-bodied Scanias, K107/8 KTX were acquired from Travelspeed Ltd (Northern Blue) by Harrogate Coach Travel, Harrogate. Further similar buses acquired were 78 (N78 PDW), 77, 93 (P177, 93 VDW) and Wright bodied Scanias 11/8 (S211, 118 TDW), the last two being acquired in July 2015. This operator later adopted the fleetname Connexionsbuses and in December 2016 acquired three Scania OmniCity saloons from Newport. These were 53/5/8 (CA52 JJZ, JKF/N) which were re-registered XNT 421, JSU 721 and UUG 384 respectively. They had been sold by 2020.

Metrobus DTG 368V is now Ensignbus 368, and is being used on the London Pride sightseeing tour. Seen in central London, it features an offside entrance door pending deployment overseas.

(Ivor Homfray collection)

B221/3 YUH passed to T R Cole (TRC Coaches) of Treorchy in 2003/4 for school contracts. Nearly ten years later B223 YUH was still looking smart when noted at Treorchy on 25 June 2013.

(John Jones)

Scania N113 (G52 FKG) is seen at Northern Blue's premises in Burnley on 2 September 2007.

(Peter Keating)

Alexander Strider-bodied Scania K108 YTX is seen turning into Low Ousegate, York, before setting off for Harrogate on 25 July 2009.

(Andrew Wiltshire)

Preservation

Compared to many municipal fleets of a similar size, there are relatively few Newport buses in preservation and only two examples that pre-date 1971.

Trams

Such was the haste to rid Newport of its outdated electric tramcars, unfortunately there were no survivors. This was the 1930s and tram preservation was something unheard in most circles. Unless an example had managed to survive in a remote location as a static caravan or store shed, then the breakers yard would be the only outcome for a redundant tramcar.

Motor buses

83 (BDW 922) a Leyland Tiger TS8 of 1938 was withdrawn from service in January 1952 and joined the ancillary fleet as a driver training bus. In May 1953 it passed to the Borough Engineers Department as a mobile workmen's cabin until 1961 when it was reduced to a chassis and cab and passed into preservation in 1962 to Newport enthusiast Mr A B Smith (later proprietor of Welsh Dragon Coaches). However, it was scrapped the following year, and so the first Newport bus in preservation was no more.

The rapid and economically essential introduction of one-man operation from the 1960s rendered many half-cab double-deckers unattractive buses after withdrawal, especially if they had open rear platforms. Only their engines were deemed to have any real value. Consequently, most of Newport's motor buses withdrawn during the 1950s, 1960s and 1970s, and which had an expired Certificate of Fitness (CoF) went straight for scrap. This meant very few survived long enough to be considered worthy of preservation. Having said that, compared to other South Wales fleets, many even more modern types of vehicle operated by Newport are not represented in preservation. Maybe the complexity of the Scanias has put people off.

The first Newport motor bus to be preserved was Leyland Atlantean 77 (KDW 77F), which was purchased in April 1981 by an enthusiast in Pontllanfraith. Unfortunately, it was damaged by fire in 1988 and later scrapped. Similar bus 82 (KDW 82F) was purchased by a Newport-based enthusiast in October 1981. Its body was scrapped in 1988 without the owner's consent and the chassis was then broken up the following year. However, in October 1990, the same Newport enthusiast purchased Atlantean 68 (EDW 68D) from Warner Motors Ltd of Tewkesbury and set about restoring it. This time the outcome was positive, and the bus eventually passed to the Cardiff Transport Preservation Group in 2007 for continued preservation.

During its relatively short spell in preservation, Leyland Atlantean 77 (KDW 77F) is seen attending the HCVS Cardiff rally in June 1983.

(Andrew Wiltshire)

68 (EDW 68D) has been preserved by the Cardiff Transport Preservation Group since 2007. It is seen at the Dock Offices providing park and ride transport for the Barry 10K event in August 2018.

(Richard Sanders)

Newport Transport re-acquired Leyland PD2 number 178 (PDW 484) in February 1983, for eventual restoration, and this project is covered in Chapter Six. The bus remains preserved with Newport Transport in 2021 and is often used for private hire events such as weddings.

Three Metro-Scanias passed into preservation. 56 passed to an individual in the Winchester area in 1989 and was eventually restored in King Alfred livery as a reminder of King Alfred's trio of Metro-Scania saloons. After two further owners it returned to the Newport area in 2007 for continued preservation. In 2021 it remains securely stored in reasonably good order, and is the subject of a long term restoration.

58 which was later renumbered 102 was retained by Newport as a preserved vehicle but was then sold to a local enthusiast in July 2006 for continued preservation. It is now stored in the Barry area awaiting restoration. Finally, former London Transport 104 was sold for preservation in 1991. It passed to the same Newport-based owner as 56, and was later broken up to provide spares for 56.

It is worth mentioning that Marshall-bodied Scania BR112 84 (JBO 84W) was withdrawn by Black Prince, Leeds in August 2001 and retained by them as a possible preservation candidate. It was however sold for scrap in May 2003. The open-top Scania N113 141 (F41 YHB) passed to the Cardiff Transport Preservation Group in 2016, and is currently kept at Barry in full running order. The Cardiff Transport Preservation Group acquired Alexander Strider-bodied Scania N113CRL 77 (P177 VDW) from Harrogate Coach Travel (Connexionsbuses) in July 2015, and this vehicle currently awaits restoration at Barry.

Three vehicles were donated to the Cardiff Transport Preservation Group in late 2017 but were found to be in very poor condition and were disposed of for scrap. These were Scania L94/Wright 10, Dennis Trident 40 and former training bus TV10, the Dennis Dart SLF. A surprise addition to the rather small ranks of preserved Newport buses was Scania OmniCity 55 (CA52 JKF), which passed to Town & District Transport Trust, Great Harwood near Blackburn in 2019 after service with Connexionsbuses.

Still in King Alfred livery, 56 (YDW 756K) is seen in September 2006 shortly after returning to Newport for continued preservation.

(Kevin Jarvis)

77 (P177 VDW) in CTPG ownership in undercover storage at Barry.

(Clive Williams)

In preservation

Fleet No	Reg No	Chassis	Body	Seating	Year	Status
178	PDW 484	Leyland PD2/40	Longwell Green	H30/28R	1958	Restored
68	EDW 68D	" PDR1/1	Alexander	H43/31F	1966	"
56	YDW 756K	Metro-Scania	MCW	B40D	1972	Part-restored
58	YDW 758K	"	"	"	"	Unrestored
141	F41 YHB	Scania N113	Alexander	046/33F	1988	Restored
77	P177 VDW	Scania N113CRLAA	"	B48F	1996	Unrestored
55	CA52 JKF	Scania OmniCity N94UB	Scania	B42F	2003	Restored

The ones that got away

77	KDW 77F	Leyland PDR1/1	Alexander	H43/31F	1968	Fire damaged
82	KDW 82F	"	"	"	"	Broken up
104	PGC 204L	Metro-Scania	MCW	B41D	1973	Broken up
10	S110 TDW	Scania L94UB	Wright	B46F	1998	Broken up
40	V140 HTG	Dennis Trident	Alexander	H47/25F	2000	Broken up
TV10	P136 LNF	Dennis Dart SLF	East Lancs	B35F	1996	Broken up

CELEBRATING FIFTY YEARS OF NEWPORT SCANIAS
1971- 2021

Bound for the Gaer estate on 30 April 1988, Metro-Scania 56 (YDW 756K) climbs Stow Hill with Dodge midibus 65 in close pursuit.

(John Jones)

MCW Metropolitan 112 (GKG 33N) in seen in the Kingsway bus station while allocated to Ringland service 8A.

(Andrew Wiltshire collection)

Cardiff bus station is the setting for this view of Marshall-bodied Scania BR112 87 (JBO 87W), just about to set off for Newport.

(Andrew Wiltshire collection)

31 (C31 ETG) is an East Lancs-bodied Scania N112 of 1986. On 19 March 1993 it heads into Newport from Moorland Park on service 16.

(John Jones)

11 (S211 TDW) is one of Newport's first low-floor buses. This Wright-bodied Scania L94UB is seen on Queensway on 23 October 2003 having worked into town from Bettws.

(Andrew Wiltshire)

Scania OmniCity 4 (YN57 FZW) was one of five vehicles to gain Pride embellishments during the summer of 2019. It is seen on 19 August on a Bettws service.

(Andrew Wiltshire)

APPENDIX 1

NEWPORT'S OVERALL ADVERT BUSES
AND SPECIAL LIVERIES SINCE 1981

Apart from the Leyland TD1 number 42 which was decorated for the Coronation in 1937, and open-top Guy Arab number 99 which received a special cream livery in May 1953 for the Coronation, no other buses received special liveries before 1981. Overall advert buses had first appeared in the UK in about 1970 with many appearing on buses in neighbouring Cardiff. However, Newport was late to adopt overall advertising and the first example did not appear until the summer of 1981.

Metropolitan 114 (GKG 35N) carried the first overall advert in the fleet from July 1981.

(Andrew Wiltshire collection)

Vehicle	Type	Description of livery	From	To	Comments
114	Metropolitan	Bona-Toggs jeans	7.81	3.83	
116	"	80th anniversary tramcar livery	8.81	9.83	
74	Metrobus	Tesco Stores	2.86	2.94	Until withdrawal
84	Scania/Marshall	Richard Crook estate agents	6.86	12.87	
78	Metrobus	Cwmbran Shopping	5.90	1991	

Marshall-bodied Scania 84 (JBO 84W) was decorated in 1986 to the order of Richard Crook, a local property specialist. It is seen entering the bus station on 3 January 1987.

(The late John Wiltshire)

78 (JBO 78W) was one of two Metrobuses to receive overall advert liveries. Here it is seen in High Street on 28 July 1990 doing its best to persuade the residents of Newport to shop in Cwmbran.

(The late John Wiltshire)

Vehicle	Type	Description of livery	From	To	Comments
88	Scania/Marshall	National Children's Home	5.91	?	Until at least 3.93
34	Scania/E Lancs	Darlow's estate agents	6.95	1.00	Until withdrawal
47	Scania/Alexander	SG Newport car dealer	5.96	2.00	
23	Scania/Alexander	University of Wales College, Newport	5.96	7.98	
49	Scania/Alexander	Cardiff Wales Airport	7.96	9.97	
51	Scania/Alexander	Premier Window Systems	9.96	10.99	
21	Scania/Alexander	Gwent Autopanels	5.97	8.99	
50	Scania/Alexander	Prince's Trust Volunteers	4.98	8.00	
23	Scania/Alexander	George Street Furnishers	8.98	?	
51	Scania/Alexander	Voodoo Zanzibar Entertainment	1.00	?	
61	Metrorider	Hartwell Newport car dealer	1.99	5.01	Until withdrawal
45	Scania/Alexander	Peter Alan estate agents	5.99	7.01	
35	Trident	SG Newport car dealer	3.00	3.05	From new
36	Trident	Acorn Recruitment	1.00	7.05	From new
37	Trident	Darlow's estate agents	2.00	1.01	From new
43	Scania/Alexander	Newport Car Auctions	10.00	1.05	Until withdrawal
37	Trident	T2 Group business skills	1.01	12.03	
85	Dart	Adult Education Classes	5.01	4.03	From new
52	Scania/Alexander	Newport Museum & Art Gallery	7.01	7.03	
52	Scania/Alexander	Newport Shops	8.03	?	
20	Scania/Alexander	Centenary tramcar livery	7.01	6.03	Until withdrawal
73	Scania/Strider	ELW learning	6.02	3.04	
49	Scania/Alexander	University of Wales College, Newport	7.02	7.03	

Scania N113 49 (G49 FKG) was another colourful overall advert this time for University of Wales College, Newport. It is seen in March 2003 about to enter the Kingsway bus station on a run from Caerleon.

(Andrew Wiltshire)

Vehicle	Type	Description of livery	From	To	Comments
54	OmniCity	Newport City Centre shopping	1.03	7.05	From new
56	OmniCity	Newport Council (Newenergy)	1.03	9.07	From new
38	Trident	Welsh Assembly Learning Grant	10.03	9.06	
31	Dart	Warburton's Bread	12.03	12.05	
41	Scania/Alexander	City Sightseeing (open-top)	4.04	2014	Until withdrawal
39	Trident	University of Wales, Newport	5.04	2006	
14	Scania/Wright	bmibaby.com	6.04	12.07	

Scania L94 14 (S114 TDW) is promoting airline bmibaby.com which operated from Cardiff Wales Airport for a number of years. It is seen at the Duffryn estate.

(Cardiff Transport Preservation Group collection)

Vehicle	Type	Description of livery	From	To	Comments
54	OmniCity	Acorn People (recruitment)	7.05	7.10	
32	Dart	Tesco Free Bus contract	10.05	10.07	All over white
32	Dart	Tesco Free Bus contract	10.07	8.10	Decorated
68	Optare Solo	Rail-link	2.08	7.08	From new
69	Optare Solo	Rail-link	2.08	8.08	From new
53	OmniCity	bmibaby.com	7.08	8.11	
55	OmniCity	bmibaby.com	8.08	6.11	
41	OmniCity	bmibaby.com	8.08	6.11	
47	OmniCity	bmibaby.com	9.08	7.11	
15	Scania/Wright	SWALEC	10.08	11.09	
37	Trident	SWALEC	10.08	9.09	
56	OmniCity	SWALEC	11.08	10.09	
57	OmniCity	SWALEC	11.08	10.09	
58	OmniCity	SWALEC	11.08	10.09	
83	Scania/Strider	Newport City Homes	3.10	6.11	Until withdrawal
307	Enviro200	World War One commemorative	7.14	12.15	
111	OmniCity	Newport Bus driver recruitment	11.17	C	Revised 2020
112	OmniCity	Newport Bus driver recruitment	11.17	C	Revised 2020
101	MAN	Newport RFC	8.18	C	
110	OmniCity	Welsh Government's Mytravelpass	5.19	C	
59	OmniCity	Welsh Government's Mytravelpass	5.19	C	
403	Enviro400	Coleg Gwent	7.19	10.20	
306	Enviro200	Newport RFC	9.19	C	

Wright Meridian-bodied MAN number 101 carries this striking livery to promote Newport Rugby Football Club. It is seen on 14 May 2019.

(Andrew Wiltshire)

Another form of advertising that became popular in the 1980s was the broadside advert that utilised the between decks panels on the sides of double-deckers and was often carried around to the front and rear of the vehicle. Newport had a number of these adverts and we have two examples.

Chartered surveyors Davis & Sons were promoting their services on East Lancs-bodied Scania BR112 number 34 (C34 ETG) when noted on 3 January 1987.

(The late John Wiltshire)

The Newport and Cwmbran Post *was a free newspaper distributed in the 1980s and 1990s. This bold advert is seen on Marshall-bodied Scania 91 (JBO 91W) as it enters the Kingsway bus station on 10 September 1987.*

(The late John Wiltshire)

Buses specially decorated for Christmas

Some were decorated with colour lights.

Period	Vehicle	
1987-91	100 (PTG 100Y)	Illuminated Santa and snowman on front of bus.
1994	45 (F45 YHB)	Illuminated Santa and snowman on front of bus.
1997	68 (L68 EKG)	Vinyls with a Christmas theme.
2001	44 (F44 YHB)	Illuminations on front of bus (new design).
2002	83 (N83 PDW)	Vinyls with a Christmas theme.
2003	44 (F44 YHB)	Illuminations on front of bus (new design).
2004	144 (F44 YHB)	Vinyls with a Christmas theme.
2009	61 (YV03 PZR)	Vinyls with a Christmas theme.
2011	35 (V35 HTG)	Vinyls with a Christmas theme.
2012	304 (YX11 AGY)	Vinyls with a Christmas theme.

Marshall-bodied Scania 100 (PTG 101Y) was quite elaborately decorated for the festive season in 1987.

(Ivor Homfray)

APPENDIX 2

LIST OF ALL PASSENGER VEHICLES OWNED

Explanation of seating codes

AB = articulated bus
B = single-deck bus
C = coach
H = highbridge layout double-deck bus
L = lowbridge layout double-deck bus with sunken upper-deck gangway
FB = single-deck bus with a full-fronted body, where a half-cab would normally be fitted
DP = bus with dual-purpose type seating
O = open-top bus
M = minibus

Numbers indicate seating capacity and for double-deckers upper deck is given before lower deck if the split is known, for example H43/31F.
F = front entrance
R = rear entrance with open platform
RD = rear entrance with platform doors
D = dual entrance/exit
T = toilet fitted

Electric Tramcars

Fleet no.	Builder	Running units	Electrical equipment	Seating	Year new	Years withdrawn
1-30	G F Milnes	Peckham cantilever	British Westinghouse 2x30hp	O33/22	1903	1930 to 1937
31-40	E. R. & T.C.W.	Brill 21E	Dick, Kerr, 2x25hp	"	1904	1930 to 1937
41	U.E.C.C.	"	Dick, Kerr, 2x35hp	Rail grinder	1906	1937
42-4	"	"	" "	O33/22	1909	1937
45-50	E. R. & T.C.W.	"	Dick, Kerr, 2x25hp	38/22	1903	1937 (a)
51-4	Brush Electrical	EE (Preston) Brill 22E bogie	EE (Dick, Kerr) 2x40hp	80	1921	1937
55-8	Hurst Nelson	EE (Preston) Brill 21E	EE (Dick, Kerr) 2x30hp	55	1922	1937

(a) 45-50 were ex London County Council (fleet numbers are unknown) in 1917.

Motor Buses

Fleet no.	Registration no.	Chassis type	Body	Seating	Year new	Years withdrawn
1-6	DW 3494/0/2/1/3/5	Karrier KY 2-ton	Short	B20F	1924	1931 to 1934
7/8	DW 4453/2	Karrier JHS	Vickers	FB30F	1925	1932 (7) 1938 (8)
9-13	DW 4768-72	"	"	"	1926	1937 (10) 1938 (others)
14-6	DW 5080-2	"	"	"	"	1938
17/8	DW 5586/7	Karrier JKL	"	B26F	1927	1939
19/20	DW 5636/7	Leyland LSC1	Leyland	"	"	1939
21-30	DW 5800-9	Leyland LSC3	Short	B32F	1928	1939
31-4	DW 6941-4	Leyland TD1	Leyland	L24/24R	1930	1944
35/6	DW 7118/9	"	"	"	"	1945
37-46	DW 7160-9	"	"	"	"	1945 to 1949
47/8	DW 7754/5	Leyland TD2	"	H24/24R	1932	1949
49/50	DW 7756/7	Leyland LT5	Weymann	B32R	"	1944
51	TJ 1514	Leyland TD2	Leyland	H24/24R	1933	1947 (a)
52-65	BDW 5-18	Leyland TS8	Weymann	B33D	1937	1945 to 1957
66-81	BDW 19-34	Leyland TD5	"	H28/24R	"	1951 to 1957 (a)
82-6	BDW 921-5	Leyland TS8	"	B36F	1938	1952 to 1957
87-91	BDW 926-30	Leyland TD5	"	H28/24R	"	1953 to 1958

(a) Ex Leyland Motors.
(b) 62 converted to B24C+24 in 5/53. Reverted to B30C in 12/53.
(c) 67 and 69 had their seating increased to 54 in 1949.

Fleet no.	Registration no.	Chassis type	Body	Seating	Year new	Years withdrawn
92-4	CDW 959-61	Leyland TD7	Weymann	H30/26R	1942	1951 to 1955
95	CDW 962	Leyland TS11	"	B36F	"	1951
96	DDW 24	Leyland TD7	"	H30/26R	"	1954
97/8	DDW 33/4	Guy Arab I 5LW	"	"	1943	1953
99	DDW 42	Guy Arab I 6LW	"	"	"	1957
100	DDW 46	Daimler CWG5	Duple	"	"	1957
101/2	DDW 60/1	Guy Arab II 5LW	Weymann	"	"	1959
103	DDW 62	Guy Arab II 6LW	"	"	1944	1959
104-8	DDW 64/6/9/71/2	Guy Arab II 5LW	"	"	"	1956 to 1959
109-12	DDW 83/110-2	Guy Arab II 6LW	"	"	"	1958/59 (a)
113-6	DDW 113-6	Guy Arab II 5LW	Park Royal	"	"	1957/58
117	DDW 117	Guy Arab II 6LW	"	"	"	1957
118	DDW 118	"	"	"	1945	1957
119-21	DDW 119-21	Daimler CWA6	"	"	"	1956 to 1966 (b)
122/3	DDW 122/3	Daimler CWD6	"	"	"	1957 to 1961 (c)
124-7	DDW 124-7	"	Brush	"	"	1958 to 1961 (c)
128	DDW 128	"	Duple	"	1946	1962 (c)

(a) 110 received a new D J Davies H30/26R body in 1956.
(b) 119 received the Weymann H28/26R body from 79 (BDW 32) in 6/55. 121 received a new D J Davies B32F body in 8/54.
(c) 123-5/7/8 received new D J Davies H30/26R bodies in 1954.

Fleet no.	Registration no.	Chassis type	Body	Seating	Year new	Years withdrawn
129-36	DDW 129-36	Daimler CVG6	Weymann	H30/26R	1947	1959/60
137-40	DDW 137-40	Leyland PD1A	"	"	1948	1960 to 1964
141-5	EDW 399-403	"	"	"	"	1964/65
1-6	FDW 51-6	Leyland PD2/3	Leyland	"	1949	1967 to 1969
7-16	FDW 41-50	Guy Arab III 6DC	Guy	"	"	1965 to 1968 (a)
17-26	FDW 841-50	Guy Arab III 6LW	"	"	1950	1967/68
27-36	GDW 94-103	Leyland PD2/3	Bruce	"	1951	1963 to 1969 (b)
37	JDW 89	Dennis Lancet	D J Davies	B38F	1954	1967
38	JDW 90	Dennis Falcon	"	"	"	1967
39-42	KDW 259-62	Dennis Lancet UF	"	B44F	"	1966/67
146	LDW 509	Guy Arab IV 6LW	"	H32/26R	1955	1969
147-9	LDW 510-2	"	"	H33/26R	"	1970/71 (c)
43-50	LDW 501-8	Dennis Lancet UF	"	B42R	1956	1963 to 1967 (d)
150	NDW 601	Daimler CVG6	"	H30/28R	1957	1970
151-61	NDW 602-12	"	Longwell Green	H33/28R	"	1969 to 1971
162	ODW 298	Leyland PD2/40	"	H33/28R	1958	1972
163-7	ODW 299-303	"	"	H30/28R	"	1972 to 1974
168-73	PDW 13-8	"	"	"	"	1971 to 1973
174-9	PDW 480-5	"	"	"	"	1971 to 1974
180-5	PDW 778-83	"	"	"	"	1971/72 (e)
51-6	PDW 992-7	"	"	"	1959	1972
57-61	SDW 133-7	"	"	"	"	1971/72 (f)
62-6	UDW 835-9	"	"	"	1961	1972

(a) 7-16 later received Gardner 6LW engines.
(b) 27/8, 31/3 are 1950.
(c) 149 is 1956.
(d) 49/50 are 1957.
(e) 184/5 are 1959.
(f) 59/61 are 1960.

Fleet no.	Registration no.	Chassis type	Body	Seating	Year new	Years withdrawn
67-71	EDW 67-71D	Leyland PDR1/1 MkII	Alexander	H43/31F	1966	1976 to 1978
72-6	HDW 772-6E	"	"	"	1967	1979
101-8	JDW 301-8F	Bristol RESL6L	ECW	B42F	"	1977 to 1979
77-84	KDW 77-84F	Leyland PDR1/1 MkII	Alexander	H43/31F	1968	1980/81
85-93	MDW 385-93G	Leyland PDR1A/1	"	"	1969	1981
94-100	PDW 94-100H	"	"	"	1970	1981

Fleet no.	Registration no.	Chassis type	Body	Seating	Year new	Years withdrawn
10-8	TDW 310-8J	Leyland PDR1A/1	Alexander	H43/31F	1971	1982/83
19-46	VDW 419-46K	Scania BR111MH	MCW	B40D	1972	1983 to 1987 (a)
47-62	YDW 747-62K	"	"	"	"	1988 to 1993
109	XDW 741K	Bedford YRQ	Duple	C45F	"	1978 (b)
110	ADW 178K	"	Willowbrook	"	"	1979 (b)
111-120	GKG 32-41N	Scania BR111DH	MCW	H44/29F	1975	1985/86
63	UTX 463S	Leyland PSU3E/4R	Duple	C51F	1978	1983
64	WTG 64T	"	"	"	"	1984
101/3-6	PGC 201/3-6L	Scania BR111MH	MCW	B41D	1973	1983 to 1990 (c)
65	DTG 365V	Leyland PSU3E/4R	Duple	C51F	1980	1985
66-72	DTG 366-72V	MCW Metrobus DR102/15	MCW	H46/31F	"	1992/93
73-81	JBO 73-81W	MCW Metrobus DR102/20	"	"	1981	1993/94
82-92	JBO 82-92W	Scania BR112DH	Marshall	H43/31F	"	1995/96
1	OBO 631X	Leyland TRCTL11/2R	Plaxton	C51F	1982	1991
93-101	PTG 93-101Y	Scania BR112DH	Marshall	H45/31F	1983	1996/97 (d)
10-8	RUH 10-8Y	"	Wadham Stringer	B42F	"	1998
2	STG 2Y	Leyland TRCTL11/2R	Plaxton	C53F	"	1995
19-26	B219-26 YUH	Scania N112DRB	Alexander	H47/31F	1985	2001 to 2003 (e)
3	B603 DDW	Leyland TRCTL11/3R	Plaxton	C55F	"	1996 (f)
27-34	C27-34 ETG	Scania N112DRB	East Lancs	H43/33F	1986	1999/2000

(a) 19 and 20 are 1971.
(b) ex A B Smith, Newport in July 1974.
(c) ex London Transport Executive (MS1/3-6) in 1978. 101 never entered service.
(d) 95 and 99 are 1982.
(e) 19-21 are 1984.
(f) Re-seated to C51F in 8/85.

Fleet no.	Registration no.	Chassis type	Body	Seating	Year new	Years withdrawn
4-9	D804-9 MNY	Dodge S56	East Lancs	DP24F	1987	1990/91 (a)
63/4	D63/4 MTG	"	"	"	"	1990 (a)
35/6, 65	E35/6/65 RBO	"	Reeve Burgess	B25F	"	1991 (b)
37/8	E37/8 UBO	MCW Metrorider MF150/90	MCW	DP25F	1988	1997
39	D474 UHC	Dodge S56	East Lancs	DP24F	1986	1990 (c)
4	XFM 203	Leyland TRCTL11/3RH	Duple	C49FT	1986	1997 (d)
41-6	F41-6 YHB	Scania N113DRB	Alexander	H47/33F	1988	2002 to 2014
47-52	G47-52 FKG	"	"	"	1989	2005
53-8	G53-8 KTX	Optare Metrorider MR09	Optare	B23F	1990	1996 to 2003
59-64	H59, 160, 61-4 PNY	"	"	"	1991	2000/01
5	J905 UBO	Leyland TRCL10/3ARZ10	Plaxton	C51F	"	2001 (e)
4-9	K104-9 YTX	Scania N113CRBAA	Alexander	B48F	1993	2004/05
68-73	L68/9,170,71,172,73 EKG	"	"	"	1994	2007
39	D478 PON	MCW Metrorider MF150/4	MCW	B23F	1987	1997 (f)
65-7	M65, 166, 67 KTG	Scania N113CRLAA	Alexander	B48F	1995	2008
74-6	M74-6 KTG	"	"	"	"	2008
78-83	N78/9, 180, 81-3 PDW	"	"	"	1996	2011/12
36	D477 PON	MCW Metrorider MF150/4	MCW	B23F	1987	1997 (g)
2	J96 NJT	Scania K113CRBAA	Plaxton	C53F	1992	2003 (h)
77/90-4	P177/90, 91-4 VDW	Scania N113CRLAA	Alexander	B48F	1997	2007 to 2012
86-9	R86/7, 188, 89 BDW	Optare Metrorider MR31	Optare	B25F	"	2005/06
3	J97 NJT	Scania K113CRBAA	Plaxton	C53F	1992	2003 (i)
10-8	S110, 211, 112-8 TDW	Scania L94UB	Wright	B46F	1998	2005 (16) 2013 to 2020 (j)

35-40	V35-9, 140 HTG	Dennis Trident MkII	Alexander	H49/30F	2000	2012 to 2018 (k)
95-9	V195, 96-8, 199 VWO	Dennis Dart SLF	"	B28F	"	2011 to 2015
54	F360 URU	MCW Metrorider MF150/108	MCW	B23F	1989	2000 (l)
31-4	Y131, 32, 133/4 YBO	Dennis Dart SLF	Alexander	B28F	2001	2011 to 2015
84/5	Y84, 185 YBO	"	"	"	"	2011 2012

(a) 4-9/63 re-seated to DP22F in 1989. 5 re-seated to B22F in 1990.

(b) 35 re-seated to B23F in 9/88.

(c) 9 ex Eastbourne Borough Transport in September 1988.

(d) ex Crosville Motor Services in 1988 and originally registered C73 KLG.

(e) 5 was later re-numbered 1 in 1993 and re-registered XFM 203 in 1997 and sold as such.

(f) 39 ex Parfitt's Motor Services in April 1994.

(g) 36 ex Cardiff Bluebird (via Cardiff Bus) in September 1996.

(h) 2 was ex Excelsior, Bournemouth, in 1996.

(i) 3 was ex Excelsior, Bournemouth, in 1997.

(j) 18 is B42F.

(k) later re-seated to H47/25F.

(l) ex Wilts & Dorset (2360) in March 2000.

Fleet no.	Registration no.	Chassis type	Body	Seating	Year new	Years withdrawn
53-8	CA52 JJZ, JKE/F/J/K/N	Scania OmniCity N94UB	Scania	B42F	2003	2016>
59/60/3/64	YN53 GGX/U/V/Y	"	"	"	"	
61/2	YV03 PZR/S	"	"	"	"	2016 (61)
19	YN04 AFU	Scania K94	Irizar	C70F	2004	2013
20-5	YN54 OCB-G	"	"	"	2005	2013
41-6	YN54 AOA-F	Scania OmniCity N94UB	Scania	B42F	2005	
48/9/51	YN07 VCK/L/O	Scania OmniCity N230UB	"	B41F	2007	
47/50/2	YN57 FZP/R/S	"	"	"	"	
1-6	YN57 FZT/U/V/W/X/Y	"	"	"	"	2019>
68-70	YJ57 YCG/H/K	Optare Solo M880	Optare	B27F	2008	2012 (a)
71-3	YJ08 PKK/N/O	"	"	"	"	2012
266/8/72	P266/8/72 PSX	Volvo Olympian YV3YNA	Alexander	H51/30D	1997	2013 (b)
276/7/9	P276/7/9 PSX	"	"	"	"	2013 (b)
101-6	CN60 FBO/V/U/Y/L/X	MAN NLF273F	Wright	B42F	2011	(c)
110-7	YT11 LUL/O/P/D/E/F/H/J	Scania OmniCity N230UB	Scania	B41F	"	2019>
301/2	YX11 CRK/U	Alexander Dennis	Enviro200 E20D	B29F	"	
303-6	YX11 AGV/Y/Z, AHV	"	"	"	"	
307-9	YX61 DUT/U/V	"	"	"	"	
310/1	YX12 DME/F	"	"	"	2012	
312-7	YX12 DHM/N/O/P/U/V	"	"	B39F	"	2012 (317)
26/7	YN06 MXU/V	Volvo B12B	Plaxton	C49FT	2006	(d)
207	FX58 ZNT	Mercedes 515CDi	Ferqui Soroco	B18F	2009	2019 (e)
400-4	SN62 AOH/O/P/W/X	Alexander Dennis	Enviro400 E40D	H45/31F	2012	
321/2	MX09 MHY/Z	"	Enviro200 E20D	B29F	2009	(f)
420-2	LN51 KXR/W/V	Transbus Trident	Plaxton	H43/31F	2002	(g)
423-5	LR02 BAO/U, BBF	"	"	"	"	2020> (g)
318/9	YX13 EGC/D	Alexander Dennis	Enviro200 E20D	B29F	2013	

(a) 69 was renumbered 74 in 7/09.

(b) 266/8/72/6/7/9 were ex Lothian (266 etc) in 2009.

(c) 101-6 were built in 2009.

(d) 26/7 were ex Woottens, Chesham, in 2012 and are named Sophie and Olivia.

(e) 207 ex White, St. Albans in 2012.

(f) 321/2 previously on loan as 222,333 until June 2013, and new to Solutions SK, Cheadle Heath.

(g) ex Metroline (TPL236/43/2, 271/2/5) in April 2013 and later had their seating reduced.

Fleet no.	Registration no.	Chassis type	Body	Seating	Year new	Years withdrawn
210	WM57 GZG	Mercedes 210	Koch	M8	2008	Returned June 2016
211	KX08 HOJ	Mercedes 511CDi	"	M11	2008	Returned June 2016
212	KX08 HOH	"	"	M12	"	Returned June 2016
213	KY15 RBX	Mercedes 516CDi		M16	2015	Returned April 2018
214	KY15 PNX	"		"	"	Returned January 2016
216-8	BL16 FZM/J/K	Mercedes City 45	Mercedes	B13F	2016	
323	KP02 PWU	Transbus Dart SLF	Transbus	B27D	2002	(a)
324/5/8/9/30	KU52 YKG/L/J/P/H	"	"	"	"	2017> (b)
326/7/31	KU02 YUE/C/D	"	"	"	"	2017> (a)
332-5	KU52 YKV/B/K/N	"	"	"	"	(b)
336	KX54 NJO	Alexander Dennis Dart SLF	Alexander Dennis	"	2004	(a)
426-9/31	KV02 USM, URS/L, USB/H	Transbus Trident	Alexander	H43/22F	2002	2019> (c)
430/2/4	KN52 NDJ/G/Y	"	"	"	"	2019> (d)
433/5/6/7	KN52 NFA, NEU/Y/O	"	"	"	"	(d)
438/9	LR52 LYC, LWF	"	East Lancs	H45/21F	2003	(e)
28/9	SV59 CHL, KX59 DLU	Volvo B12BT	Plaxton	C65FTL	2009	(f)
219	KV18 WFT	Mercedes 516CDi		B19F	2018	
220/1	HK67 EFD/E	Ford Transit	Ford	M16	2018	
222/3	HN18 VHK/T	"	"	"	"	
224	BL67 ELU	"	"	"	"	
225/8/30	HV17 KVK/F/J	"	"	"	2017	orig: 238/1/7
226/7/31	HV18 GVP/O/T	"	"	"	2018	231 orig 234
232	HV18 GWA	"	"	"	"	orig: 235
229	HN66 UDO	"	"	M17	2016	orig: 236
440	KV02 URM	Transbus Trident	Alexander	H43/22F	2002	(h)
Z01	YK66 CBC	Yutong E12LF	Yutong	B38F	2017	(i)
Z02-8	YD70 CFE-G, CFJ-M	"	"	B37F	2020	
Z09-15	YD70 CHG/H/J-L/N/O	"	"	"	"	
351/2	BV19 LPA/C	Volvo B8RLE	MCV eVoRa	B42F	2019	(j)
405-7	SK70 BUO, SK70 BUP, YX70 0LA	Alexander Dennis	Enviro400 MMC	H47/35F	2020	

210-4/6-9 were leased from Dawson Rentals commencing October 2014 (210), May 2015 (211/2), July 2015 (213/4), June 2016 (216-8) and March 2018 (219).

220-32 were leased from Dawson Rentals in August 2018. 351/2 were owned by the Welsh Government. 405/6 were leased from Dawson Rentals in January 2021.

(a) All new to Armchair, Brentford.

(b) All new to Thorpe, Wembley. 330 via Yellow Star, Haverhill. 323/4/6/9/31-6 were rebuilt to B27F before entering service.

(c) 426/7 ex Courtney, Finchampstead; 428 ex Geldards, New Farnley; 429 ex GSAL Transport, Alwoodley, 431 ex Webberbus, Bridgwater, all in 2017, and all new to Connex London and had subsequently worked for Abellio London.

(d) 430/2/3/45/6/7 ex Abellio London in 2017 and new to Armchair, Brentford.

(e) 438/9 ex CT Plus in 2017.

(f) 28/9 ex Stagecoach Western Buses (54071/61) in 2017.

(g) 221-32 all acquired from Dawsongroup rentals in 2018.

(h) 440 ex McLure, Elderslie, in 2018 and new to Connex London.

(i) ex Pelican Engineering, Castleford in August 2019.

(j) ex Stagecoach Red & White (21351/2) in 2020.

APPENDIX 3

FORMER BUSES USED AS DRIVER TRAINING VEHICLES

Fleet no.	Reg. no.	Chassis type	Body	From	To	Comments
44	DW 7167	Leyland TD1	Leyland	2/49	8/50	
57	BDW 10	Leyland TS8	Weymann	6/53	1/54	
59	BDW 12	"	"	4/56	5/57	
61	BDW 14	"	"	9/55	4/56	
65	BDW 18	"	"	1954	6/55	
72	BDW 25	Leyland TD5	"	6/54	1/56	
80	BDW 33	"	"	7/51	7/53	
83	BDW 922	Leyland TS8	"	1/52	5/53	
84	BDW 923	"	"	6/55	7/55	
85	BDW 924	"	"	4/56	6/57	
90	BDW 929	Leyland TD5	"	1/56	6/57	
97	DDW 33	Guy Arab I	Weymann	7/53	6/54	
101	DDW 60	Guy Arab II	"	3/59	9/59	
103	DDW 62	"	"	3/59	9/59	
105	DDW 66	"	"	11/58	2/59	
110	DDW 110	"	D J Davies	9/59	9/61	
111	DDW 111	"	Weymann	9/59	12/60	
112	DDW 112	"	"	5/58	11/58	
118	DDW 118	"	Park Royal	7/57	5/58	
137	DDW 137	Leyland PD1A	Weymann	1/65	1968	
138	DDW 138	"	"	12/60	10/64	
140	DDW 140	"	"	9/61	1/65	
143	EDW 401	"	"	11/64	3/69	
2	FDW 52	Leyland PD2/3	Leyland	4/69	3/72	
5	FDW 55	"	"	7/69	2/72	
71	EDW 71D	Leyland PDR1/1	Alexander	3/78	2/82	Renumbered T1 in 10/79
164	PDW 100H	Leyland PDR1A/1	"	3/82	3/82	Previously 100 in main fleet
174	XGM 450L	Leyland PSU3/3R	"	4/91	12/02	(a)
117	RUH 17Y	Scania BR112DH	Wadham Stringer	2/00	10/04	Previously 17 in main fleet
176	E881 YKY	Leyland TRCTL11/3ARZ	Plaxton	7/02	8/07	(b)
172	W833 PWS	LDV Convoy	LDV	7/03	?	Re-numbered TV3 in 3/07 (c)
9	K109 KTX	Scania N113CRB	Alexander	10/04	10/07	
TV7	J232 NNC	Volvo B10M-60	Van Hool	2/07	6/11	(d)
TV10	P136 LNF	Dennis Dart SLF	East Lancs	7/07	2/16	To CTPG in 11/17 (e)
TV8	WV06 CNF	Ford Transit	Ford	7/07	?	(f)
61	YV03 PZR	Scania OmniCity N94UB	Scania	2/16	C	

Prior to 1979, most vehicles did not carry any fleet numbers while in the training bus fleet.

(a) 174 acquired from Morris Travel, Pencoed, and had been new to Central S.M.T. (T150) in 9/72.

(b) 176 acquired from Ensign, Purfleet, and had been new to Luton & District (109) in 5/88.

(c) 172 was new to LDV Ltd, Birmingham in 5/00.

(d) TV7 was acquired from Western Greyhound Ltd, Summercourt, (as DSU 107), and had been new to Shearings Ltd, Wigan, in 2/92 as J232 NNC.

(e) TV10 was acquired from Ensign, Purfleet, and had been new to Stuart Bus and Coach Co Ltd, Hyde in 12/96. It was only ever used as a training bus by Newport.

(f) TV8 was new to Flightform, Halifax, in 4/06. It carried a special Christmas livery in December 2012 and towed a sleigh.

DEMONSTRATORS AND OTHER VEHICLES
TAKEN ON LOAN/LONG TERM HIRE

Supplier	Reg. no.	Chassis type	Body	Seating	Year new	From	To	Comments
Karrier Motors	?	Karrier WL6/1	?	?	1927	7/27	-	(a)
Leyland Motors	TJ 1514	Leyland TD2	Leyland	H24/24R	1933	3/33	9/33	Purchased in 9/33 as 51
Daimler	GHP 259	Daimler CVD6	NCB	H30/26R	1947	1949	-	(b)
"	PHP 220	Daimler CVG6	NCME	H33/28R	1954	7/55	8/55	(b)
"	SDU 711	"	Willowbrook	H37/29RD	1956	6/56	-	(b)
"	7000 HP	Daimler CRD6	Weymann	H44/33F	1960	6/63	-	(b)
Leyland Motors	SGD 669	Leyland PDR1/1	Alexander	H44/34F	1963	6/63	-	
Daimler	565 CRW	Daimler CRG6LX	"	"	1964	4/65	5/65	(b)
Leyland Motors	KTD 551C	Leyland PDR1/1	Park Royal	H43/31F	1965	11/65	-	
Daimler	CVC 124C	Daimler SRC6	Marshall	B50F	"	8/66		(b)
A.E.C. Ltd	FGW 498C	AEC Swift MP2R	Willowbrook	B53F	"	8/66		
Leyland Motors	STB 957C	Leyland PSUR1/1R	"	"	"	10/66		
MCW Ltd	VWD 452H	Scania BR110MH	MCW	B31D	1969	6/70	7/70	(c)
Seddon Motors	ABU 451J	Seddon Pennine RU	Pennine	B45D	1970	11/70	12/70	
Hestair-Dennis	SHE 722S	Dennis Dominator	East Lancs	H45/32F	1977	7/78	8/78	(d)
Bournemouth Transport	ERU 401L	Ford Transit	Strachan	B16F	1973	11/79	2/80	
Leyland Motors	FHG 592S	Leyland Titan B15	Park Royal	H47/28F	1975	3/79	4/79	
Scania (GB) Ltd	CDC 816	Scania CR112	Scania	B38T	1980	3/80	-	Left-hand drive vehicle (e)
Tayside Regional Council	CSL 602V	Volvo B55-10	Alexander	H44/31D	1980	5/80	-	Not operated
Brighton Transport	OAP 17W	Dennis Dominator	East Lancs	H43/31F	1981	11/81	-	Not operated
Merseyside PTE	?	Leyland ONTL11/1R	ECW	H47/31F	1981	11/81	-	Not operated
Hestair-Dennis	Un-reg	Dennis Lancet	Wadham Stringer	?	1981	1/82	-	Not operated
Leicester City Transport	PJU 90W	Dennis Falcon HC	Duple	B51F	1981	2/82	-	Used on contract work
Shaw & Kilburn	ABH 760X	Bedford YMQ	Wright	B45F	1982	2/82	-	Not operated (f)
Leyland National Co	GCK 430W	Leyland National 2	NL116L11A/1R	B49F	1981	2/82	4/82	Not operated (g)
Volvo/WS	JSJ 435W	Volvo B58-56	Wadham Stringer	B47F	1981	3/82	-	Not operated (h)
Scania (GB) Ltd	EMJ 560Y	Scania BR112DH	East Lancs	H46/32F	1982	8/83	10/83	Used on contract work (i)
Chesterfield	PNU 122K	Leyland PDR1A/1	Roe	H42/29D	1972	11/83	-	Used on contract work (j)
Kirby-Kingsforth	A112 RMJ	Scania K112CRS	Plaxton	C49FT	1983	4/85	-	Hired to cover a shortage

(a) Used on a service from Newport station to the Royal Agricultural Show at Tredegar Park from 5-9/7/27.
(b) GHP 259, PHP 220, SDU 711, 7000 HP, 565 CRW and CVC 124C were on loan from Transport Vehicles (Daimler) Ltd, Coventry.

(c) VWD 452H on loan from Metro-Cammell-Weymann Ltd, Birmingham. It could carry 29 standee passengers.

(d) SHE 722S was on loan from Hestair-Dennis Ltd, Guildford but was owned by South Yorkshire PTE (522).

(e) This vehicle was on loan from Scania but was owned by Swedish operator Kalmar Omnibusförening U.P.A., Kalmar.

(f) ABH 760X on loan from Shaw & Kilburn Ltd (dealer), Hemel Hempstead.

(g) GCK 430W was on loan from Leyland National Co, Lillyhall but was owned by J. Fishwick, Leyland (12). Not used after 17 March 1982.

(h) This vehicle was on loan from Volvo (Great Britain) Ltd, Irvine and Wadham Stringer Ltd, Waterlooville.

(i) To cover for Scania 89 which returned to Scania for repairs.

(j) Received on loan in exchange for a Scania saloon which went to Chesterfield for evaluation.

Supplier	Reg. no.	Chassis type	Body	Seating	Year new	From	To	Comments
Nottingham	D121-3 URC	Dodge S56	Reeve Burgess	B25F	1987	5/87	>	(a)
Thamesdown	D401 TMW	"	"	DP25F	1987	8/87	9/87	
Scania (GB) Ltd	C112 JTM	Scania K112CRS	Berkhof	C49FT	1985	6/87	7/87	
NCME	D312 RVT	Dodge S56	NCME	B22F	1986	7/87	-	Not operated
Ipswich BT	C200 WGV	"	East Lancs	B21F	1986	8/87	10/87	
Thamesdown	C753 FMC	Leyland TRCTL11/3RH	Duple	C49FT	1986	7/88	9/88	(b)
"	E405 YMR	Renault S56	NCME	B25F	1988	7/88	9/88	
South Wales Transport	KEP 829X	Leyland National 2	NL116AL11/1R	DP44F	1982	5/89	-	(c)
Scania (GB) Ltd	F113 JPP	Scania K113CRB	Van Hool	C53FT	1988	6/89	-	Private hire/ contract work
"	F380 JTV	Scania N113DRB	Alexander	H47/33F	1989	8/89	9/89	Private hire/ contract work
Bournemouth	G50 BEL	Mercedes 811D	Wadham Stringer	B31F	1989	1/90	2/90	
Nottingham	G166 RRA	Mercedes 709D	Reeve Burgess	B25F	1990	3/90	4/90	
Optare Ltd	G842 LWR	Optare Metrorider Mr09	Optare	B23F	1990	4/90	-	
VL Bus	H47 NDU	Leyland Lynx	Leyland	B50F	1991	10/91	-	(d)
Optare Ltd	G837 LWR	DAF SB220	Optare Delta	B49F	1990	11/91	-	
Plaxton	H912 HRO	Scania N113CRB	Plaxton Verde	"	1991	11/91	12/91	
Dennis SV Ltd	J110 SPB	Dennis Lance	Alexander	B52F	1992	2/92	-	
"	K740 YPJ	"	"	B47F	1993	5/93	6/93	Not operated (e)
Volvo Bus (GB)	K114 PRV	Volvo B10B-58	NCME	B51F	1993	6/93	-	
Yorkshire Rider	K110 HUM	"	Alexander	"	1993	6/93	-	Not operated
West Midlands	F668 YOG	MCW Metrorider MF150	MCW	B23F	1988	1/94	4/94	(f)
Hughes (dealer)	K536 RJX	DAF MB230	Van Hool	C51FT	1993	6/95	10/95	
Optare Ltd	M925 TYG	Mercedes 0405	Optare Prisma	B49F	1995	7/95	-	
Volvo Bus	M918 MRW	Volvo B6L	Wright	B36F	1995	8/96	9/96	
Optare Ltd	P447 SWX	Optare Excel L1150		B42F	1996	9/97	10/97	
Scania Bus & Coach	Unreg	Scania L94	Wright	B40F	1998	-/98	-	Not operated (g)
Optare Ltd	V235 LWU	Optare Solo M850	Optare	B30F	1999	11/99	-	(h)
Plaxton	V680 FPB	Dennis Dart SLF	Plaxton	B29F	1999	11/99	-	(i)

(a) 123 returned to Nottingham in 5/87, 122 in 7/87 and 121 in 10/87.

(b) C753 FMC had been new to British Airways plc, Heathrow (CC8010).

(c) KEP 829X on loan for assessment of its "kneeling facility".
(d) H47 NDU was on loan from VL Bus, Warwick, but was owned by Nottingham City Transport (750).
(e) K740 YPJ had a Cummins 6C/211 engine, and was not actually registered while with Newport.
(f) F668 YOG was used on a new free bus service from the Bus Station to the Royal Gwent Hospital.
(g) This bus was in First Glasgow livery and was inspected at the depot.
(h) V235 LWU was used on the free bus service from the Bus Station to the Royal Gwent Hospital.
(i) V680 FPB was used on a new free bus service from the Bus Station to the Royal Gwent Hospital.

Supplier	Reg. no.	Chassis type	Body	Seating	Year new	From	To	Comments
Alexander	W194 CDN	Mercedes 814D	Alexander	B27F	2000	6/00	8/00	(a)
Scania Bus & Coach	X94 UBC	Scania L94UB	Wright	B40F	2001	8/01	-	Not operated
Volvo Bus	X645 RDA	Volvo B7TL	East Lancs	H47/29F	2001	12/01	-	
Scania Bus & Coach	YP02 AAN	Scania L94UA	Wright	AB59D	2002	3/02	-	Road tested only
"	Unreg	Scania OmniCityN94UB	Scania	?	?	3/02	5/02	Was this an Omnicity? (b)
Mercedes	Unreg	Mercedes Citaro	Mercedes	B??D	?	3/02	-	Red livery; road tested (c)
"	Unreg	"	"	B??F	?	5/02	-	White livery; road tested
Volvo Bus	Y814 BOJ	Volvo B7L	Wright	B40F	2001	4/02	5/02	
Ensign (dealer)	DMN 20R	Dennis Dart SLF	Marshall	B37F	1997	6/03	-	Not operated
"	ATK 154W	Leyland AN68B/1R	East Lancs	O43/28D	1980	6/03	7/06	New to Plymouth City Transport (d)
Evobus (UK) Ltd	BX05 UVZ	Mercedes Citaro 0530	Mercedes	B42F	2005	1/06	4/06	(e)
Scania Bus & Coach	YN55 RCY	Scania OmniCityN94UB	Scania	B42F	2005	2/06	-	Used on contract work
Optare Ltd	YJ55 BLX	Optare Tempo X1200	Optare	B42F	2005	2/06	-	Used on contract work
"	YJ56 APY	Optare Solo M880	"	B28F	2006	1/07	2/07	Used on contract work
Plaxton ?	AU07 AFV	Plaxton Primo	Plaxton	B28F	2007	5/07	-	Used on Tesco free bus service
Alexander Dennis	SN56 AYA	Alexander Dennis	Enviro200	B29F	2007	10/07	-	Not operated
Optare Ltd	YJ57 EHU	Optare Versa V1100	Optare	B35F	2007	10/07	-	Used on Tesco free bus service
Mistral (dealer)	MX04 VLP	Optare Solo M850	"	B29F	2004	12/07	2/08	(f)
"	MX56 NLG	"	"	B28F	2006	12/07	2/08	(f)
Scania Bus & C.	YN07 LFU	Scania OmniLink K94	Scania	B45F	2007	2/08	3/08	Road tested (g)
"	YN07 EXP	Scania OmniCity N230UB	"	B41F	2007	3/08	6/08	Not operated
Optare Ltd	YJ57 EHE	Optare Versa V1100	Optare	B38F	2007	3/08	-	Not operated (h)
Evobus (UK) Ltd.	BN09 FWS	Mercedes Citaro 0530	Mercedes	B42F	2009	6/09	-	
Scania Bus & C.	YR09 GXP	Scania OmniLink 270UB	Scania	B54F	2009	11/09	-	3-axle bus
"	YR10 BBO	Scania OmniCity N230UD	"	H45/31F	2010	6/10	-	
Alexander Dennis	SN59 AWX	Alexander Dennis	Enviro400	H41/29F	2009	8/10	-	
"	YX59 BXW	"	Enviro200	B29F	2009	9/10	-	
Scania Bus & C.	YS10 XBO	Scania OmniLink K230UB	Scania	B46F	2010	9/10	10/10	(i)
Mistral (dealer)	MX11 EGY	Wright Streetlite WF	Wright	B37F	2011	4/11	5/11	

Supplier	Reg. no.	Chassis type	Body	Seating	Year new	From	To	Comments
Scania Bus & Coach	YT11 LPN	Scania OmniLink K230UB	Scania	B46F	2011	6/11	-	
Evobus (UK) Ltd	BF60 OEZ	Mercedes Citaro 0530	Mercedes	B39F	2011	8/11	-	
Alexander Dennis	SN09 CGX	Alexander Dennis	Enviro300	B39F	2009	4/12	12/12	
"	YX61 DOU	"	Enviro200	B39F	2011	4/12	6/12	Temporary fleet number 320
MAN, Swindon	WX12 EKO	MAN 14.250 Citysmart	Caetano	B37F	2012	4/12	5/12	
Scania Bus & C.	YN54 AHP	Scania OmniCity CN94UB	Scania	B42F	2004	5/12		(j)
Mistral (dealer)	MX09 MHZ	Alexander Dennis	Enviro200	B29F	2009	6/12	6/13	Later 333
"	MX09 MHY	"	"	"	"	1/12	6/13	Later 222
Scania Bus & Coach	YT11 LSE	Scania OmniCity N230UD	Scania	H45/31F	2011	7/12	4/13	
Evobus (UK) Ltd	BF60 OEZ	Mercedes Citaro 0530	Mercedes	B39F	2011	7/12	8/12	
Alexander Dennis	YX61 DOU	Alexander Dennis	Enviro200	B39F	2011	12/12	7/14	Temporary fleet number 320
"	YN62 AAK	Scania K230UB	Enviro300	B43F	2012	12/12	1/13	
"	YX59 BZL	Alexander Dennis	Enviro200	B29F	2010	1/13	6/13	As 555
"	YX59 BZM	"	"	"	"	1/13	6/13	As 444
"	YX59 BZN	"	"	"	"	1/13	-	Intended to be 666 (k)

(a) W194 CDN was loaned by Alexander due to the late delivery of the Dennis Darts on order.

(b) This was road tested in March and again in May 2002. May have been the bus later registered YU02 GGZ by Scania.

(c) May well have been the bus which became LV02 UUC.

(d) Used to launch a Newport sightseeing open-top bus tour in 7/03, and retained as a spare vehicle.

(e) BX05 UVZ was used in service for a period in January and again in April 2006 with a conductor.

(f) Both on loan pending delivery of new Optare Solos (68-73). Only MX56 NLG was used.

(g) On loan as warranty cover for the Omnicity saloons in the fleet. This bus was also used on the Tesco free bus service and for driver training.

(h) YJ57 EHE on loan as warranty cover for the Solo midibuses (68-73) but was not used.

(i) Used for Ryder Cup shuttles and on service 30.

(j) On loan from Scania Bus & Coach to cover for repairs to Omnicity 113. Owned by Nottingham (216).

(k) YX59 BZN was returned to Alexander Dennis unused.

Supplier	Reg. no.	Chassis type	Body	Seating	Year new	From	To	Comments
Volvo Bus	BF62 UYM	Volvo B7RLE	MCV	B44F	2012	1/13	2/13	
MAN, Swindon	WX12 EKO	MAN 14.250	Caetano	B37F	2012	3/13	4/13	Citysmart model
"	WX13 GHN	MAN 18.270 Ecocity	"	B43F	2013	3/13	5/13	CNG Gas bus
Alexander Dennis	YT13 YUK	Scania K270UB	Enviro300	B42F	2013	8/13	10/13	CNG Gas bus
Mistral (dealer)	MX12 CGE	Alexander Dennis	Enviro200	B29F	2012	2/14	3/14	(a)
"	MX10 KNR	"	"	"	2010	2/14	3/14	(a)
Evobus (UK) Ltd	BU14 SZC	Mercedes City 45	Mercedes	M13	2014	7/14	-	Trialled on route 62
Days Rentals	CU13 JFA	Ford Transit	Ford	M14	2013	8/14	9/14	Used as a shuttle bus

Supplier	Reg. no.	Chassis type	Body	Seating	Year new	From	To	Comments
Days Rentals	CU13 JFJ	Ford Transit	Ford	M14	2013	8/14	9/14	Used as a shuttle bus
Evobus (UK) Ltd	BT15 KLZ	Mercedes City 45	Mercedes	M13	2015	3/16	4/16	
"	BP65 JOV	Mercedes Tourismo	Mercedes	C53FT	2016	4/16	-	Used for private hire
"	BP14 FJZ	Mercedes Citaro O295	Mercedes	B41F	2014	3/16	4/16	
Volvo Bus	BN64 CNY	Volvo B8RLE	MCV	B45F	2014	3/16	4/16	
Alexander Dennis	YX65 RKK	Alexander Dennis	Enviro200 MMC	B41F	2015	4/16	-	
Evobus (UK) Ltd	BT66 TZE	Mercedes Citaro O295	Mercedes	B41F	2016	4/17	5/17	
Dawson Rentals	LT02 ZZU	Dennis Trident	Plaxton	H39/24F	2002	8/17	?	As 1003
"	KV02 USS	"	Alexander	H43/27F	"	8/17	11/17	As 1005
Ensignbus	PJ02 PZK	Volvo B7TL	East Lancs	H45/20D	"	9/17	?	As 1010
"	PJ02 PZE	"	"	H45/23D	"	9/17	10/17	As 1012
"	V336 LGC	"	Plaxton	H43/22F	2000	9/17	?	As 1011
Dawson Rentals	PN03 UMK	Dennis Trident	"	H41/23D	2003	9/17	1/20	Used as a source of spares
Ensignbus	Y133 HWB	"	Alexander	H47/27F	2001	10/17	11/17	As 9734
"	Y134 HWB	"	"	"	"	10/17	11/17	As 9733
"	Y136 HWB	"	"	?	"	?	?	As 9736
"	LR52 VMO	Volvo B7TL	Plaxton	H39/20D	2002	11/17	3/18	As 1013
"	LR52 BNK	"	"	"	"	11/17	4/18	As 1014
Dawson Rentals	HV66 PYH	Ford Transit	Ford	M16	2016	8/18	8/18	Allocated 225 but not used
"	HV66 PYU	"	"	"	"	8/18	8/18	Allocated 228 but not used
"	HN16 VDO	"	"	"	"	8/18	9/18	Allocated 229 but not used
"	HV17 KVG	"	"	"	2017	8/18	9/18	Allocated 230 but not used
"	HV66 RAU	"	"	"	2016	8/18	8/18	Allocated 232 but not used
"	HV66 PYW	"	"	"	"	8/18	9/18	Allocated 233 but not used
"	HV17 KVM	"	"	"	2017	8/18	9/18	Allocated 239 but not used
"	LR52 KVV	Dennis Trident	Plaxton	H45/28F	2003	9/18	10/18	
"	KV02 URM	"	Alexander	H43/22F	2002	9/19	1/19	As HV04. Later purchased (440)
Pelican Eng	YK66 CBC	Yutong E12F	Yutong	B38F	2017	10/18	11/18	Later purchased 8/19
Evobus (UK) Ltd	BF68 ZHB	Mercedes Citaro O295	Mercedes	B41F	2018	1/19	-	Hybrid bus
Dawson Rentals	KN52 NEF	Dennis Trident	Alexander	H43/22F	2002	10/19	?	Gold livery
"	LR52 BOF	Volvo B7TL	Plaxton	H??F	2002	10/19	11/19	Red livery
Pelican Eng	YG18 CVS	Yutong E10	Yutong	B31D	2018	4/20	?/21	Red livery as DEM4

(a) Hired to cover for Scania OmniCitys out of service.

BIBLIOGRAPHY

Books

Newport Trams	Colin Maggs	Oakwood Press 1977
Trams and Buses of Newport 1845 to 1981	D B Thomas & E A Thomas	Starling Press 1982
Newport Transport 80 years of service	EA Thomas	Newport Borough Council 1981
Alexander Coachbuilders	Gavin Booth	Transport Publishing Co 1980
Park Royal Coachworks	Alan Townsin	Transport Publishing Co 1980
The Weymann Story Part 2 1942-1966	John A Senior	Venture Publications 2012
Guy Motors Ltd and the Wulfrunian	R N Hannay	Transport Publishing Co 1978
Air Dispatch Ltd and Bruce Coachworks Ltd of Cardiff	Glyn Bowen	CTPG 2002
Dennis – 100 Years of Innovation	Stewart J Brown	Ian Allan 1995
PSV Circle fleet history	PG10 Newport Transport Ltd and predecessors	PSV Circle 2009
PSV Circle supplement	PG10A	PSV Circle 2011
The Best of British Buses series (see below)	Alan Townsin	Transport Publishing Co
Leyland Titans 1927-1942, Leyland Tigers 1927-81, Utilities, Post-war Titans 1945-1984 and Post-war Daimlers 1942-1981		

Magazines etc

Buses Illustrated/Buses
Commercial Motor (various articles from very old copies)
The archives and records of Ivor Homfray
The archives and records of the late Dave B Thomas
The archives and records of the late Chris Taylor
The archives and records of John Jones
The archives and records of the Cardiff Transport Preservation Group

47 (YDW 747K), a Metro-Scania, inbound at the junction of St. Julian's Avenue and St. Julian's Road on 19 March 1983.

(John Jones)